The Spanish Ambassador's Suitcase

Stories from the Diplomatic Bag

MATTHEW PARRIS
AND ANDREW BRYSON

PENGUIN BOOKS

PENGUIN BOOKS

Published by the Penguin Group

Penguin Books Ltd, 80 Strand, London WC2R ORL, England

Penguin Group (USA) Inc., 375 Hudson Street, New York, New York 10014, USA

Penguin Group (Canada), 90 Eglinton Avenue East, Suite 700, Toronto, Ontario,
Canada M4P 2Y3 (a division of Pearson Penguin Canada Inc.)

Penguin Ireland, 25 St Stephen's Green, Dublin 2, Ireland (a division of Penguin Books Ltd)

Penguin Group (Australia), 707 Collins Street, Melbourne, Victoria 3008, Australia
(a division of Pearson Australia Group Pty Ltd)

Penguin Books India Pvt Ltd, 11 Community Centre, Panchsheel Park, New Delhi – 110 017, India

Penguin Group (NZ), 67 Apollo Drive, Rosedale, Auckland 0632, New Zealand
(a division of Pearson New Zealand Ltd)

Penguin Books (South Africa) (Pty) Ltd, Block D, Rosebank Office Park,
181 Jan Smuts Avenue, Parktown North, Gauteng 2193, South Africa

Penguin Books Ltd, Registered Offices: 80 Strand, London WC2R ORL, England

www.penguin.com

First published by Viking 2012
Published in Penguin Books 2013
005

Typeset by Jouve (UK), Milton Keynes
Printed in Great Britain by Clays Ltd, St Ives plc

ISBN: 978–0–241–95708–0

www.greenpenguin.co.uk

MIX
Paper from
responsible sources
FSC
www.fsc.org **FSC™ C018179**

Penguin Books is committed to a sustainable
future for our business, our readers and our planet.
This book is made from Forest Stewardship
Council™ certified paper.

PENGUIN BOOKS

THE SPANISH AMBASSADOR'S SUITCASE

Matthew Parris worked for the Foreign Office and the Conservative Research Department before serving as an MP. He joined *The Times* as a parliamentary sketchwriter in 1988, a post he held until 2001. He now writes as a columnist for the paper, and in 2011 he won the Best Columnist Award at the British Press Awards. His acclaimed autobiography *Chance Witness* was published by Viking in 2002.

Andrew Bryson is a radio journalist working in the BBC's Business and Economics Unit. He can usually be found working behind the scenes as a producer on BBC Radio 4's *Today* programme and Radio 5 Live, and occasionally in front of the microphone.

Their first volume of diplomats' despatches, *Parting Shots*, is published by Penguin.

Contents

Introduction

'A kind of gilded vagabondage'

'Good temper, good health and good looks,' wrote Sir Ernest Satow; 'Rather more than average intelligence, though brilliant genius is not necessary.'

Sir Ernest, Queen Victoria's Envoy Extraordinary and Minister Plenipotentiary to Japan for the last five years of the nineteenth century, was listing the qualities a successful senior British 'diplomatist' (as they called it then) requires. His book, *A Guide to Diplomatic Practice* (1917), became standard reading within the Foreign Office and is still read today – though his recommendation that diplomats should have an independent income can now be ignored.

'Science is not necessary,' he adds; 'Geography, beyond elementary notions, is not of great value. The diplomatist will acquire what geographical knowledge he needs of the country to which he is appointed while residing at his post.'

The ideal diplomat should be 'a straightforward character', Sir Ernest concluded. Such an officer needed 'A mind trained by the study of the best literature, and by that of history. Capacity to judge of evidence. In short, the candidate must be *an educated gentleman*. These points cannot be ascertained by means of written examinations.'

If the marks of competence are as Satow describes them, readers of this book may agree that British diplomats have measured up well since he wrote. Whatever he thought of written examinations, it's fair to say that, more than any other country in the world, Britain's ambassadors have been assessed by their fellow diplomats at least (though not only) on the quality of their prose. Style always mattered in the Foreign Office. As I explained in *Parting Shots*, the forerunner to this book, I learned early as a young Foreign Office trainee that a successful diplomat was importantly judged on the quality of his drafting: not just the content, but the vigour, the clarity, the descriptive power, the style – and (in the right circumstances) the humour too.

These are the very attributes that, we hope you'll agree, are to be found flowering abundantly in the despatches that make up this book. Compiling and researching our second collection of diplomatic writing has been great fun, not least because we allowed ourselves a much wider range of sources. Whereas every item in *Parting Shots* was a valedictory despatch – written by an ambassador departing a post – the despatches in this new book are far more eclectic. In Chapter 1, 'Protocol Department', you will find a hoard of miscellaneous comic masterpieces, sent from all sorts of different times and places. In so far as these 'funnies', as they are known in Whitehall, share a common thread, it is the pomp and ceremony of diplomacy; and the absurdity that goes with it.

Chapter 2 is a collection of despatches which are in one sense the opposite of valedictories, but actually have much in common with them, First Impressions despatches being sent at the beginning of a posting, of course, rather than at the end. In the best of these reports ambassadors turned their unfamiliarity with the local scene to their advantage.

The final chapter, 'Envoi', takes in a few previously over-looked valedictories in which ambassadors departing a post summed up what they had learned about the host country – and lessons too for their bureaucratic and political masters back in Whitehall and Westminster. The valedictory was (until banned by embarrassed ministers and civil servants in 2006) a traditional way of letting off steam, and saying what had perhaps been unsayable while the ambassador was still in post.

Almost all the entries in this book are despatches. Most are traditional diplomatic despatches: letters both signed and drafted by ambassadors in post, and formally addressed to (but only in a minority of cases actually read by) the Foreign Secretary of the day. An ambassador would typically write only one or two despatches a year (the rest of his post's 'reporting' being by letters, telegrams and, increasingly, emails between colleagues) and the despatch of a despatch was an indication of the importance and interest the ambassador attached to the subject: an interest it was hoped (not always realistically) that colleagues back in Whitehall would share.

What exactly is a 'despatch'? Let the Foreign Office answer that question itself, as it does in some Office notes we found at the National Archives, dating from the early 1980s:

3.2   DESPATCHES

3.2.1   The despatch is the most formal method of communication. It is sent by or in the name of the Secretary of State to a Head of Mission, Minister, Acting Head of Mission, Head of Post, Officer Administering the Government of a Dependent Territory or the Governor of an Australian State. It is sent from a Head or acting Head of a Post to the Secretary of State, or on some matters, between a Mission and its subordinate Posts.

3.2.2   A despatch is usually confined to one subject. It is written in a clear, simple style, without courtesy phrases in the text, and the addressee is referred to throughout as 'you'. Normally, paragraphs are numbered and a file reference given. References to previous correspondence are given in full. Appropriate security classifications and privacy markings are used. Recipients of copies of the despatch are listed in the last paragraph. Further specific guidance is given in paras 3.3 to 3.6.

3.2.3   The despatch opens with 'Sir' or 'My Lord' and closes:

I am, Sir,

yours faithfully

It is addressed simply by name and place, e.g.

Sir Nicholas Henderson, GCMG PARIS

The Rt. Hon. Dr David Owen, MP LONDON

Our book of valedictory despatches, *Parting Shots*, was accompanied by two series of programmes for BBC Radio 4. The success of both the book and the radio programmes took my co-editor, Andrew Bryson, and me by surprise. We had certainly been confident that poking around in a forgotten corner of diplomatic archives would amuse and entertain a minority audience; but such was the quality, the humour, the wisdom and sometimes the outrageously *un*diplomatic tone of the valedictories we unearthed through word of mouth, Freedom of Information and the National Archives at Kew, that both book and broadcasts gained a far wider audience than we had expected. And people seemed to enjoy reading gems of Foreign Office draftsmanship, and to have approved.

Approval came, not least, we found (again to our surprise), from serving and former members of the Foreign and Commonwealth Office (FCO) itself. Essays that had been crafted to impress were now impressing an intelligent readership they had never anticipated – and their authors, many of them men-of-letters-*manqués*, were pretty chuffed about that.

As a result, correspondence, calls and emails started to come in. 'I seem to remember that old Archie wrote a corker from . . . where was it? . . . something-or-other-*stan*, wasn't it?' Or 'Why don't you try to track down a marvellous bit of comic writing from our ambassador in . . . Algiers, I think it was . . . about a ludicrous flight into the Sahara and a Spanish ambassador (was it?) with a mysterious and incredibly heavy suitcase? The despatch was circulated right round the Office at the time . . .' and 'There was this fantastic pen-portrait of Göring – sometime before World War II – can't recall from whom – our man in Berlin, obviously – or exactly when . . .' Our former Prime Minister Sir John Major reminded us of a hilarious British Embassy telegram from Moscow, describing the lengths to which diplomats had gone to arrange the transit by railway of a horse given to him by the President of Turkmenistan.

And so began part two of Andrew Bryson's sleuthing work: a hunt for documents half-remembered and imperfectly described, some comical, some vivid pen-portraits of countries and individuals, some heavy with prophecy, some triumphantly right, some horribly wrong . . . all of them essays that deserve rereading, and many of them models of wisdom, humour or style.

The research process for this book was much the same as for *Parting Shots.* It was at the National Archives at Kew that we found most of the despatches in this collection. After thirty years most despatches are declassified and sent to Kew, where anyone can read them. These files, in which sit the despatches alongside further correspondence and memos sent between the embassy and officials at the Foreign Office in Whitehall, make for fascinating reading, especially the remarks scribbled in pencil or pen in the margins by senior politicians – some of which we've quoted in this book.

Andrew made more Freedom of Information requests (ninety-eight this time, against sixty-five for the first book; the hit rate was lower because not all ambassadors wrote First Impressions despatches – but the quality of what we found when we did score a hit was striking). He did a great deal more research in the National Archives too, going through all the new files that were declassified at the beginning of 2011 for 1980; and, this year, those declassified for 1981.

Not least in the appeal of reading these reports is that they were never intended for prying eyes. Most were classified documents (categorized as 'Restricted' or 'Confidential' – sometimes 'Secret') which only those inside the Foreign Office, government ministers and other privileged individuals in the higher echelons of Whitehall were permitted to read – and of course only those that had passed the relevant security vetting procedure.

A great many of these despatches were written in what we have come to consider the 'golden age' of despatch-writing between 1965 and 1975 when Britain still had a Diplomatic Service fit for an empire but no longer had the empire. Our diplomats counted among their number the brightest in the land; but one has the sense that back then British ambassadors had rather more time on their hands than they do today; time enough, for instance, to compose works as long, as dense and as brilliant as Sir John Russell's 1967 First Impressions report from Rio (pp. 179–90).

Modern diplomatic writing may be less showy but its very newness packs a punch. The scattering of despatches in this collection from the 1990s and 2000s have a currency and relevance all of their own. Whereas older generations of diplomats would peck away at the embassy typewriter, an antique which required them to underline words to represent italics, modern diplomats sally forth with word processors. With the advance of technology despatches are no longer sent as typed or printed documents but rather as tele-letters (secure emails); and they sit awaiting discovery not on a dusty library shelf but on a computer server. Naturally the Foreign Office keeps this material under close control. Unlike at Kew where the main problem is simply too much information, official material written after 1981 is currently unavailable unless you ask for it, and your Freedom of Information request had better be specific if it is to stand any chance of success. The print-outs we received in response to our FOI requests would arrive in the post redacted – that is to say, with sensitive sections blacked out in thick marker pen. What made it into the book is what survived the censors' pen. Researchers in later decades will be able to see the full versions of these despatches once they finally arrive at Kew. Tomorrow's historians will have a shorter wait, however, than today, with the thirty-year period being cut to twenty years.

In November 2010 – shortly after *Parting Shots* was first published – Wikileaks began releasing 250,000 confidential US diplomatic cables, the content of these leaks and the methods used to obtain them attracting intense interest and controversy. *Parting Shots* and this new collection are more modest undertakings, but they do have their similarities with Wikileaks. Unlike Julian Assange, however, we've gone through official channels to obtain properly vetted copies of diplomatic reports. Doubtless there exists sensational material we might be unable to obtain in this way, but our experience has been that the authorities are pretty grown-up about withholding things and do not do so for trivial reasons; we've occasionally been surprised at the release to us of some quite seriously embarrassing material, but never material that would prejudice national security. A couple of times, on seeing (through other sources) pre-redacted versions of material we received in redacted form, I've understood the reasons for redaction.

What follows is a magpie collection. Not all are of equal quality, but the best are truly outstanding. In my view the 1934 despatch from our ambassador in Berlin, Sir Eric Phipps, describing a day in the forest with Herman Göring, is the finest despatch we found, sending shivers down the spine even as one winces at Phipps's unkind humour; and it is, too, a work of minor prophecy. This is diplomatic writing at its very best. But even the worst here are worth reading for the insight they give into just how wrong an ambassador – with all the experience, contacts and research available to him – can sometimes be.

There's one quality, however, very few of these despatches lack: penmanship. Senior British diplomats really knew how to write.

They wrote (at their best) with a beautiful balance between economy and style. In the Foreign Office prose for which as a young entrant I was encouraged to aim, a workmanlike functionality was prized equally alongside a certain understated classiness. Every word, every paragraph, would whisper 'top drawer'. There was an understated confidence, a smidgeon of cynicism and a suggestion of buried humour. It was the language of the very best kind of courtier: high-calibre, at its most powerful quite spare, practical and to the point, but delivered with grace and subtlety; prose that could wink but would never leer, hint but never hammer home, tweak tails but seldom draw blood. The mood is convivial but never gushing.

Lofty rhetoric was despised – the sort of thing politicians do. Strings of adjectives were not encouraged. Mysticism was disapproved of. Arguments of idealism and incantations to Destiny were treated with suspicion. To this day, British diplomats tell against themselves, but with a secret pride, the story of Sir Oliver Franks, who was HM Ambassador to the United States of America from 1948 to 1952.

One evening in 1948, shortly before Christmas, the British Embassy in Washington received a telephone call from a US radio station asking to interview the ambassador for its holiday programming. Franks was told that the radio station was doing the same with the other embassies, and he duly answered their questions about international affairs and other matters. At the end they asked him what he would like for Christmas, and thanked him for contributing to the programme.

Franks thought nothing of it until he turned on the radio on Christmas Eve and heard the broadcaster announce that they had asked three leading foreign ambassadors to share with listeners what they would like for Christmas.

The Russian ambassador had said he wanted 'peace on earth and understanding between nations'. The French ambassador had said he wanted 'a brighter future for humanity and for the spread of freedom throughout the world'. The British ambassador had said: 'That's ever so kind of you – a small box of crystallized fruit would be lovely.'

You can imagine the company in which this anecdote would be related, to an amused chuckle. Such is the company into which the despatches that follow are intended to draw their reader: a worldly but civilized company; a circle of the best and the brightest among whom it was implicitly understood that we chaps were but intelligent observers of a world in which our capacity to transform was severely constrained, but we might here or there readjust a detail or two. We were a Rolls-Royce of a cadre, we thought, in the faintly disappointed service of a country that probably wanted only a Vauxhall. The language of these despatches breathes as much. Foreign Office prose was once described as 'the last respite of the English subjunctive'.

This is drafting that does not hope for too much from the world and subtly denigrates those who do. There is, in truth, a trace of something smug here, and the false modesty can grate: but the style is never unreflective, never thoughtless, never unmindful that things could be a little better or a little worse and that the difference matters. Above all, never too much zeal.

Note that last sentence. The best sort of British diplomat would not reproduce the original French ('Surtout pas trop de zèle') or cite Talleyrand by name. That would be showy. Instead he would assume his audience's easy acquaintance with the source, indulging himself and his readers thereby in a little discreet mutual flattery.

Apart from a few routine obsequities towards the Foreign Secretary to whom the despatch is formally addressed, British politicians are almost completely disregarded in these letters, or treated as a peripheral nuisance. That more or less mirrors the ethos in which I worked, and I've no reason to suppose it has changed.

Something that has changed is our modern and welcome intolerance of racist language and racist opinion. There are some frankly embarrassing remarks, usually meant in jest, to be encountered in these pages, but we've on the whole left the material in place – as being indicative of another era (though Ronald Burroughs's jokes about black skins in his famous Algerian despatch on pp. 94–103 did test our patience. They aren't even very funny).

Towards the Office (as we called it) in London, readers may sometimes detect the false servility that knows respect is called for but does not feel it. A senior diplomat abroad doubts that his colleagues in Whitehall entirely understand his situation or sympathize with his difficulties; doubts they are giving his views or reports the attention or credence they deserve; and suspects they think they know it all already from secondary sources while treating lightly the gold dust of a first-hand report offered by their man in post, on the ground, in harness and in daily contact with the realities.

He fears they think he's 'gone native' (suffering from what Kenneth East, departing Iceland in 1981 – see pp. 348–9 – described as '"clientitis" – that blurring of the vision in which one's hosts are increasingly seen at their own valuation'). He thinks that in international affairs they're so focused, back in London, on the immediate British interest that they've lost sight of the longer-term benefits of the good relations with a friendly and promising country: a place he can tell them all about if only they would listen.

He may have, however, no stars in his eyes about the natives, and many of these despatches attest to that. Our ambassador's 1970 pen-portrait of President Bongo of Gabon is rescued from calumny only by wit. In *Parting Shots* a handful of the valedictories we published caused, by their modern publication, quite a stir in the countries criticized. A 1984 despatch by the British High Commissioner in Ottawa opining on the 'moderate' ability of the populace ('One does not encounter here the ferocious competition of talent that takes place in the United Kingdom') briefly became national news in Canada when we uncovered it with a Freedom of Information request. A much older despatch from Thailand caused an even bigger stink. Sir Anthony Rumbold signed off from Bangkok in 1967 by saying of the Thais that 'they have no literature, no painting and only a very odd kind of music' and that among the rich, after gambling and golf, 'licentiousness is the main pleasure of them all'. Our man in Bangkok in 2009 felt obliged to issue a press release after local media picked up on the story. 'My own views differ from my predecessor of 42 years ago,' said HM's thoroughly modern Ambassador Quinton Quayle, who avowed his love of the country's culture, landscape and people: 'The country for me certainly lives up to its brand name – Amazing Thailand.'

Mercifully for the book that follows, President Bongo is now dead, so there should be no comeback there. Sir John Russell's 1967 description of the steamy and dysfunctional country that Brazil then was – as being like 'the United States . . . if the South had won the Civil War' – is so obviously out of date that no offence will surely be taken today. And let me assure Barbadians that 'This windblown island of boredom' (I quote our sometime High Commissioner – see p. 324) describes the Barbados of 1967, not today. I hasten, too, to remark that John Robinson's bleak and bitter prospectus for the Algeria he found in 1974 has not really come to pass, though I still find the despatch perceptive. So Andrew Bryson and I can hopefully sleep safely in our beds after publication.

Andrew, who has done all the work, will deserve the slumber. He and I have not sought to give this collection any sort of thematic shape. Instead, to stop the book becoming one unremitting barrage of diplomatic prose, we've gathered the material into three chapters, whose rationale – should you wish to challenge it in the particular – I will not even attempt to defend, but simply here describe.

～

'Protocol Department' (Chapter 1) needs the most elaboration. Many but not all of these despatches are funny, and intentionally so. Typically they draw their humour from the ridiculous situations created by diplomatic protocol; so ridiculous (and a serious point is often being made here) that the diplomat decided the incident was worth describing to a wider Office audience than his own staff.

Not every entry in this section is a despatch; some of the funniest were simply letters written from one diplomat in the field to a colleague with whom he was friendly back in London. Even these, however, often tended to stick to the standard despatch format, with numbered paragraphs and a mock-formal tone, which often contrasts to great effect with the ludicrous events described. There's an echo of public-school giggling in a lot of this.

When we talk about 'protocol' we mean the word defined in its broadest sense: from etiquette to silly costumes to formal processes, arcane ceremonies, foot-dragging, grandstanding and pedantry: all of them part – sometimes an integral part – of the business of diplomacy. The observation of correct diplomatic etiquette is deemed so important that there is in the British Foreign Office, and in the foreign services of other countries, a unit dedicated to it, from which this chapter takes its name. It is the job of the Protocol Department to advise British diplomats on the accepted practice. A British High Commissioner in Africa wants to know the correct drill for the funeral of a former President: should he attend in person? – and how attired? – or simply send condolences? And an ambassador in the Middle East wants to know how he might politely decline a gift offered to Her Majesty the Queen by a wealthy but somewhat suspect sheikh, without causing a diplomatic incident – or should he accept? When they dispense their advice, the FCO's protocol experts rely on precedent – because things should be done the correct way, which is as they have been done before; and because breaking a precedent or setting a new one could make things difficult further down the line.

Diplomats can find themselves bound by many such rules and precedents, although things have relaxed a little since the 1950s, when Marcus Cheke's *Guidance on Foreign Usages and Ceremony, and Other Matters* (1949) was the bible distributed to new FCO recruits. Cheke's tome had dos and don'ts for every social and professional situation, governing how a diplomat should behave among his colleagues in the British Embassy as well as with foreigners, and how his wife should act too. Protocol and good manners were imperative; if a diplomat found himself faced with two alternatives, 'one easy but appearing somewhat over-familiar, the other respectful but appearing somewhat pompous or old-fashioned', Cheke's advice was always to choose the latter. 'If his wife is hesitating whether to appear at the beach picnic of the Counsellor's wife (who has been most friendly to her) with or without stockings,' wrote Cheke, 'let her (if she is unable to telephone and ask) wear stockings.'

I recall on joining the Service in the mid-1970s being given a slim introductory guide to 'Diplomatic Service Etiquette', which included the advice that on a social occasion a serving male officer desirous of seating himself on a sofa or one of a line of adjacent chairs should never so position himself that a senior officer (or the wife of a senior officer) would – if also desirous of a seat – have no choice but to sit beside him.

Nowadays things are not quite so stuffy and formal, but many of Cheke's rules still stand – indeed, many FCO recruits in recent years to whom an old copy of the book is made a gift as a joke by friends or family say they find themselves turning to it for real advice in the end. A 2005 guide by the US State Department called *Protocol for the Modern Diplomat* contains passages which could (and some probably do) come straight from Cheke: concerning the necessity of official calls to make introductions, sample seating plans for formal dinners, and the order in which diplomats should step on board the deck of a ship (ambassador first, naturally). And woe betide the US diplomat who thinks embassy social functions are for socializing. 'When you attend social functions that the ambassador and other high ranking U.S. officers are also attending, you should arrive approximately fifteen minutes early ... remember to eat before leaving home ... Leave a party at a reasonable hour, no matter how much fun you are having' while, at the same time, observing the golden rule: 'Do not leave before the guest of honor.'

On official business, as opposed to the cocktail circuit, protocol enters another league altogether. One formal set-piece which occurs time and again in these despatches is the presentation of credentials by an incoming ambassador to the Head of State. The Head of Mission must be accredited by the host government before ambassadors may represent their country in any official business at the Foreign Ministry. He or she must be acceptable to that government, which will have been notified of a proposed candidate for any ambassadorial vacancy in advance, so that any reservations may be lodged. The acquiescence of the receiving state is signified by its granting what is called *agrément* to the appointment. It is rare but not unheard of for *agrément* to be refused.

Letters of credence (and recall) follow a standard text,

identifying the diplomat as the representative of Her Majesty the Queen and empowering him or her to speak for her. The amount of time given by the Head of State for the tête-à-tête component of the ceremony is jealously watched and recorded by ambassadors, as an indicator of how important Britain is seen in comparison with other nations. Protocol, however, dictates that no official business should be discussed in these conversations but that the exchanges should be cordial. The ceremony complete, the ambassador is deemed accredited and, according to protocol, gains the protections, privileges and immunities accorded to the Diplomatic Corps.

The Diplomatic Corps is a key concept: when used of a single country it is the collective term for all diplomats, from every country, accredited to that host government. Despite their different nationalities and origins, these itinerant envoys in fact have more in common with one another than the vast majority of officials with whom they might deal in the host country. Diplomats practise the same profession, of course, and attend the same functions: be they the formal state affairs of the host government, or the social merry-go-round of the National Day receptions each ambassador holds at his embassy. In many of these despatches the British ambassador will refer to ambassadors from other countries posted in the same capital as his 'colleagues', a term laden with meaning (the casual observer might have expected 'competitors' instead). In a way, therefore, the Corps functions like a trade association.

Protocol is easy to mock and diplomats mock it all the time, but in fact they do take it rather seriously – and not without reason. There is much formality in national and international affairs, and people need to know their place.

Samuel Pepys in the 1660s describes an occasion when rivalry between the ambassadors from France and Spain over which sovereign – and thus which ambassador – had precedence at a British state occasion, led to two footmen being killed. Breaches of protocol are to be avoided at all costs lest they be misinterpreted as a deliberate slight against the ambassador and, through them, their Head of State.

Protocol has at its heart an acknowledgement of hierarchy, and diplomats use precedence as a straightforward way of organizing the corps without causing ugly scenes. For ambassadors, precedence is determined by the order in which they presented their credentials to the Head of State; on many social occasions whoever has been in post longest has precedence over all the others. This rule crops up to comic effect in the 'Spanish Ambassador's Suitcase' despatch. Of course behind closed doors states still jostle for power, and superpower diplomats pack a bigger punch than diplomats from small states, no matter how long they have been in post; but on the surface at least the system of precedence helps maintain order.

British diplomats within these pages come with a wide range of titles each marking a different degree of importance within the Office, and between the countries involved. Until the late twentieth century, for instance, Britain sent ministers, not ambassadors, to lesser powers, and they worked out of legations not embassies. The names and the titles always signified something: hence the various titles here – Consul-General or Chargé d'Affaires where the regime in power was not officially recognized by Her Majesty's Government (HMG) or diplomatic relations were otherwise politically complicated or incomplete, or where a more junior diplomat was minding the shop in the absence of a fully fledged Head of Mission. Consuls are usually senior diplomats abroad whose function is to look after the interests of their own nationals who may need help in the country in question; and we sometimes maintain consuls in large cities that are not capitals, as well as in the capital itself. If you get robbed in Barcelona, it is to the British Consul that you should address your requests for help.

Where the host country is a member of the Commonwealth, the Head of Mission is called a high commissioner, not ambassador. The even more arcane label of Extraordinary and Plenipotentiary was used to indicate that a diplomat had full powers to negotiate treaties and the like in the name of the Queen. 'His/Her Excellency' is an honorific given to both ambassadors and high commissioners.

As an indication of how seriously issues of protocol are taken in diplomacy, papers declassified in January 2012 show how the Foreign Secretary and Britain's Ambassador to France had to get involved when French officials complained about the relative size of the chairs proposed for President Giscard d'Estaing and Margaret Thatcher to sit on at a 1981 summit. The issue, raised 'quite seriously' by the French, was that Thatcher's chair had arms, while the chair intended for the French President did not.

The reader will have gathered that 'Protocol Department' is really a ragbag of a category, by whose title we also include the logistics, the nuts and bolts, the whys and wherefores of a senior diplomat's life abroad. Readers may, for a start, wonder how and in what form all these despatches reached London: a question I'll try to answer now.

'Needs must . . .' and a few of the letters you'll find in this book were sent as telegrams via the FCO's very extensive Diplomatic Wireless Service. But the medium of choice was a proper, typed letter on pale blue Foreign Office crested paper, which reached London by the relatively secure means of the Diplomatic Bag. Let Humphrey Trevelyan in his book *Diplomatic Channels* (1973) describe a world before what he calls 'the central ceremony of embassy life' was elbowed aside by today's electronic despatches. Lord Trevelyan had been Ambassador to Egypt (1955–6), Iraq (1958–61), the Soviet Union (1962–5) and High Commissioner in Aden (1967) before he wrote this:

The central ceremony of embassy life [is] . . . the ritual of the diplomatic bag. It is an expensive and complicated operation. Someone buried in a London attic tenuously connected with the Foreign Office takes a hundred retired service officers – or whatever the number is – pours in a bag of airline schedules, stirs vigorously and allows the mixture to simmer gently till ready. Enormous ingenuity is shown in routing the Queen's messengers so as to cover the largest number of posts with the smallest number of colonels. In sensitive areas they travel in pairs so as to avoid being raped on the way. The rhythm of embassy life centres on the bag and it is advisable for outsiders to give the embassy a wide berth on bag day . . . it is not advisable, though not unknown, for an ambassador to use his diplomatic bag to enhance his salary by conducting profitable and illegal currency deals, or selling duty-free cigarettes on the black market . . . But the British are not guilty of these peccadilloes. A British head of chancery guards the virginity of his bag like a mid-Victorian chaperone at an attractive maiden's first ball.

These bags, incidentally, have by custom been sewn, repaired and laundered in Wandsworth Prison in south-west London. Some of our closest allies have used our own facilities for the transmission of their bags. The Canadians have. By some ghastly error in 1991 Canadian diplomatic bags still full were sent for laundry. A British minister was called to the House of Commons to make an Emergency Statement on the fiasco – an occasion the gravity of which was undermined from the start by Mr Speaker's commenting that some of the 'Foreign Office's briefs' might have been in the laundry ... but let the parliamentary sketch I wrote for *The Times* of 6 December that year speak for itself:

'PUBLIC WASHING OF PRIVATE GRIEF'

Where will political fortune take Mark Lennox-Boyd – Home Secretary, Chancellor, who knows? But of this we may be sure: however famous he may become, nobody will ever forget that Thursday in December, way back in 1991, when he had to handle the Diplomatic Bag and Prison Laundry Affair.

Or it may be (merit is not always rewarded) that he sinks back into the friendly obscurity of the Tory backbenches, praised for his quiet but capable service, and knighted after twenty years. But of one thing we may be certain: though the rest be forgotten, everyone will remember how, as junior Foreign Office minister, he drew the short straw and manned the dispatch box for the Diplomatic Bag and Prison Laundry Statement. Readers may know what happened. Empty diplomatic bags are washed at Wandsworth Prison laundry. Some sent there recently were not empty.

And that's all – except that the incident sparked the funniest Westminster episode for years. For much of twenty wonderful minutes the whole Chamber was quite literally helpless with laughter.

Mr Lennox-Boyd rose. To picture him, imagine a tall, slim, slightly dishevelled fellow in his early forties: the sort who, despite intelligence and breeding, might not notice that a collar was frayed, a shoe scuffed, or a shave overdue. A sallow man with dark hair, Mr Lennox-Boyd has a courteously hesitant manner and always looks vaguely preoccupied. If ever he should be subject to violent passions, he never permits them to disturb an air of quietly anxious concern. His mildly sorrowful look would equip him well for the profession of undertaker's assistant in a cut-price funeral parlour. But he is a junior Foreign Office minister and the Dominion of Canada had lost their correspondence in the Wandsworth Prison laundromat, and the Opposition had found out, and Mr Lennox-Boyd had to explain. We couldn't stop laughing.

'Mr Speaker, I must get the answer out!' he pleaded. Apparently the Canadians use our bags for some of their own traffic. 'On this occasion the Canadian bags in question had been inadvertently included in such a consignment' and sent to Wandsworth.

Containing what? Were secret by-pass plans for Moose Jaw now in the public domain? Were local election results in Saskatoon common knowledge among prison officers? Were the sensitive points of

Belgo-Canadian relations a subject of gossip with bank-robbers, the details of Alcan's balance sheet exposed to comment among recidivist kerb-crawlers? Struggling through gales of laughter, an expression of the utmost dolefulness on his worried face, Mr Lennox-Boyd staggered on . . .

'Steps were immediately taken to recover the diplomatic mail and to investigate the incident.' And, quite abruptly, he sat down.

What? Was that all? 'More! More!' the House shouted. But there was no more. Lennox-Boyd sat on the green bench, staring intensely at his shoes.

For Labour, Gerald Kaufman now pretended that this was a Home Office matter and he had expected the Home Secretary to handle the statement. Was it true, he asked, that 'an interval of several days elapsed between the discovery and the search?' How much material was still missing? How much of it was sensitive? With each new bogus question the laughter grew. The Speaker tried to stop it, insisting that this was 'an important matter' [cries of No!]. To no avail.

'Can you say if a watch was in the missing material? What guarantees can you provide that other metal objects cannot find their ways into prison in the way that this did?'

The watch was a new element in the mystery. There were cries of 'oooh!' and 'aah!'. Mr Lennox-Boyd's feet became the objects of his renewed scrutiny. 'Was the Home Secretary informed? Why has the Government not made this public?' Mr Kaufman has a talent for dignifying the ludicrous, but even he could not keep a straight face now, and he sat down, grinning.

'Is he aware,' intoned Sir Peter Tapsell, 'that Prince Metternich left Vienna disguised in a laundry basket? This incident is in the highest diplomatic traditions.' Dared the minister smile? The faintest of grins hovered, briefly, on Mr Lennox-Boyd's troubled face.

Such are the snakes and ladders of FCO logistics. By those who knew the ropes, the internal structures of diplomatic life tended to be taken for granted in the report and analysis that ambassadors framed for Foreign Secretaries. But their existence was understood and acknowledged, and underlies much that you won't find in the despatches themselves. Take, for instance, the endless round of entertaining and being entertained our senior diplomats have to endure. 'A diplomat these days' (wrote Peter Ustinov) 'is nothing but a headwaiter who's allowed to sit down occasionally.' When they complain about their demanding social calendar, diplomats know better than to expect much sympathy from outsiders. 'Much rubbish,' wrote Paul Wright, in his book *A Brittle Glory* (1986), 'is written and talked about diplomatic entertainment:

... the alleged glamour of gold chairs, caviar, champagne and glittering jewels and of state secrets falling from the pretty but careless lips of the Prime Minister's mistress. Much indignation is generated by the supposedly artificially high lifestyle necessarily adopted by our diplomats in order to suborn and seduce the foreigner ... The reality is quite the contrary, as anyone will vouchsafe who has sat through innumerable meals, struggling to keep going conversations of stupendous dullness, or has hung about at cocktail parties clasping a sweaty glass and trying to avoid the Olympic-class bores of which the profession has its share.

Wright, who was Ambassador to the Democratic Republic of Congo and later Lebanon (from where he wrote a lively First Impressions despatch – see pp. 287–8) nevertheless saw the utility of such encounters:

Shared social occasions, however painful, do in the end produce familiarity and, in some cases, intimacy . . . [T]he ice gets broken or, more important, is prevented from forming. Moreover, indiscretions have been known to filter through the noise and smoke and to have been recognised as important when discreetly reported back; or if deliberately let slip, as I have done on more than one occasion, have been picked up and acted upon in exactly the way hoped for. Much of this is possible on a social occasion, little of it elsewhere.

The cuisine can be as important as the conversation. 'A good cook,' comments François de Callières in his 1716 *The Art of Diplomacy*, 'is often an excellent conciliator.' And as Michael Shea describes in *To Lie Abroad* (1996), even when the conversation is all about the food, diplomacy can triumph.

My Ambassadress in Bonn in the late Sixties, the invincible Lady Roberts, at a time when Franco-British iciness over de Gaulle's refusal to allow our entry to the EEC was at its most frozen, left a dinner party at the French Residence with the calculating words directed at her hostess: 'Thank you for a wonderful evening, my dear. Such a pity about the soufflé.' This was no mere catty remark. This was serious. The two ladies, and it reflected on their husbands' relationships as well, hardly spoke again.

But mishaps occur in even the best-regulated of Residence dining rooms, as happened in the 1970s to Norman

Reddaway, ambassador father to an ambassador son, David. In *To Lie Abroad* Shea explains that sometimes a culinary catastrophe can be turned, with the right butler, into an opportunity. David Reddaway of the British Embassy in Ankara recalls such an event in Warsaw when his father was Ambassador to Poland:

As the butler entered the room carrying a salver with three sizeable legs of lamb for the main course, he caught his toe on the carpet and fell full length. The legs of lamb rolled onto the floor. My mother watched ashen faced . . . as the butler gathered them up and disappeared. Uneasy conversation resumed . . . within ten minutes, however, the butler reappeared. He was carrying a tray with a number of roast duck, which he served with due aplomb to the gratified amazement of the guests. As soon as the guests had left, my mother . . . asked the butler to explain the miracle . . . the answer was simple. The Swedish Ambassador, who lived next door, had also been giving a dinner that evening; and his cook had been kind enough to let our household serve their duck. What . . . had the Swedes eaten instead? 'Why,' replied the butler without batting an eyelid, 'they had our lamb.'

The challenges of managing domestic staff in the lives of ambassadors and spouses have been an iceberg of which but a tip surfaces in diplomatic archives. The experience of Sir William Hayter, Second Secretary in Shanghai, 1938–40 (described in *To Lie Abroad*), is an indication:

[Sir William and Lady Hayter had an] enormous staff, the No. 1 boy and No. 2 boy, the cook and the learner cook, the amah, the coolie, the gardener, the chauffeur, most of them with large families (the No. 1 boy had two wives). Quei, the No. 1 boy, was a remarkable character. He had been the head servant in the flagship of the flotilla of British gun-boats which patrolled the Yangtse. He had found his position an excellent one for organising opium-smuggling up and down the river. When this was detected he was dismissed, whereupon he withdrew all Chinese labour from the gun-boats, thus effectively immobilizing them. 'Face' clearly precluded his re-employment in the flagship, but was saved by the provision of a suitable situation for him in the Embassy, which being immobile provided less scope for opium-smuggling.

No better description of a career, domestic as well as political, in the Diplomatic Service, will be found than that captured in the last five words of a commentary by Sir Hughe Knatchbull-Hugessen, whose despatch from the Baltic States is on pp. 90–94. 'This is,' he says:

... the most unfaithful of careers. At comparatively regular intervals the diplomat is called upon to express simultaneously his immeasurable grief at leaving his old post and his unlimited joy on arriving at his new one. I had to express these twin sentiments on one occasion in the presence of natives of both ... Life (for diplomats) is ... a kind of gilded vagabondage.

～

'A kind of gilded vagabondage': diplomatic prose of the highest order. Sir Hughe's observations take us neatly to the second and third chapters of this book. 'First Impressions' means exactly that; and is the name the Office itself gave to the despatch which by tradition a new ambassador sent back not too long after arriving. Such despatches are, as Sir John Russell put it, 'an essentially subjective account of how the country first strikes the writer'. In the 1960s Russell was himself a writer of brilliant if rather wordy despatches – among his FCO contemporaries we might call him the Tolstoy of the telegram age.

The best First Impressions have much in common with the best travel-writing. These despatches were sent, by custom, after about three months in a new post. That was thought long enough for the ambassador to have taken a good look and formed an initial opinion of the principal personalities – but not so long that by the time pen was set to paper the authenticity of the first response would have faded, to be replaced by less intuitive judgement.

Unlike the now-banned valedictory, First Impressions despatches are still sent today. In fact, I understand that they thrive, not least because the current Foreign Secretary, William Hague, apparently has an appetite for frank diplomatic reporting in considered prose rather than just sofa-based remark. (Mr Hague told me in 2011 that on becoming Foreign Secretary he had inquired whether the ban of valedictories could be lifted, and the missive perhaps be given better protection, where appropriate, against exposure. The answer had been that it could not.)

Where the valedictory despatch was the parting shot, an ambassador's first despatch was his opening salvo: a chance to set the agenda, to set the parameters of his post, to define what success and failure would look like in the context of his new posting and before embarking on his work; an opportunity to put his stamp on the role before others did it for him.

'I had better write this now' is a sentiment frequently expressed in these despatches, the author concerned his

First Impressions might become considered or second thoughts unless he commits them quickly to paper. It's a sentiment that implies (I think usefully) that lack of experience, lack of familiarity, has a value all in itself: a fresh pair of eyes on the problem. Today's business argot has a term for people like this: 'valuable virgins'.

Not all First Impressions are of value for their naivety, however. Some of the country studies in this collection are astonishingly considered and knowledgeable – read, for example, Sir John Pilcher's erudite despatch from Tokyo on pp. 159–69.

Revealingly, ambassadors often seem to try to get the measure of their new post by comparing it to the post from which they've just shipped out. The FCO likes to be even-handed in the way it distributes assignments: everyone takes a turn and everyone gets their share of both tough and cushy posts; so a couple of years listening to gunfire outside the residency in Freetown might earn you some time in tranquil Luxembourg for your next post. And vice versa. 'After pacifist, neutral, affluent, Socialist, birth-controlled Sweden,' writes Ian MacKenzie (p. 173), 'Korea presents an extreme contrast. Magpies are about the only thing the two countries have in common'). Maurice Eaden in Karachi (pp. 321–3) finds surprising parallels between war-torn Pakistan and sleepy Belgium.

More than any other diplomatic missives, except perhaps valedictories, First Impressions stand a decent chance of reaching the desks of ministers. But their authors know how little time politicians have to spare and how many other reports and priorities their despatch competes with in the minister's red box. So they deploy descriptive colour as a device, like a peacock's tail, to draw the audience in.

The reader hooked, the despatch then invariably moves on to matters more profound, grown-up – and, all too often, dull. For the benefit of our readers, in researching and editing these despatches we have tried to excise the seriously boring bits while keeping the bait. Many entries are in fact short extracts from within despatches, as opposed to abridged versions. The very best writers here, however, managed to make even their serious writing a pleasure to read – and plenty of these make their way into the book. We've given the longer entries due prominence by including the letter-headings as they appeared in the original despatch, but we've omitted these from the shorter entries. Further inconsistencies in the way despatches appear on the page stem from periodic advances in the communications technology ambassadors used to write them (among which email stands out as a particularly retrograde step, aesthetically speaking).

Finally it's worth noting that, as he or she drafts a First Impressions despatch, a new ambassador knows there's a good chance reactions will be read with an open mind: by senior colleagues and perhaps ministers keen to see what the new ambassador makes of a posting, and whether they seem to be shaping up to the task. Once an ambassador gets a reputation – as being anti- or pro-French, for instance, labels which both have been pinned frequently on British ambassadors in Paris over the years – they know that that reputation will become a prism through which their subsequent analysis will be interpreted. So they try hard to make their first unclouded effort hit the target. And, as you will see, it shows.

~

'Envoi' was a term of art in diplomatic prose. In poetry an envoi is a short stanza at the end used either to address the reader or to comment on the preceding verses. In valedictory despatches some ambassadors would confine their outspokenness to this final section, having devoted the remainder to more serious, immediate and matter-of-fact commentary on policy issues relating to the post they were departing. Then, finally, they would (variously) let fly, shed a metaphorical tear, shake a wise head or try to sum up what it had all meant to him or her. It's an opportunity, too, for ambassadors to give their successors some useful advice: at its best a distillation of wisdom acquired in post; and at any rate a few helpful hints on the obvious pitfalls; whom and what to cultivate; and whom and what to avoid.

In *Parting Shots* we may have deluded ourselves that we had all but exhausted the FCO's treasury of valedictory despatches. Not so. More were recommended to us and Andrew Bryson's further searches through both the National Archives and Freedom of Information uncovered some nuggets. Not all confined their un-pulled punches to a few paragraphs of Envoi at the end.

From Stockholm our outgoing ambassador, Sir Jeffrey Petersen, drew a portrait of 1980's Sweden as 'a leisured, antiseptic society' (p. 352). Writing in the same year our man in Oslo, Sir Archie Lamb, had plainly hated Norway (pp. 355–6). Cambodia (concluded Sir Leslie Fielding, in a marvellous phrase in 1966) was 'more of a retinal sensation than a coherent picture' (p. 362). Baroness Park, leaving Hanoi in 1970 as Consul-General (she was actually a very senior spy), observed that to Vietnamese Communists, 'some pigs [are] more equal than others' (p. 373).

Our final despatch is from the Vatican. Geoffrey Crossley, departing both the Holy See as HM Envoy Extraordinary in 1980, and a lifetime's career as a diplomat, tries to sum it all up.

He does so, as do almost all the diplomats whose essays follow, better than I can. So without further ado, read on.

Matthew Parris
Derbyshire
September 2012

1. Protocol Department

Oman

'Music itself is regarded by many as sinful'

JOHN PHILLIPS,
CONSUL-GENERAL TO THE SULTANATE OF OMAN,
AUGUST 1960

John Phillips's despatch comes from a long tradition of good-natured moaning in the Diplomatic Service whenever bureaucrats in London issue blanket instructions to overseas missions in disregard of local applicability. Every foreign post, large or small, has to fulfil these edicts, regardless of the endlessly variant local circumstances and no matter how trivial the need.

The Foreign Office wrote to Phillips in Oman following a request from the Admiralty Office. Clerks there were conducting an audit of sheet music for the 200 or so different national anthems played by Royal Navy ships when visiting friendly ports. The stock check was instigated after a band aboard a ship accidentally played the wrong national anthem, causing the Foreign and Commonwealth Office (FCO) embarrassment.

Oman, with its deep harbour and friendly sheikhs, was strategically important to Britain's interests in the Persian Gulf. But it was hardly in the top league of diplomatic posts. It was therefore to no one's surprise that when Admiralty officials delved in their files in search of the score to the National Salute to the Sultan of Muscat and Oman, they returned almost empty-handed. The clerks could lay their hands on only one version, transcribed for a wind instrument. The Foreign Office duly sent the sheet music to the Consul-General in Oman, telling him to turn musical detective and verify it.

Six weeks later Phillips sent the following despatch back to the Foreign Secretary and instantly entered FCO folklore.

At first glance the account given in the despatch reads like that of a subordinate dutifully fulfilling orders. But on closer inspection the Consul-General is actually blowing a raspberry to his faraway taskmasters, mocking at every turn the Whitehall tendency to centralize and standardize. Phillips put into the diplomatic bag bound for London along with his despatch a broken gramophone record with a recording – could it but be played – of the National Salute.

The despatch may be short but it was no rush job. According to one retired diplomat, Oliver Miles, Phillips's registry clerk 'sealed and unsealed that damn bag' as many as four times 'so that the Consul-General could change a comma' in the despatch, and make other last-minute tweaks. Phillips was quite right to do so, says Miles, 'because it made his career'.

The despatch leaked, and found its way into Time magazine on 14 November 1960 under the headline 'Sultan's Salute'. There was a leak inquiry (conducted with more urgency than usual – the Sultan himself was known to read Time), which never found the culprit.

Time's story concluded: 'The Foreign Office had no comment, but a Navy man said admiringly: "They do write good letters down in Muscat." '

L 1752/2 *Foreign Office and Whitehall Distribution*

MIDDLE EAST (GENERAL)
September 1st, 1960

NATIONAL SALUTE TO THE SULTAN OF MUSCAT AND OMAN

Mr Phillips to Lord Home (Received September 1st)

SUMMARY

Difficulty in verifying a B♭ clarinet score in a country where none can read music and music itself is regarded by many as sinful.

(NO. 10. CONFIDENTIAL) *Oman,*
August 17, 1960.

My Lord,

I have the honour to refer to Your Lordship's despatch No. 8 of the 29th July, in which you requested me to ascertain, on behalf of the Lords Commissioners of the Admiralty, whether the B♭ clarinet music, enclosed with your despatch, was a correct and up to date rendering of the National Salute to the Sultan of Muscat and Oman.

I have encountered certain difficulties in fulfilling this request. The Sultanate has not since about 1937 possessed a band. None of the Sultan's subjects, so far as I am aware can read music, which the majority of them regard as sinful. The Manager of the British Bank of the Middle East, who can, does not possess a clarinet. Even if he did, the dignitary who in the absence of the Sultan is the recipient of ceremonial honours and who might be presumed to recognize the tune, is somewhat deaf.

Fortunately I have been able to obtain, and now enclose, a gramophone record which has on one side a rendering by a British military band of the 'Salutation and March to His Highness the Sultan of Muscat and Oman'. The first part of this tune, which was composed by the Bandmaster of a cruiser in about 1932, bears close resemblance to a pianoforte rendering by the Bank Manager of the clarinet music enclosed with Your Lordship's despatch. The only further testimony I can obtain of the correctness of this music is that it reminds a resident of long standing of a tune, once played by the long defunct band of the now disbanded Muscat Infantry, and known at the time to non-commissioned members of His Majesty's forces as (I quote the vernacular) 'Gawd strike the Sultan Blind'.

I am informed by the Acting Minister of Foreign Affairs that there are now no occasions on which the 'Salutation' is officially played. The last occasion on which it is known to have been played at all was on a gramophone at an evening reception given by the Military Secretary in honour of the Sultan, who inadvertently sat on the record afterwards and broke it. I consider however that an occasion might arise when the playing might be appropriate; if for example, the Sultan were to go aboard a cruiser which carried a band. I am proposing to call on His Highness shortly at Salalah on his return from London, and shall make further enquiries as to his wishes on the matter.

I am sending a copy of this despatch, without enclosure to His Excellency the Political Resident at Bahrain.

I have the honour to be Sir,
J. F. S. PHILLIPS

~

Chad

'Our Man In Chad Isn't'

JOHN WILSON, HM AMBASSADOR TO THE REPUBLIC
OF CHAD, SEPTEMBER 1970

This despatch marks the moment British diplomacy conjured up a curious and fleeting paradox: John Wilson's appointment as Britain's first London-based ambassador.

Long ago the Diplomatic Service, which was comprised of ambassadors and other diplomats living overseas, was entirely distinct from the Foreign Office, staffed by Whitehall mandarins. The joke that a fully fledged ambassador could operate day to day from London, thousands of miles from the people to whom he was supposed to be representing HMG, would clearly have struck the FCO's funny bone.

As Wilson realized, the novelty of his predicament was a product of the jet age. The FCO has long rotated its diplomats between posts overseas and spells at home in Whitehall, and nowadays of course senior diplomats and ministers would think nothing of jumping on a plane for a whistlestop tour to negotiate with their foreign counterparts. The Foreign Office has repeated Wilson's experiment since, but only infrequently, and the London-based ambassador remains a rare breed today. When representing their country, the FCO still expects its honest men (and women) to lie abroad.

John Wilson went on eventually to become High Commissioner to Canada, by which time he had succeeded his father to the barony as Lord Moran. He acquired during his career a reputation for amused candour. His 1984 valedictory, featured in our first volume of despatches (noting the parochialism of Ottawa politics, and the absence, as Wilson saw it, of a 'ferocious competition of talent' in Canada) caused some controversy there when we published it.

CONFIDENTIAL

FOREIGN AND COMMONWEALTH OFFICE
DIPLOMATIC REPORT NO. 424/70

JWD 25/1   *General Distribution*

CHAD
3 September, 1970

APPOINTMENT OF HER MAJESTY'S FIRST
LONDON-BASED AMBASSADOR, AND THE
PRESENTATION OF HIS LETTERS OF
CREDENCE TO PRESIDENT TOMBALBAYE

The British Ambassador in Chad to the Secretary of State for Foreign and Commonwealth Affairs (Received 3 September)

British Embassy to Chad,
c/o Foreign and
Commonwealth Office,
6 August, 1970.

Sir,

Last Monday, as usual, I was at work in the Foreign and Commonwealth Office. But on Tuesday I flew to Fort Lamy in Chad, 3,000 miles away in the middle of Africa, taking with me hastily prepared credentials, a speech and a morning coat. On Wednesday I called on the Chadian Minister of Foreign Affairs, the chief foreign representatives in Fort Lamy and the United Nations representative. On Thursday morning I presented my credentials to President Tombalbaye and, just over an hour later, flew back to Europe. On Friday I was again at my desk in the office.

This curious exercise in instant diplomacy was the outcome of a decision that, for the first time, the Head of a Political Department in the office should be appointed additionally as Ambassador to one of the countries for which his Department was responsible. Her Majesty's late Ambassador in Yaoundé covered five African countries – Cameroon, where he resided, and, as non-resident Ambassador, Gabon, Equatorial Guinea, Chad and the Central African Republic. Mr Edden told the Department that he thought that these five countries were too many for one Ambassador to cover adequately ... [He] suggested that, in default of any better arrangement, the Head of the West African Department might be proposed as non-resident Ambassador based in London ... [T]he Government of Chad promptly agreed and proposed that the arrangement should come into force without delay.

To me therefore fell the honour and privilege of being the first member of the Diplomatic Service to be appointed as one (albeit certainly the least) of Her Majesty's Ambassadors while continuing to serve as Head of a Department in the Foreign and Commonwealth Office. This is an experiment and, as such, it has taken most people by surprise. It is a new departure, reported by one newspaper under the appropriate headline, 'Our Man In Chad Isn't'. It is too soon to say whether the arrangement is a practicable, sensible and economical one, but I shall do my best to make it so.

In the notes I recorded after a visit to West Africa in February 1969 I stressed the constant need to remember the prodigious gulf between European theory and African reality. Nowhere is this gulf wider than in Chad. We, for example, work by the clock. For Africans life is timeless and haste is unknown. I arrived last Tuesday in response to a summons from the Chadian Government, who had asked me at very short notice to present my credentials between 15 and 30 July and had agreed to the proposal that I should do so on 29 July. I rashly assumed that I should be given on arrival a programme of calls and a firm appointment at the palace. I was indeed met by the Chief of Protocol, but it soon emerged that he had made no plans at all, and that we had to start from scratch. A great deal of tactful prodding of Chadian bureaucrats was therefore called for . . .

Next morning I saw the Minister for Foreign Affairs, M. Baroum, who was on holiday but came into the office specially to receive me. I was told later by the German Ambassador that M. Baroum nurses racial anti-white prejudices, but I must say that he received me with great cordiality and that we had an agreeable conversation. Most of the rest of the day I spent seeing other people in Fort

Lamy ... By the evening, however, we were still without news of any appointment with the President. I was told by my new colleagues that I might be summoned at five minutes' notice or alternatively that I might have to wait for several weeks, a prospect that filled me with alarm. More prodding took place, but the lamp of hope burnt low. That night, however, a message came that I was to present my credentials at 10 a.m. next day and I retired to bed in a mood of unreasoning euphoria.

On Thursday morning the timing began to slip. The Chief of Protocol rang to say that the time was now to be 10.30 and that he would fetch me at 10.15 or 10.20. A motor cycle escort arrived, the commander of which came up to my room and asked if I could tell him where we were going. I said I thought the President's Palace, but that it was scarcely for me to say. At 10.15 I was on the steps of my hotel in a morning coat. 10.20 passed, then 10.30. No car appeared. The motor cycle escort departed. Time passed. A herd of long-horned cattle were driven by. It began to rain. The little group on the hotel steps settled down into a torpid state. 10.40, 10.45 passed. My return flight was at 12.35. I surrendered to a feeling of despair. The words of the old song came back to me:

'There was I, waiting at the church,
. . . left me in the lurch.'[1]

There was no more we could do. The rain had stopped, but Africa, and Chad, seemed to have won.

Then, astonishingly, the escort reappeared, with a car bringing the Chief of Protocol, who explained the delay as due to the shower. Proudly the chauffeur pressed a button and the car roof opened. My flag (which, luckily, I had remembered to bring out from London) was fixed to the wing, and we set out. All seemed splendid again. Being driven slowly through the streets of Fort Lamy, past the acacias and oleanders, escorted by motor cycles, with even French officers having to salute and a cheer going up from some Nigerian students at sight of the British flag, I again thought that our troubles were at an end. But optimism is always premature in Africa. At that point the heavens opened in a cloudburst worthy of the tropics. The rain descended in a solid sheet. The chauffeur prodded a button, but the roof refused to close again. The Chief of Protocol wrung his hands and exclaimed 'O là là' any number of times. Through the deluge I sought to assure him that he must think nothing of it and that, as an Englishman, I was entirely used to wettings.

I arrived therefore at the palace, through a double line of guards in red and blue with drawn sabres, in the condition of a sponge, with a steaming morning coat, a smell of wet serge, and water running off both elbows. The Chief of Protocol made ineffectual attempts to dry me with a handkerchief. So I advanced and delivered my speech under the klieg lights while the cameras whirred. President Tombalbaye stood motionless with a rigid and forbidding expression on his face. I thought at the time that he was seeking to make an impression of dignity, strength and independence, but on reflection I think he was probably determined not to be the first to burst out laughing at the spectacle of this bedraggled Ambassador emerging like a newt from the waters and proceeding to declaim a formal address. He replied to my speech in very much the same terms as my own – indeed I thought I recognised some phrases out of mine, conveniently appropriated, no doubt, by those who had had to draft the reply. I then handed him my credentials and Mr Edden's letter of recall.

Afterwards I had a conversation with the President, who was relaxed and agreeable and seemed to me to be alert, realistic and shrewd ... He spoke of the administrative reforms being instituted in the country (by the French) and of the importance of trained administrators. Speaking with some feeling, he said that the situation was altogether different in the former British colonies in Africa. Britain had really trained their peoples for independence, whereas 'we', he observed, 'started from zero' ...

So, after photographs, I departed, driving to the airport in my sodden morning coat and, I imagine, leaving behind a damp patch on the President's sofa.

I came away with an impression of friendliness and goodwill, of a desperately poor country with some of the world's highest prices, on the border between the desert and the rain forest, still dominated by French soldiers, French administrators and rapacious French businessmen – 'the last French colony', as the United Nations Representative called it. The French have sadly neglected it for the 70 years they have run it since they defeated and slew the Sultan of Bornu and cut the country off from Nigeria, despite its romantic associations for them with Generals de Gaulle and Leclerc.[2] When the French Chargé d'Affaires was describing to me the great effort France was making in the administrative field, with 600 experts in the country, I wondered what the French had been doing since 1900 and why it was necessary to mount a crash programme now ...

I am sending copies of this despatch to Her Majesty's Representatives at West African posts, in Libya, the Sudan and Ethiopia, to the Chargé d'Affaires at Her Majesty's Embassy in Paris, to Her Majesty's Ambassador in Washington and to the Permanent Representative to the United Nations in New York.

I have, etc.,
JOHN WILSON.

1. *There was I . . . in the lurch*: A music-hall favourite popularized by the singer Vesta Victoria (1873–1951). 'Waiting at the Church' was also sung in 1978 at a TUC conference by the Prime Minister, Jim Callaghan, to convey that there wouldn't be a general election that year.
2. *Generals de Gaulle and Leclerc*: In 1940, while Marshal Pétain was collaborating with the Nazis, Chad became the first French colony to declare its support for Charles de Gaulle's Free France. Under General Leclerc, Chadian and French troops fought Italian soldiers in Libya before marching 1,500 miles to join Montgomery in Tripoli. Chadian soldiers also won distinction in European theatres of war; in 1945 the Régiment de Marche du Tchad were among the Allied troops who captured Hitler's Berghof at Berchtesgaden, a mountain hideaway where the Nazi leader spent much of the war.

∾

Russia

'We all feel like that, Reggie, now and then'

SIR ARCHIBALD CLARK KERR, HM AMBASSADOR TO THE
SOVIET UNION, APRIL 1943

A hoary old favourite in Whitehall and Westminster, but not every reader will have encountered this unashamedly vulgar document. In recent years, Sir Archibald Clark Kerr's marvellous one-pager from Moscow to his friend Lord Pembroke in Whitehall has gained considerable currency, not to say notoriety, on the internet. It first came to light long before that, having been published in 1978 in the Spectator and in the Far Eastern Economic Review. Though often suspected to be the FCO's equivalent of an urban myth, it's almost certainly genuine. Donald Gillies, the ambassador's biographer, attests to its existence.

The central character in the despatch appears elsewhere, too, in Clark Kerr's private papers. Douglas Stuart, a former BBC correspondent in Austria, still has the great man's actual calling card (embossed 'Secretaire de l'Ambassade de Turquie'), which had been left at the British Embassy. 'On my return to Vienna,' he wrote, 'my wife put [it] in our scrapbook with a simple paper covering on which she wrote, "For Adults Only". This was intended to warn off our children. It didn't.'

Clark Kerr had the distinction of serving as ambassador to three global powers: China, Russia and, lastly, America; and was raised to the peerage in 1946 as Baron Inverchapel. In the USSR during the darkest days of the Second World War he formed a firm friendship with Stalin. Clark Kerr recalled his chats with the Soviet leader as the chief 'delight' of his time in Moscow.

LORD PEMBROKE,
FOREIGN OFFICE,
LONDON

6 April 1943

My Dear Reggie,

In these dark days man tends to look for little shafts of light that spill from heaven. My days are probably darker than yours, and I need, my God I do, all the light I can get. But I am a decent fellow, and I do not want to be mean and selfish about what little brightness is shed upon me from time to time. So I propose to share with you a tiny flash that has illuminated my sombre life and tell you that God has given me a new Turkish colleague whose card tells me that he is called Mustafa Kunt.

We all feel like that, Reggie, now and then, especially when spring is upon us, but few of us would care to put it on our cards. It takes a Turk to do that.

Archibald Clark Kerr

⁓

'The next time we want to import a horse to Russia it will be a doddle'

LAURA BRADY, THIRD SECRETARY AT HM EMBASSY
MOSCOW, OCTOBER 1993

In October 1993 the main event in Moscow was a bloody constitutional crisis that culminated in tanks shelling the Russian White House. The stand-off between parliament and Boris Yeltsin's troops demanded the full attention of most foreign diplomats in Moscow.

Laura Brady, a junior diplomat in the British Embassy in Moscow, had a different problem to deal with. It involved some large melons, the Moscow railway – and an unusual fiftieth-birthday present given to John Major by the President of Turkmenistan, a newly de-Sovietized state on the periphery of what had until recently been the USSR.

On an official visit to London earlier that year, President Niyazov presented Mr Major with a framed photograph of a horse called Maksat. Turkmenistan was justly proud of its wonderful Akhal-Teke stallions, and Niyazov was fond of making gifts of them to foreign leaders. Diplomatic correspondents on newspapers inevitably dubbed the practice 'equine diplomacy', after China and its globetrotting panda-envoys.

That evening Major took the book with him to his audience at Buckingham Palace. The Queen told him Turkmen stallions were much prized as breeding stock, and that she herself had been given one some years before. A single Akhal-Teke was worth £30,000. The Prime Minister was persuaded not to look a gift horse in the mouth, so to speak – although protocol meant he could hardly have refused such a present, anyway.

But the horse was still in Turkmenistan and the only route out was through Russia. The Foreign Office soon established that the French Ministry of Foreign Affairs shared their predicament, because President Mitterrand had also been offered a stallion. An Anglo-French plan was hatched. The two horses were to be sent with local grooms by train to Moscow. On arrival the Third Secretary at the British Embassy was to meet them, in liaison with the French horse attaché. Once in Moscow the horses were to enter quarantine before their eventual transit to the UK and France. A stable was waiting for Maksat in the Household Cavalry.

Laura Brady therefore spent this crucial juncture in modern history battling with the bottom rung of Russian bureaucracy in order to take successful delivery of a pair of thoroughbreds. Several days' train travel across the vastness of the rapidly crumbling Soviet empire had done little to improve the temper of the two Akhal-Teke, a notoriously skittish breed. Brady, however, had simply to take care of the customs and excise formalities. What could possibly go wrong?

A copy of the telegram Brady wrote at the end of her resulting ordeal was released to us in response to our FOI request in 2011. It is a testament to the effectiveness of the Freedom of Information process, and to the rectitude with which it is applied at the Foreign Office that this wonderful and still quite recent telegram was released to us with only the most minor amendments – identifying marks and names, shown here as redactions. We know, because we do in fact have a complete copy of the original document, obtained by other means. We shall, however, observe the FCO's redactions.

In 1993, Brady's telegram was circulated around Whitehall and read with pleasure – not least by John Major, who sent a personal reply congratulating her on her resourcefulness. Brady's account is evidence if evidence were needed of the difficult and unglamorous nature of much of the work of junior Foreign Office staff abroad – contrary to the stereotype.

Eventually the horse did reach Britain. A military career was not to be, however. After a short trial the Household

Cavalry found him too frisky for ceremonial work – which worked out quite well for the stallion, who was put out to stud at an equestrian centre in Wales. Since then his excellent genes have also won him sporting laurels: he is a champion endurance racer, the Turkmeni record holder over one and one and a half miles on the flat, and a British show champion. Maksat still lives happily in Carmarthenshire as we write.

HORSES: THE DEFINITIVE END OF AN ERA

As I reported to you on the telephone today, the Turkmen horses have arrived in Moscow. They are now in the quarantine stables, no doubt reliving the excitement of the last week. The last few hours leading up to this momentous event are as follows.

On Tuesday morning I got an excited phonecall from [REDACTED] of the Russian Horse Society (RHS). He had found the horses' carriage. The reason he had not been able to find it the day before was because the carriage hadn't been there. The Turkmens had got the day wrong and the train had only arrived on Monday night, not Sunday night. [REDACTED] said that the Railway Authority's vet had already inspected the horses and passed them as fit. We were now free to begin the customs formalities. We phoned the [REDACTED] Diplomatic Customs Post in northern Moscow and were given an appointment for one o'clock.

At one o'clock we presented ourselves at the customs office. Apart from two mangy dogs and a receptionist the place was deserted. The receptionist told us that it was lunch time. We should return at three o'clock. We explained our mission, pleading the case of two poor Turkmen horses that had been standing up in a railway carriage for four and a half days. This elicited in response the sad tale of the Finnish ambassador's parrot, the only other living thing that had fallen in to the hands of the [REDACTED] Diplomatic Customs Post during her memory. The receptionist, an animal lover and close to tears at the thought of the parrot, relented and led us through a maze of ceiling-high packing cases in the enormous warehouse. And there we found the staff of the [REDACTED] diplomatic customs post playing poker.

Fifteen dollars poorer but with the customs formalities completed we hotfooted it to the station accounts office in south Moscow, arriving there at 16.45. We presented the vet's certificate of fitness and our stamped customs declaration. We were told that staff had stopped work to get ready to go home at 17.00. Nothing could be done until the following day. We again trotted out the pitiful story of the horses. The soft-hearted and enormously fat clerk relented. But after one glance at the papers on her desk and a quick twiddle on the office abacus she announced that we owed the Russian Railway Authority eight and a half million roubles. We explained that the Turkmens had paid for the transport in advance. She replied that they had added up the figures wrongly and we had to pay the balance. We pointed out that the Turkmens had provided their own railway carriage for the journey. They did not want the carriage back. Could we not come to some arrangement? After some deliberation her boss finally agreed. But now it was after five o'clock. We would have to return the next day.

At 08.30 Wednesday morning we were all back at the accounts office. Could we now have the bit of paper that would allow us to drive out of the freight yard with the horses? In principle, yes, said the fat clerk. In practice, however, no. As the horses had been at the station for 24 hours they would have to be seen again by the vet. The vet was in her office adding-up extremely slowly a long list of figures on a calculator with dodgy batteries. The numbers kept fading, at which point she began again at the top of the list. We waited an hour. The vet then pushed across the table a signed declaration saying that she had inspected the horses again and that they were fit. All without leaving her desk. For this we paid precisely R7,614.

At 10.00 we got to the station itself. Within 20 minutes we had the horses loaded into the horse-box. I thought that we were ready to go. But out of the railway carriage the three grooms, who had travelled with the horses, began to carry countless sacks of potatoes, onions, carrots and at least 200 large yellow melons. One groom explained that as Turkmenistan had no post 1992 banknotes they were forced to bring wares to sell in Moscow to be able to buy the return ticket to Ashkhabad. The groom also told me how they had lost some of the melons when armed bandits had broken into their carriage at a rural station in Kazakhstan. The bandits had been disappointed to find no cash at all amongst the three grooms. The main cargo (the horses) had been unwilling to dismount from the train and make off into the Kazakh darkness. So the robbers had made off with as many of the legendary Turkmen melons as they could carry.

As the last few sacks of vegetables were loaded alongside the horses we made our way to the office of the head of the freight department of the station to get the document allowing us to leave the station with our 'freight'. He told us that we had to return to the accounts department to arrange for a sticker to be stuck on the carriage saying that the freight had been removed and that the carriage was ready for disinfection. We trooped back to the accounts department. It was 11.40. Predictably they were again packing up their papers in order to begin the lunch break on the dot of 12.00. We found the fat clerk who abandoned the woman she was dealing with (giving as explanation the same pitiful story of how long the horses had been standing up that we had given her the day before). We paid R5,084, for which we received a little old lady armed with the aforementioned sticker. We accompanied her back to the railway carriage. She took one look inside and screeched that she was not going to stick her sticker on such a dirty carriage full of horse manure. We would have to remove it. And no, we were not allowed to put it in the station dustbins. She stomped back to the accounts department. By this time the French horse attaché was getting hysterical.

I contemplated putting the manure in the boot of my car and taking it back for the roses at the residence. But we didn't have a spade, and the amount of manure produced by two highly-strung horses over a period of five days is considerable. Luckily the melons again came to the rescue. Bribed with several particularly large ones the driver of an engine was persuaded to shunt the carriage a couple of miles down the track where the offending material was unceremoniously scraped out on to the track. The carriage was returned to the freight yard, the sticker was stuck and we were allowed to leave the station. The horses are now installed in the quarantine stables. The e.t.a. in London will thus be early January.

On an administrative note, the breed papers for our horse, Melekoosh,[1] were apparently presented to the Prime Minister by President Niyazov[2] himself. Before Melekoosh

leaves Moscow they will have to be sent here so t̶
can be incorporated into his 'passport'. I took photog̶
throughout the day and will forward to you copies fo̶
household cavalry. I will be in touch about any oth̶
points that arise. I have made some useful contacts over
the last few days so the next time we want to import a
horse to Russia it will be a doddle.

SIGNED . . . [REDACTED]

1. *Melekoosh*: John Major's horse was actually called Maksat. The name
Melekoosh on the breed papers denoted the stallion that sired him.
2. *President Niyazov*: A brutal and vainglorious dictator, Saparmurat Niyazov, ruled Turkmenistan from 1991 until his death in 2006.
He renamed the months of the year after members of his family and
national heroes. One statue of the President, twelve metres tall and gold-
plated, rotated every twenty-four hours so as to always face the sun.

∾

Ethiopia

*'Flunkeys in red, orange and green livery, gilded state
coaches, and champagne'*

WILLIE MORRIS, HM AMBASSADOR TO ETHIOPIA,
NOVEMBER 1972

*Nowadays the name Haile Selassie is pronounced most
often by men in dreadlocks. In the 1930s, Jamaican follow-
ers of the Rastafari sect settled on the belief that the
Emperor of Ethiopia, a country 7,000 miles away, was the
Second Coming incarnate. The die was cast. When in 1966
he visited Jamaica he was greeted at the airport by some*

100,000 members of the sect hailing him as the reborn Jesus, a title which, despite the pleas of the Jamaican government, he never abjured.

An other-worldly quality never seemed far from the imperial throne. Sir John Russell, one of Willie Morris's predecessors who served in Addis Ababa from 1962 to 1966, described Ethiopia as: 'a country which has two hundred thousand and fifty priests and thirty one doctors, the priests teaching a doctrine that the earth is flat and who are about to worship St Pontius Pilate's day'.

In 1972, when Morris arrived in Addis, Haile Selassie was well into his fourth decade on the throne. It is no surprise that the ambassador found the atmosphere there strange. A reading of Evelyn Waugh's Black Mischief (1932) had primed him to expect a touch of the ridiculous, too. A satire on Ethiopia, the novel sees Emperor Seth of Azania bent on dragging his country up by its bootstraps with a Ministry of Modernization.

Willie Morris is no Waugh but his subject was without modern parallel. This is a rambling despatch, going frequently off at a tangent to reminisce on other bizarre episodes in Morris's and others' careers, as well as comparisons with Waugh. Back in Whitehall, the Third Room will have found the writing self-indulgent; but nobody will have committed the thought to paper.

'No doubt modernisation will in the end do away with the Evelyn Waugh aspects of the country,' wrote Simon Dawbarn from the Foreign Office in London back to Morris, after reading the despatch. 'But this seems bound to take a very long time, and in the meanwhile it is nice to know that not too much has changed.'

Dawbarn and Morris were not to know, but when Morris presented his credentials to Haile Selassie in 1972, *the Emperor's reign had less than two years left to run. He was deposed by a Soviet-backed junta called the 'Derg' led by Mengistu Haile Mariam, who turned Waugh's Azania into a one-party Communist state of an exceptionally brutal kind. King Faisal of Saudi Arabia, another redoubtable monarch who features in the despatch, was assassinated the following year. This despatch deserves reading not only for its exoticism but also – in retrospect – for its melancholy.*

CONFIDENTIAL

BRITISH EMBASSY,
ADDIS ABABA,
25/56   9 November 1972.

The Right Honourable
Sir Alec Douglas-Home KT MP
etc etc etc

Sir,

ON ARRIVING IN ETHIOPIA

I have the honour to report that, in accordance with the instructions in your despatch of 11 October 1972, I delivered to the Emperor on 1 November the Letters addressed to Him by Her Majesty The Queen accrediting me as Her Majesty's Ambassador Extraordinary and Plenipotentiary at Addis Ababa and announcing the recall of my predecessor. My arrival had been timed with the hope that I would be able to attend the Coronation Day celebrations and the Opening of Parliament on 2 November; I was therefore in the nick of time . . . My first three days of official existence in Ethiopia were therefore quite busy, and, given the Ethiopian Government's penchant for dressing up, I felt by the end of them that I could have profited from a short training course with Danny la Rue in the art of quick costume changes: my uniform and white tie have already been worn as much here as during the previous twenty years in the less dressy places to which I have been accustomed.

The credentials ceremony was 'as described by my predecessor' (that <u>leitmotif</u> of reporting on Ethiopia). It was punctual and dignified. I was fetched to the Palace by the Vice Minister of Court and, having inspected a smartly turned-out Guard of Honour, I was presented, after three ceremonial bows, to the Emperor by the Minister of Court. After presenting my Letters, I was introduced to the Minister for Foreign Affairs and the Minister of the Interior, and in turn I presented four members of my staff to the Emperor. I was then invited to sit and had ten minutes of friendly but very formal conversation . . .

In new surroundings one instinctively gropes for the familiar with which to make comparisons and draw contrasts; in my case the comparisons have to be with Saudi Arabia, my last post, and with the Ethiopia I have previously known – that of Evelyn Waugh. Though King Feisal is ten years younger than Haile Selassie, he is visibly ageing, and the Emperor's features are less ravaged than his. The Emperor's are certainly those of an old man, yet they are not all that different from the pictures which were so familiar when those of my generation were first becoming aware of international affairs 37 years ago. Both rulers have great presence and dignity, but the Emperor gives the impression of a serenity and repose which are absent in the great Saudi worrier. (I mean 'worrier'.) I think this impression may be deceptive, when I recollect that, while Feisal was sowing his wild oats, and even before, Ras Tafari was with craft and ruthless energy already establishing control of his ramshackle empire; that in his eighth decade he has established himself so improbably as doyen among the present generation of African leaders, and that in his own country even yet no dog barks in his presence.

When it comes to ceremony, the contrast between Wahhabi puritanism and this court of flunkeys in red, orange and green livery, gilded state coaches, and champagne, could not be more complete. King Feisal, when I presented my credentials to him, wore a double breasted jacket over his <u>thob</u>. It is the incongruity between the ceremony, based on nineteenth century European courts, and the Afro-Ethiopian milieu that brings Evelyn Waugh to mind. It was a Waugh touch that when the Emperor seated himself between President and Mrs Tolbert[1] at the Opening of Parliament last week, he waited in dignified silence for fifteen minutes while someone went to fetch the gracious speech which everyone had forgotten to bring along. On the occasion of that coronation 42 years ago, the visiting Royal Marine band drank champagne for breakfast, luncheon, tea and dinner all the way from Djibouti. I note that it is still served almost as regularly on all royal occasions. And at the actual Coronation ceremony, Waugh noted that 'there was plenty of room for all, except, as it happened, for the Abyssinians themselves'. As, sandwiched between the cars of His Excellency from Reykjavik (Long live Icelandic–Ethiopian friendship!) and Her Excellency from Trinidad and Tobago, one looks through the car window at the mixed racial features and variegated dress of the

Ethiopians in the street (some of them earning a few extra cents by carrying pictures of President and Mrs Tolbert, or yesterday, even more improbably, of King Baudouin and Queen Fabiola[2]) then the Ethiopians in the street seem very far removed from the charade in which one is taking part. It must take quite an effort to cross the divide.

Returning to this most beautiful of Embassy compounds, I am also reminded of that fictional predecessor, the Envoy Extraordinary in 'Black Mischief', who took such care to insulate himself from the unpleasantness going on outside its happy life. I can now see his temptation. Perhaps it is as well that there exists one feature of this charming Embassy that I do not immediately take to. By a tradition too hallowed for me to think of breaking it, my predecessors' names and dates are carved and gilded on the grey stone pillars in the front hall, suggesting some graveyard or memorial to the glorious departed. Faced when I come home with this memento mori, I still find myself humming the old A. and M. hymn

'A few more years shall roll
A few more seasons pass . . .'

(Fortunately, it has disappeared from the modern hymn books, and I cannot accurately complete my quotation[3] with the warning of the narrow grave that awaits me, too.)

I have the honour to be

Sir

Your obedient Servant
Willie Morris

1. *President and Mrs Tolbert*: William Tolbert, President of Liberia 1971–80.
2. *King Baudouin and Queen Fabiola*: Baudouin I reigned over Belgium, 1951–93. In the 1870s his great-great-grandfather King Leopold II seized the Congo, an area seventy-six times the size of Belgium, as his personal domain. Millions of Congolese died in the decades that followed through forced labour, shootings and disease. The quite staggering brutality of Belgian colonial rule was hardly likely to have endeared Baudouin to the man on the African street.
3. *complete my quotation*: Dawbarn had someone in the Department ('diligent as ever') look up Morris's lines for him, and the full text was sent back to Addis Ababa: 'Then we shall be with those at rest / Asleep beyond the tomb.'

~

Sierra Leone

'I am now entitled to 10 wives'

PETER PENFOLD, HM HIGH COMMISSIONER TO THE
REPUBLIC OF SIERRA LEONE, JUNE 1998

On the surface this appears to be a cheery tale. The High Commissioner writes of a memorable return to his post in Sierra Leone after a spell in London. But the events surrounding this anecdote were extremely serious. Far from blowing his own trumpet out of vanity, in this despatch Penfold was in fact trying to shore up his reputation against formidable odds.

Penfold addressed his report to his bosses in the West Africa Department in Whitehall, but he also copied it – classified as 'unrestricted', allowing for further distribution – to eleven other diplomatic posts, including Bonn and New York. Penfold's peers and colleagues across the Diplomatic Service could learn that the people of Freetown held him in high esteem.

Though the account is highly readable, some of the humour in this telegram comes across a little forced. This is unsurprising given the nature of the 'Other preoccupations' that had been demanding the High Commissioner's attention, and presence, in London. For the very events that made Penfold a hero on the African street were to ruin his Foreign Office career.

At issue was the markedly proactive role the High Commissioner had played in helping restore democracy in Sierra Leone. In 1997, thugs from the Revolutionary United Front were on the streets hacking people to death. When the democratically elected President Kabbah fled the country, Penfold was at his side, and in the months that followed the High Commissioner worked to return Kabbah back to power.

In doing so Penfold chose to cooperate with Sandline International, a mercenary organization which provided weapons to help the government-in-exile oust the rebels. These were choppy waters for a diplomat, and they proved to be Penfold's undoing. Sierra Leone was subject to a UN arms embargo, which the High Commissioner suddenly found himself accused of contravening.

The subsequent controversy, known as the 'Arms to Africa' affair, provoked an official inquiry. Penfold was back in Freetown by the time Sir Thomas Legg published his report. Legg exonerated the Foreign Secretary, Robin Cook, and his senior officials, while criticizing Penfold. The High Commissioner was blamed for giving Sandline's plans 'a degree of approval which he had no authority to do'. But the episode also highlighted management failures within the FCO, and Tory MPs railed against the 'monstrous injustice' they saw in the report that made Penfold the 'fall guy for everyone else's shortcomings'.

Sierra Leone was a dangerous post, and Penfold was accompanied in his duties there by a team of Close Protection Officers from the Royal Military Police (RMPs). After 1998 the situation in Freetown continued to deteriorate. The following year UN peacekeepers were deployed and eventually British combat troops, who finally defeated the rebels.

Penfold could have expected one more big job in the Diplomatic Service before retirement. Returning to London in 2000, he applied for sixteen posts but did not get any of them, and left the Foreign Office shortly afterwards.

SUBJECT: RETURN OF HIGH COMMISSIONER

I have been asked by the department to send a report about my return to Freetown (c/f FCO teleletter dated 15 June). Other preoccupations have prevented me from doing so until now.

I returned to post on Sunday 14 June . . . We were given clearance to fly direct from Conarky to Hastings airport, on the outskirts of Freetown. We landed around 11 a.m. On arrival we were greeted by representatives of government and the civil societies, accompanied by the Defence Adviser and the Close Protection team. A number of Sierra Leoneans, including members of the S L Women singing, cheering and carrying placards and banners. In a short ceremony in the customs hall of the airport, I was appointed an honorary Paramount Chief by the Paramount Chief of the Western Area, Chief Naimbana. I was presented with a ceremonial suit and hat made from local cloth and a staff of office made of wood and brass, and given the name 'Chief Komrabai Penfold'.

We then drove in cavalcade to Freetown, and along the way there were people, including schoolchildren and various organisations, carrying placards, welcoming my return, praising Britain and the British Government and waving Union Jacks and the Sierra Leone flags. At the PZ roundabout in Freetown, I was transferred to a specially made hammock with a wooden awning painted as a Union Jack. A hammock is the traditional way for Paramount Chiefs to travel. We processed through the streets of Freetown with a throng of cheering and singing Sierra Leoneans, estimated to be several thousands, waving flags and banners, up to the Law Courts Building alongside the Cotton Tree in the centre of Freetown.

After thanking the 4 bearers of the hammock I was carried to the steps of the Law Courts from where a ceremony was arranged in front of the assembled crowds. Speeches were delivered . . . interspersed with prayers and singing . . . In my remarks, partly delivered in Krio, I thanked the people for their warm welcome and for all their support in recent weeks. I told them that I was privileged to accept the appointment of Paramount Chief on behalf of Her Majesty, the British Government and the British people. (I understand that this is the third time that someone from Britain has been appointed a Paramount Chief – The Queen and Prince Philip were appointed during their visit to Sierra Leone in the 70s). I noted that their reception was a clear indication of the gratitude to the British government and people for their role in restoring democracy to Sierra Leone and promised that we would continue to help where we could to develop a peaceful and prosperous democratic society.

I finally reached the residence, where some of the organisers of the rally and members of the local staff joined me for drinks. President Kabbah later telephoned to welcome me back. (He now addresses me as 'Chief!')

My appointment as 'PC Komrabai Penfold' has several implications, on which I may need to seek official advice :-

a) I understand that I am now entitled to 10 wives. I have reported this to my wife, who now also has an official title of 'Yabomposse'. It is her duty to choose them for me. But what is the position over married allowances?

b) The hammock has been presented to me for my official travel, but what is the official mileage rate for travel by hammock? How many porters am I allowed?

c) I am checking about my seat in Parliament alongside my fellow Paramount Chiefs, but as a Chief I am entitled to select a group of tribal hunters, and, under President Kabbah's plans for the recruitment of the new army (on which I will be reporting separately), I will have to select candidates from my Chiefdom. Can I use the Close Protection team for this? . . .

d) The RMPs will be writing to Longmoor[1] to seek advice on the drills for close protection when escorting hammock travelling High Commissioners.

e) The DHC[2] would welcome guidance on substitution pay for Paramounts Chiefs. He will require an extra porterage allowance for the hammock!

PENFOLD

1. *Longmoor*: Training area in Hampshire used by the Royal Military Police Close Protection team.

2. *DHC . . . porterage allowance*: DHC is Deputy High Commissioner. The FCO is famously stingy in the porterage allowances paid to lower ranks for luggage taken abroad.

~

Brazil

'Weary figures in dripping tails and sodden ribbons wandered forlornly under the rain searching for their vanished cars'

SIR JOHN RUSSELL, HM AMBASSADOR TO THE
FEDERATIVE REPUBLIC OF BRAZIL, MARCH 1967

Sir John Russell was famous in the Foreign Office for his witty, florid despatches, brilliantly composed and rather self-indulgent. Below are two fine examples. The first, an account of the inauguration of a new President of Brazil, made Russell's reputation. The second, the better for not being over-worked, is a less formal set of notes written the following month, describing an airborne sight-seeing trip the ambassador endured over the jungles of northern Brazil. This gives a sense of the vastness and variety of the country.

The 1967 inauguration in Brasilia of President Costa e Silva was a state occasion where pageantry and pomp came undone, thanks to disorganization and a downpour. Despite the air of farce, for Whitehall the inauguration was no laughing matter; London had sent a Foreign Office Minister, Lord Chalfont, as Special Representative of the Queen. On both sides national pride was at stake and decorum was important.

The visit was a fiasco. This could have damaged the career prospects of the Ambassador, who was supposed to ensure things went smoothly. Instead, Russell rather cleverly seized the initiative by – instead of slinking embarrassedly away – trumpeting the farce and penning a warts-and-all account of every disaster that befell the delegation on their trip through the Canaries, Rio and Brasilia. Implicitly the reader absorbs the impression that none of this was the Ambassador's fault – which it almost certainly wasn't. In London, the despatch was 'printed' – FCO-speak for a widespread official circulation across Whitehall. In the file a senior clerk notes that Russell's account 'so well brings out the mixture of magnificent achievement and hopeless incompetence of the Brazilian character'.

Having found success with his early efforts from Rio (see also his First Impressions on pp. 179–90), Russell kept on writing funny despatches from Brazil and from Madrid, his next posting – a habit which began to irritate some colleagues: 'increasingly tedious', remarks a diplomat on the receiving end.

CONFIDENTIAL – GUARD

<u>THIS DOCUMENT IS THE PROPERTY OF HER BRITANNIC MAJESTY'S GOVERNMENT</u>

AB 1\2   *Foreign Office and Whitehall Distribution*

BRAZIL
29 March, 1967
Section 1

PRESIDENTIAL INAUGURATION:
BRASILIA 1967

Sir John Russell to Mr Brown. (Received 29 March)

(NO 12. CONFIDENTIAL) *Rio de Janeiro,*
23 March 1967

Sir,

I have the honour to report on the visit paid last week to Brazil by the Minister of State for Foreign Affairs and Lady Chalfont on the occasion of the inauguration of President Costa e Silva.

I hope that the Minister of State feels that the experience was worth the discomfort. Both were startling. But I take consolation from the reflection that it is important to us to have a Minister handling our affairs in London who has seen for himself the extraordinary range in the human endeavour of this country.

If agents of Fidel Castro or some other bitter enemy of the Brazilian regime had taken over the programme, they could not have devised a performance better calculated to discredit Brazilian claims to a place amongst the advanced and efficient countries of the world. The arrangements were chaotic and deplorable. It is indeed hard to reconcile the genius which created the near-miraculous city of Brasilia with the grotesque confusion that attended almost every moment of last week's ceremonies. But in that contradiction of extremes, I am told, lies the charm of Brazil.

Brazil has long been proud of her Foreign Service: it is indeed recognised throughout the world as a well staffed, trained and directed example of its kind. And yet last week it fell flat on its face in the puddles of Brasilia with a splash which has left a sadly tarnished image on the unlucky spectators. Brasilia is the most modern and the best planned city in the world: there is not a traffic light or a right-angle intersection in the whole place: yet on Wednesday night the authorities managed to tie up the Presidential guests in one long, snarling, binding traffic jam. The Brazilians are the most polite and hospitable of people: yet they managed to give their guests the impression that no one was interested in their welcome or their welfare.

The arrival of Lord and Lady Chalfont (accompanied by Mr Paul Buxton of the Foreign Office) was only too true to what turned out to be subsequent form. The British United VC-10 developed engine trouble an hour this side of the Canaries and had to turn back to Las Palmas, where the party waited all day for a relief aircraft. They thus did not get to Rio until nearly midnight on Monday, the 13th of March, instead of breakfast time that day as planned. This unfortunate initial reverse not only meant the loss of all the official engagements arranged for that day, including a large Ministerial lunch party at my house, but also deprived the visitors of any chance of seeing Rio. However, as the city was blanketed all day in tropical rain, they did not really lose much. After a short night here we left the Embassy at 8 o'clock the next morning, Tuesday the 14th, to catch the special aircraft to Brasilia. Here the visitors received their baptism of Brazilian incompetence. Together with 69 other Special Missions, we waited 3 hours and 20 minutes: we waited on the tarmac of the military airport, at a temperature of 90°F. and a humidity of 90 per cent: we waited without chairs, without drinks, without parasols, without information and without apologies. But all things have an end and eventually we took off and had an agreeable flight to Brasilia . . .

The next morning Wednesday, the 15th of March, we started with a pleasant short round of sightseeing: but our troubles soon began. After being waved half way round the city by the traffic police, we eventually ploughed our muddy way on foot into the Congress, where three or four thousand more guests had been invited than the building could possibly accommodate. The space reserved in the gallery had long since been invaded. Eventually we fought our way, elbows and knees, to a position in the gangway at the rear of the floor where, by holding on tightly to the backs of the last row of seats in front of us, we were able more or less to see and hear the ceremony of swearing in the new President and Vice-President.

Emerging buffeted but still buoyant from the Congress, we walked across to the Planalto Palace to witness the handing over of the presidential authority. Here we were herded into a roped-off section at the back of the floor, from where we could neither see nor hear anything that was going on. There was no public address system and the words of the ceremony were lost in the roar of Brazilian conversation all round us. At this point my Swedish colleague left the palace in a rage, and I heard my Norwegian colleague threatening the Chief of Protocol that he would advise the King of Norway to cancel his imminent visit. But tempers were to become more frayed than this before our longest day was out.

At 4.30 that afternoon Lord Chalfont and the delegation took part in a short and reasonably well-organised ceremony at which the Special Missions were presented to the new President. The Minister of State read out the message of greeting from Her Majesty The Queen: also the message from the Government of New Zealand. (The unhappy Special Ambassador of Trinidad and Tobago had not received his credentials but, on my advice, handed over a heavily sealed empty frog-footman envelope, which did just as well.) ... The Americans presented a complicated and hideous silver writing set: the Japanese handed over what looked like a Jack-in-the-box: some other Orientals gave the astonished President a sort of yo-yo ...

After supper we returned to the hotel to struggle into our white ties. And then our troubles really began. My wife and I and Mr and Mrs Sheridan were lucky in that our car only took one hour to cover the four miles from the hotel to the Alvorada Palace where the President was giving his great reception. It was raining heavily, there appeared to be practically no police attempting to control the traffic and the vast avenues so brilliantly designed by the greatest urbanists of our day for the unimpeded flow of practically any number of vehicles were within a few minutes choked with traffic driving every way regardless of direction. Even the President got stuck: and eventually, fought his way through to his own reception an hour late. Lord and Lady Chalfont took two and a half hours to make the journey. It speaks well for their endurance and good humour that they then joined the reception: a large number of delegations simply stayed in their cars and went straight on round and back home. Amongst those who thus cut the party were the Swedes and the Dutch, the French led by the former Gaullist Minister M. Jacquinot, the Pakistanis, and the Americans led by the former Governor Brown of California. But the party was worth seeing, if only for the real beauty of the ladies' dresses. And one could only feel sorry for Dona Yolanda, the wife of the new President, when the unabated rain drowned out the beautiful supper which she had prepared in the Palace gardens. But a child of three could have told her that it was bound to rain.

At this point I felt that patience and good manners risked defeating the wider purposes of diplomacy. I accordingly sought out the Vice-Chief of Protocol and told him in clear and cogent terms that Her Majesty The Queen did not often send Ministers of the Crown to represent her abroad and that, when she did, she assumed that they would be treated with some attention and consideration. Lord Chalfont had now been kicked around (in some instances literally) for 24 hours and I felt that, unless rapid and adequate steps were taken, he would return to London in a mood somewhat less than gruntled. The Vice-Chief took the hint: and a few minutes later Lord and Lady Chalfont were summoned to the Presidential presence . . .

This tattered day was now at last drawing to its tattered close. Weary figures in dripping tails and sodden ribbons wandered forlornly under the rain searching for their vanished cars. We found ours after an hour and forty minutes. But fate had one sweet in store for us. The Spanish Special Mission was led by the Head of General Franco's military household: this splendidly bemedalled figure, in a beautiful white uniform and scarlet sash, pardonably tired and perhaps a little unobservant, mistook the ornamental water in front of the Palace for the gleaming wet pavement and stepped right into it, disappearing with dignity up to his Golden Fleece. This restored the evening for me. 'Gibraltar to you!' I thought as we climbed into the car for home . . .

For all its reverses and discomforts, I hope that Lord Chalfont will feel that his visit was worth while. From this Embassy's point of view it was eminently rewarding.

The Brazilians were much flattered by this attention from Her Majesty The Queen; whilst on his side I believe that Lord Chalfont found the occasion interesting and his hosts friendly and alert, for all the grotesque incompetence of their organisation. The pity is that they had to demonstrate it so blatantly for all the world to see.

But then Brazil is like that: great brilliance at the top, apathy and sloth in the lower levels, endless good humour throughout.

I have, &c.
JOHN RUSSELL.

~

'One thousand miles from anywhere in any direction'

SIR JOHN RUSSELL, HM AMBASSADOR TO THE FEDERATIVE REPUBLIC OF BRAZIL, MAY 1967

<u>Notes by H.M. Ambassador, Rio de Janeiro, on North-East Brazil: June 20 to 29, 1967.</u>

<u>Rio – Brasilia – Manaus – Belém – Recife – Paulo Afonso – Petrolina – Salvador – Rio.</u>

<u>10,750 kilometres (6,735 miles): 35 hours flying time . . .</u>

<u>Tuesday, June 20.</u>

<u>Rio to Brasilia</u>: 2 hrs. 40 mins: 900 km.

<u>7 p.m. Santos Dumont Airport</u>. Punctual take-off in 'Avro' of Brazilian Air Force.

A motley crew: 9 Ambassadors: a U.N. representative: various journalists: the Minister of the Interior: the Director

General of 'Sudene' (the North-East Development Agency): our three bear-leaders named respectively Makarios, Abuyaghi and Rudolf Valentino: one gentle retired Ambassador, Afranio de Mello Franco (his first time north of Rio!): the President of the Federal Housing Bank: the Editor of 'Cruzeiro' magazine: various hangers-on.

Much jovial seat-hopping and beginning-of-term banter. I feel we should sing 'Lord behold us with thy blessing' . . . I hide behind 'Brazilian Adventure,'[1] but Rudolf Valentino has a strong sense of duty: he perches on the arm of my seat: 'It is very well, Yes? We have a beautiful voyage?' 'Yes, Mr Valentino, it is very well, we have a beautiful voyage,' I reply, gazing doubtfully down into the inky Brazilian night.

Mr Abuyaghi (who must have started life as a citizen of one of the sleazier cities of Asia Minor, perhaps Aleppo) is wearing Old Etonian cuff-links. He reminds me of Mr Loukoumian in 'Black Mischief'.[2]

A disgusting T.V. dinner. We plod slowly on through the night.

9.40 p.m. Brasilia.

Drinks at our Beau-Geste[3] 'staging post': then early to bed in the familiar second-class semi-comfort of the Hotel Nacional.

Wednesday, June 21

Brasilia to Manaus via Belém – (2,800 kms: 8 ½ hours)

5 a.m. call.

A delicious peeled orange for breakfast but Allah protect

the unwary pilgrim who calls for a boiled egg! That really throws the 'Nacional'.

6 a.m. Class gathers punctually at the airport: slightly subdued, as always on the first day of term. Back into the 'Avro'. Seats, of an unrivalled discomfort, by the well-known British firm of Procrustes[4] Ltd. The Avro is too slow for those distances: but, we hope, safe . . .

6.30 a.m. take-off.

Dawn over the high veldt . . . Somewhere below us to the West lies Bananal, the largest alluvial island in the world. And somewhere again West of that the bones of Colonel Fawcett, last heard of on May 30th 1925. He was 60 then: so he must be 102 now. (And tonight, as Mr Todd said in 'A Handful of Dust', we will start 'Little Dorrit'.[5])

Four and a half hours over scrub-forest: finally our first sight of the Amazon Delta.

11 a.m. Belém.

Unscheduled stop to refuel: the Brazilian Air Force are disturbed by the recent loss up here of a C.47 and are taking no chances.

The usual scruffy Brazilian airport: but delicious hot fried crabs in the buffet, washed down with an appalling white cane-alcohol of a truly industrial proof . . .

3.20 p.m. Off again: due West along the Amazon, just South of the Equator. A long, pleasant afternoon (except for the excruciating discomfort of the Avro's seating): road and sleep: and look down at an unchanging world of green jungle and turgid brown waters: like 'the great grey-green, greasy Limpopo River, all set about with fever trees'.[6] Not a sign of human life.

After a jolly, gossipy start my companions relax; and sleep. The Italian Ambassador wears both braces and a belt. (He is a near-albino: are all albini pessimists?)

<u>7.15 p.m. Manaus:</u> population: 174,000: – capital of the State of Amazonas (which is larger than the whole of Europe less only Germany: or, as John Gunther[7] puts it – the area of Mexico, and the population of Milwaukee).

Manaus is an exotic extravaganza. One thousand miles from anywhere in any direction . . .

[T]he immortal soul of Manaus is its Opera House . . . a magnificent, florid monument to the Second Empire: a piece of 'bel canto' in Aberdeen granite and gilt and plush and ormolu, marble from Carrara, the curtain by Visconti, the ceiling painted by de Angelis who did the Municipal Theatre in Rio; seating 1,200: the stall fauteuils wicker-backed and wicker-seated against the perspiring heat, with slides under them for opera-hats. (What is the plural of gybus?) At the back the jungle reaches in with hungry green fingers to the stage-door, whilst from the front terrace you look straight out across the enormous expanse of the Rio Negro, a sheet of water as broad as the Solent at Cowes. (And even then you are 11 miles up from the Amazon proper.) . . .

The Booth Line still connects Manaus, twice a month, to Liverpool. Manaus cannot be reached from anywhere at all by road . . . As the crow flies (if any crow were so rash) Rio is more than 3,000 miles away to the South: the nearest Brazilian city is Belém, 1,000 miles due East on the Atlantic: the same distance and another six days due West upstream the Booth Line steamers take you to Iquitos in Peru: British Guiana is a mere 500 miles North – through totally impenetrable jungle: the 'Boa Vista Highway' stops despondently at the 10th kilometre stone, brought to an abrupt halt, by a solid green wall of palmetto and liana.

We have an Honorary Consul here, whose real (though it can hardly be full-time) job is local Manager of the Bank of London and South America. I beat the telegram, sent him five days earlier from Rio to announce my visit, by a full day.

But for me Manaus will always be the Opera House in the Jungle – a thing of rich Victorian beauty and pathos in this tiny rubber-sick town, rotting on its mud-bank in the heart of the world's greatest primaeval forest. The Opera House: and the Amazon River, inviolate by dam, bridge, tunnel or fixed ferry in the whole 4,000 miles of its course down to the Atlantic Ocean.

(If turned into Texas, the Amazon would flood the whole place one inch deep in a day: John Gunther.)

Thursday, June 22.

Manaus to Recife: via Belém and Fortaleza: 3,500 kms: 10 hrs.

7.30 a.m. take-off.

From a few hundred feet up the confluence of the clear black Rio Negro with the muddy Amazon is momentarily interesting. Then four hours back again down the Amazon to Belém, all over solid jungle.

No wonder they cannot find the C.47 which disappeared here six days ago. Eventually they found the wreck: with five survivors. Pure incompetence to lose it: great persistence to find it; real skill and courage to get the survivors out.

Endless swamp and forest: little timber of any value, and that economically inextricable.

The classic 'Green Hell', untouched by civilisation, its only inhabitants a few Indian tribes, living off fish and game, wandering stark naked as they did four hundred years ago – surviving only if they avoid all contact with the white man: but fortunately they seem to realise that this to them is the deadliest animal of all. Thanks to this commendable precaution there are still about 70,000 Indians surviving in their wild or 'bravio' state out of the 3 or 4 million who were happily living in Brazil when the first white man intruded.

11 a.m. Belém: pop: 450,000: capital of State of Pará (which exceeds the total area of England, France, Belgium, Italy and Portugal).

The Englishman's grave, where he made his fortune: but where he also left his fevered bones.

Ghosts of the Rowing Club, the Tennis Club, the Skittles Club in the moat of the old Portuguese fort. Everything in Belém was built by us – the docks, the waterfront, the railway station: this last is a thing of Gothic-Industrial beauty to rival King's Cross: the sleepers are of Scotch fir, the cast iron balconies and staircases were imported whole from Liverpool. (There were British trams running in Pará before the first tram ran in Manchester.) Only the splendid Opera and the Customs House predate us ... Everything else was made by us: the very pavements are of Aberdeen granite, brought in as ballast in the westward empty rubber ships: the shut and dead Grande Hotel, from the roof-tiles to the urinals in the Gents' washroom, is decked in black slate imported from South Wales ...

In boom days there were 200 English families here: their children went home (by Booth Line) to school in England, as it was nearer than Rio.

Belém still has a certain melancholy charm – more than Dar-es-Salaam, less than Mombasa.

All too short a time to see the town: driven briefly round by our active and well-informed Consul (hon.) Bolivar Kup Esq. Lunch at the Air Force Base, which took two hours to be served to 75 people by two women with one spoon – never have so many been served so slowly by so few ...

On the airfield two Catalinas: date – 1938? A beautiful air-craft, like some great streamlined dragon-fly: and ideal for the Amazon.

A glimpse from the air of the island of Marajó in the delta: the island is slightly bigger than Belgium.

12.30 p.m. take-off.

Fuel stop at Fortaleza.

7 p.m. arrive Recife: pop. 921,000: capital of Pernambuco.

Lodged at the Grand Hotel: very second-rate and grubby: evening off: early and wearily to a hard bed.

<u>Friday, June 23.</u>

<u>Recife</u>

Wake to a light rain on a dirty unattractive town, caught between two worlds: a smelly riverfront, the harbour rapidly silting up: the main bridge permanently closed: the centre of life seems to be the rubbish-strewn market where the only commodity on sale today, St. John's Eve, is fireworks.

Recife, I am reliably informed, boasts 40,000 registered prostitutes. I can well believe it. There cannot be much else to do.

A soft muggy climate like Singapore: and a really 'mean' temperature. Little worth seeing: altogether rather charmless ...

3.30 p.m.

Meeting of SUDENE Council ('Superintendence for the Development of the North East'): the Superintendent, General Euler Bentos, in the chair. We attend as guests. A surprisingly business-like performance. Main item on agenda naming of firms to qualify for tax-exemption on investment in North-East. 'Intoxication with music of own voice department' strongly represented: and the stabbing forefinger of equatorial oratory.

As later unkindly revealed on television, the Italian Ambassador catches up with lost sleep. I stay, heroically, open-eyed, if glazed. A long hot session, but not uninteresting ...

After a very official supper at the Governor's Palace we go off hoping for gaiety and local colour to the São João fiesta at the Portuguese Club. Sedate and dull: even the young of Recife seem rather old. In the hotel they are very up to date and have television: this evening it is showing 'Desert Victory'. I find my bed standing in a flood from the air-conditioner: but l calculate that I shall still be above high-water mark at 7 a.m.: so hopefully to bed with the St. John's Eve firecrackers popping away below my window; like a quiet night in Tombstone, Arizona.

Saturday, June 24:

Recife, via Boa Esperança to Paulo Afonso: 1450 kms: 7 hours: DC. 3.

Depart Recife 8 a.m.

Today is to be a day in the country and we have been told accordingly to dress 'desportivo'. Interpretation of this instruction varies widely: the French Ambassador wears a white cotton beret, avec 'chemise flottante'; the Italian is in shiny black alpaca, but has insouciantly discarded his tie: the Dutchman is very pukka in belted and brass-buttoned shirt, club scarf and desert boots looking more than ever like a motor-car salesman on the Great West Road: Makarios appears in a Pompey football jersey: Mr Abuyaghi sports a hunting costume which would have aroused comment in Sherwood Forest.

D.C. 3: seats much more comfortable than 'Avro': (great loss of face for British Aviation and for me). Four hours over the 'sertão' – not jungle anymore, but upland scrub . . .

Boa Esperança to Paulo Afonso.

Three hours' flight over forest: dusk as we fly in: much relieved at last to see landing lights on strip by power station: short drive to Company's guest-house.

After an excellent dinner I notice that all the Brazilian members of the party have quietly disappeared one by one, leaving us foreign guests to our own devices. Unworthy suspicions of riotous night-life with local Indian ladies are dispelled when we realise that our hosts have simply slipped off upstairs to hog the single rooms. We are thus left to dispose ourselves three to a room on the ground floor. Germany, Belgium and Holland move in together: Italy and France next door: kindly inviting me to take the sixth bed with them.

And so we entered the Common Market!

India is left to doss down with Poland and Czechoslovakia. India turns stuffy. Remembering his country's attitude of unctuous disapproval during the recent Middle East crisis, we told him happily: 'As you vote, so you sleep!' India is not amused.

France and Italy are two rather maidenly old gentlemen: but at least neither snores.

Paulo Afonso: Sunday, June 25.

Out early to look round. The guest-house is a large, pleasant, stone-built sort of Swiss chalet. The dripping garden is full of rubber trees, hibiscus, poinsettia, golden mohur, a copper plum, those revolting 'kaki', giant aspidistra – and all the lush sub-tropicals of which you get so tired in this country . . .

Paulo Afonso via Petrolina to Salvador: 800 km: 2 1/4 hrs . . .

Back to Petrolina for lunch at the Governor's mother's house . . . This is the last stage of our trip and there is a hilarious end-of-term atmosphere. We should sing 'Lord dismiss us with thy blessing'.

A tremendous meal, served by the Governor's sisters and cousins and nieces, with wonderful local dishes and excellent French wines.

Makarios has put a mango on top of his glass to keep the flies out of his Chateauneuf du Pape. Mr Abuyaghi, plainly smelling his stable, is working with single-minded concentration on cane-alcohol and Pouilly Fuisse, evidently an effective mixture. Funny hats and speeches. A 'Lolita' band from Petrolina high school plays a vaguely familiar tune on green plastic mouth-pianos: enquiry reveals that it is 'a Scotch song called Timperary'. The Governor's mother, aged 84, has gone to sleep . . . Rudolf Valentino is pursuing the conductor of the band round the garden. Mr Abuyaghi sings quietly to himself in Arabic. The Italian Ambassador pleads sunstroke and makes a dash for the Gents.

Finally Makarios calls plane-time and we sway dizzily out into the blinding sunshine and the cheering populace of Petrolina, who greatly approve of nine ambassadors at high noon in paper hats.

3.45 p.m. off, on my last lap, to Salvador.

1. *'Brazilian Adventure'*: Peter Fleming's book, published in 1933, was a first-hand account of an expedition tracing the steps of Colonel Percy Fawcett, who had vanished into the Brazilian jungle eight years previously. Russell said that in 1967 this remained the most up-to-date travel literature available for his trip.
2. *'Black Mischief'*: Evelyn Waugh novel, 1932. See also Willie Morris's despatch, p. 57.

3. *Beau-Geste*: Literally, a gesture or sacrifice which is noble, but futile. Also the title of a 1966 Hollywood film in which the French Foreign Legion defended a fort against Tuareg attacks.

4. *Procrustes*: In Greek mythology, Procrustes was a rogue metalsmith who invited unwary travellers to sleep the night on an ill-sized iron bed – and then either stretched or amputated their limbs to fit.

5. *Mr Todd ... 'Little Dorrit'*: From Evelyn Waugh's 1934 novel, *A Handful of Dust*. Wandering delirious in the Brazilian jungle, the protagonist Tony is rescued by a Mr Todd, who then keeps him captive, reading aloud the complete works of Dickens for Todd's entertainment, until the end of his days.

6. *'the great grey-green, greasy Limpopo River ... fever trees'*: From 'The Elephant's Child', one of Rudyard Kipling's *Just So Stories* (1902). The Limpopo is in central-southern Africa.

7. *John Gunther*: American journalist (1901–70).

<hr>

~

Germany

'A big, fat spoilt child'

SIR ERIC PHIPPS, HM AMBASSADOR TO GERMANY,
JUNE 1934

In your editors' view this despatch is in a league of its own, placed there not only by Sir Eric's psychological insight and powerful prose but by the circumstances of history.

British ambassadors are expected from time to time in their reporting to compose pen-portraits of important politicians in the countries in which they are posted. Often vivid personality studies, these descriptions help ministers and more senior diplomats in London prepare themselves for important face-to-face meetings on overseas visits as well as helping policymakers anticipate political responses.

Eric Phipps acquitted himself of this duty with exceptional aplomb in his June 1934 letter to the Foreign Secretary. Known to historians of the Nazi era simply as the 'Bison despatch', it describes a day in the countryside with one of the twentieth century's most infamous political figures.

Hermann Göring was Commander-in-Chief of the Luftwaffe and the founder of the Gestapo. In the Nazi hierarchy, Göring stood second only to Hitler. In a speech to the Reichstag in 1939 on the outbreak of war the Führer designated the General his successor 'should anything befall me'.

When Phipps wrote his despatch in 1934, Göring was merely Minister of Civil Air Transport, but the Ambassador was not fooled, correctly attributing (as did others) hostile intent to German rearmament. It was only a year later that Hitler repudiated the Treaty of Versailles, unveiling the Wehrmacht; and the aeroplanes that Phipps memorably describes here as Göring's 'winged toys' were repainted with military decals. Acting as flying artillery to fearsome Panzer tanks, Göring's Luftwaffe went on to score a string of decisive victories in the blitzkrieg campaigns in Poland, France and Russia in the early years of the Second World War, and bombed many British cities into rubble.

When Hitler became Chancellor in 1933 he made Göring Prime Minister of Prussia. Göring kept the title – to which Phipps refers at the beginning of the despatch – as an honorific when Hitler scrapped the devolved Prussian administration two years later, in the cause of a united Germany.

General Field Marshal Göring did not start as a slob. Phipps does not need to remind his expert readership of

Göring's talent but today we do need to remind ourselves (as the last paragraph of the despatch so chillingly hints) that the buffoon the ambassador describes did also have outstanding ability. He was once himself an ace fighter pilot, trim and athletic, but by the 1930s he was obese. As well as the General's physical appearance, Phipps's portrait in this despatch bears witness to some of the unpleasant character traits which have since become associated with Göring, notably his extravagance and greed.

Göring built up a large personal fortune, some of it from confiscated Jewish property, and in 1933 acquired the country estate where Phipps was invited, along with other ambassadors, to witness the wonders of Germanic country life. At Schorfheide Göring enjoyed playing the aristocrat, decorating the walls with coats of arms and ceremonial swords, which he had made up for him.

The General's fetish for costume, so vividly captured in Phipps's despatch, is backed up by other contemporary accounts. Witnesses attest to Göring meeting subordinates dressed in a toga, and relaxing in medieval hunting garb. The Italian Foreign Minister, Galeazzo Ciano, recalled Göring wearing on one occasion a fur coat of the kind that 'a high grade prostitute wears to the opera'.

Arriving in Berlin in 1933, Phipps took a strong dislike to the Nazis[1] and in his reporting back to Whitehall sought to portray them in as negative a light as possible. His hostility towards the regime (which was by no means uncontroversial at that time) did not escape the notice of the Nazis. An aide to Von Ribbentrop, the Foreign Minister, thought the British ambassador was 'inspired by a hatred of the Nazis, if not for the German people in general'. Hitler thought 'Sir Phipps was a thug'.

This approach made Phipps less effective as Ambassador, and the Prime Minister, Neville Chamberlain, eventually had him recalled. By 1936, according to a senior official in Downing Street, Phipps had 'no telephone line to Hitler, who despises him'.

Göring, on the other hand, had become quite useful to Phipps towards the end, despite the ambassador's obvious distaste for the man. Phipps wrote back to London that he had developed 'very helpful points of contact with General Göring, who is an old army officer with few Nazi proclivities in his saner moments'.

Even today, apologists point out that Göring was never as ardent an anti-Semite as Heinrich Himmler, for example, or Joseph Goebbels, and that the General's enthusiasm for Hitler's war-making was mainly of the professional – rather than ideological – kind. But the judges at Nuremberg, where Göring was tried after the war, were far from convinced. According to their judgment:

> There is nothing to be said in mitigation. For Göring was often, indeed almost always, the moving force, second only to his leader. He was the leading war aggressor, both as political and as military leader; he was the director of the slave labour programme and the creator of the oppressive programme against the Jews and other home races, home and abroad . . . His guilt is unique in its enormity. The record discloses no excuses for this man.

At Nuremberg, Göring was sentenced to death, but escaped execution by suicide, swallowing cyanide in October 1946, on the night before he was due to hang.

[C 3911/3911/18]   No. 102.

Sir E. Phipps to Sir John Simon.—(Received June 21.)

(No. 696.)   *Berlin, June 13, 1934.*

Sir,

I HAVE the honour to inform you that General Göring, Prussian Prime Minister and 'Head Ranger of the Reich' ('Reichsjägermeister'), was so good as to invite Lady Phipps and myself last Sunday, the 10th June, to visit the new bison enclosure in the Schorfheide, about 70 kilom. from Berlin.

We arrived at our destination at 3 o'clock in the afternoon by motor, being shown the last part of the way by keepers posted at all cross-roads. Our host, as usual, was late, but eventually arrived in a fast racing-car driven by himself. He was clad in aviator's garments of india-rubber with top boots and a large hunting-knife stuck in his belt. The American, Italian and French Ambassadors, Herr von Papen, General Blomberg, the Minister of Finance and Countess Schwerin von Krosigk were also present, the number of guests amounting to about forty.

General Göring opened the proceedings by a lecture delivered to us on the outskirts of the bison enclosure in a stentorian voice with the aid of a microphone. He celebrated the beauties of the primeval German forest, in which roamed the primeval German animals, and announced his intention of reconstituting such a forest, ensuring to the animals the necessary forest peacefulness and to the German citizen the possibility of glancing at primitive German animals in German surroundings.

On the conclusion of General Göring's address, three or four cow bison were driven towards a large box containing the bull bison. A host of cinematograph operators and photographers aimed their machines at this box preparatory to the exit of the bull. Those who, like myself, have seen the mad charge of the Spanish bull out of his 'torril' looked forward to a similar sight on this occasion, but we were grievously disappointed, for the bison emerged from his box with the utmost reluctance, and, after eyeing the cows somewhat sadly, tried to return into it. This part of the programme, therefore, did not fulfil our expectations.

The guests were then taken for a long drive across the Schorfheide in open carriages, General Göring heading the procession, accompanied by the wife of the Italian Ambassador in a small vehicle drawn by two powerful horses. After about an hour we alighted at a spot between some swamps, where General Göring made another address on the beauties of bird life. After a further drive we got into our motors again, which had been sent on to meet us, and General Göring disappeared alone at breakneck speed in his racing-car. Some twenty minutes' motor drive brought us eventually to the shooting-box which General Göring has just completed building for himself, overlooking a lovely lake. Our host met us here in a costume consisting of white tennis-shoes, white duck trousers, white flannel shirt and a green leather jacket, with the large hunting-knife still stuck into his belt. In his hand he carried a long harpoon-like instrument, with which he punctuated the further address that he then proceeded to deliver, expatiating on the beauties of his shooting-box and all the purely German materials of which it had been made. We were then taken through every room. The chief ornament in the

living-room was a bronze medallion of the Führer, but opposite to it was a vacant space, reserved for the effigy of
Wotan.[2] A tree grows in the living-room, presumably ready
to receive the sword to be placed there by Wotan and eventually to be removed by Siegfried[3] or General Göring.

After this an excellent and purely Germanic collation was
served at small tables in the open air and presided over most
amiably by the actress, Fräulein Sonnemann,[4] introduced
by our host as his 'private secretary'. By this time it was past
7 o'clock and we were about to take our leave, but were told
that the *pièce de résistance* was yet to come.

The concluding scene in this strange comedy was enacted at a lonely and very beautiful spot some 500 yards
distant, overlooking the lake, where a mausoleum has been
erected by General Göring, to contain, as he told us in his
final and semi-funeral oration, the remains of his Swedish
wife[5] and his own (no mention was made of Fräulein
Sonnemann). Under an oak tree General Göring planted
himself, harpoon in hand, and celebrated to his guests,
drawn up in a semi-circle round him, the Germanic and
idyllic beauties of these Germanic surroundings. The
mausoleum was placed between two German oak trees
and flanked by six Druidical (but Germanic) sarsen stones
reminiscent of Stonehenge, which itself must be Germanic
though we do not know it. The stones are to have various
appropriate marks engraved upon them, including the
swastika, but no sign of the Cross. The only blot in an
otherwise perfect, and consequently Germanic, picture was
the tombstone itself, which is made of Swedish marble; but
this could not be avoided, as General Göring explained to
me apologetically, for it was the original tombstone on his
wife's grave in Sweden. 'She will rest here in this beautiful

spot, where only swans and other birds will come; she will rest in German earth and Swedish stone. The vault will serve for all eternity, as the walls are 1 metre 80 centimetres thick.'

On the return walk to our motor General Göring told me that the interment will take place on the 20th June in the presence of numerous detachments of the S.A., S.S. and Reichswehr, and also a number of aeroplanes. At times he stopped and drew me pictures in the sand with his harpoon of the mausoleum as it will look years hence, when newly-planted German trees will flank it yet more worthily. The whole proceedings were so strange as at times to convey a feeling of unreality; but they opened, as it were, a window on to Nazi mentality, and as such were not, perhaps, quite useless. The chief impression was that of the almost pathetic naïveté of General Göring, who showed us his toys like a big, fat, spoilt child: his primeval woods, his bison and birds, his shooting-box and lake and bathing beach, his blonde 'private secretary', his wife's mausoleum and swans and sarsen stones, all mere toys to satisfy his varying moods, and all, or so nearly all, as he was careful to explain, Germanic. And then I remembered there were other toys, less innocent, though winged, and these might some day be launched on their murderous mission in the same childlike spirit and with the same childlike glee.

I have, &c.
ERIC PHIPPS.

1. *Phipps took a strong dislike to the Nazis*: Our commentary here draws on an excellent study by Peter Neville. Entitled 'The Foreign Office and Britain's Ambassadors to Berlin, 1933–39', this essay can be found in Gaynor Johnson's *The Foreign Office and British Diplomacy in the Twentieth Century* (Routledge, 2005).

2. *Wotan*: The pagan god Wotan was in vogue in 1930s Germany. Nazi youth sacrificed sheep for him on the solstice. In a 1936 essay, the psychologist Carl Jung diagnosed Wotan as 'a fundamental attribute of the German psyche, an irrational psychic factor which acts on the high pressure of civilization like a cyclone and blows it away'.

3. *Siegfried*: The third opera in Wagner's *Ring* cycle. The eponymous hero kills a dragon and then breaks Wotan's spear with a blow from his sword. As in the Excalibur myth, the sword was embedded (this time by the great god Odin, in a tree) and only the chosen one could pull it out.

4. *Fräulein Sonnemann*: Göring did in fact make an honest woman of Emma Sonnemann, his 'private secretary', the following year. In 1938 Emma bore him a daughter, and to celebrate Göring ordered 500 of his Luftwaffe pilots to fly a salute over Berlin. Had it been a boy, Göring said, he would have ordered twice that number.

5. *Swedish wife*: After the First World War, Göring found work as a commercial airline pilot in Sweden, where he met Baroness Carin von Kantzow. It was love at first sight, even though she was five years his senior and already had a husband (albeit estranged) and a child. Carin returned to Munich with Göring and they married in 1922. She liked Hitler and would often entertain him and other Nazis at the Göring home. Göring was heartbroken when Carin died from heart failure in 1931, following a bout of tuberculosis.

∽

The Baltic States

'One in Three, and Three in One'

SIR HUGHE KNATCHBULL-HUGESSEN, HM ENVOY
EXTRAORDINARY AND MINISTER PLENIPOTENTIARY AT
RIGA, TALLINN AND KOVNO, 1930S

The Book of Common Prayer was the inspiration for Sir Hughe Knatchbull-Hugessen's elegant complaint about the difficulties of what is known in the Diplomatic Service as the system of Multiple Representation. From 1930 to 1934 Knatchbull-Hugessen was minister to Latvia, Lithuania and Estonia (at the time Britain sent ambassadors only to great powers, where she maintained embassies; lesser countries had to make do with 'ministers', working out of 'legations'). The letter he sent colleagues in the Foreign Office recounting this experience was titled 'One in Three, and Three in One' – as in the Father, the Son and the Holy Ghost.

A take-off of the Athanasian Creed (Quicunque vult – 'whosoever wishes [to be saved]') Knatchbull-Hugessen's letter suddenly started doing the rounds again in the Foreign Office sixty years later, when the Soviet Union fell to bits. Newly independent states were springing from the wreckage, among them the very same Baltic trio Knatchbull-Hugessen had once found himself stretched across, each requiring some sort of British diplomatic presence on the ground or at least near by. An entirely new generation of diplomats faced anew the challenge of covering several states from one base. A 1992 despatch by Richard Samuel, the new British ambassador in Latvia, ably portrays the sense of a logistical puzzle every bit as hard as the logic of the Catholic Trinity (see pp. 313–16).

The cleverness of Knatchbull-Hugessen's parody will have been especially apparent to a generation to whom the wording of the Athanasian Creed was either familiar or at least to hand. But even readers hazy about the original text will appreciate the way he echoes the metaphysics and the rhythm of Church language.

A few years after Knatchbull-Hugessen wrote his creed, his career reached its peak (in so far as it was all downhill thereafter) when he was ambassador in wartime Istanbul. While the diplomat was taking a bath, his valet stole a set of *keys to his safe, and wasted no time in selling the contents to the Nazis. Impressed by this sudden windfall of intelligence, the Germans gave him the code name Cicero. Over the next two years, as the unwitting Knatchbull-Hugessen dutifully refreshed the contents of the safe, Cicero copied and passed on to the Nazis everything from precise details of Allied bombing raids to an outline of the D-Day landings.*

Quicunque Balt

Whosoever will be saved, before all things it is necessary that he hold the Baltic post.

Which post, except a man keep for a few years, without doubt he shall go to Bogota or La Paz everlastingly.

For the Baltic post is this, that we have one Minister in three capitals and three capitals in one Minister.

Everyone confounding his person and dividing his substance.

For there is one Minister for Lithuania, one Minister for Latvia and one Minister for Estonia.

But the Minister for Lithuania, for Latvia and for Estonia is all one; the uniform uncomfortable and the travelling almost eternal.

Such as Riga is, so is Tallinn and so is Kovno.

But Kovno in particular is uncreate and incomprehensible.

As also Riga is a Legation, Tallinn is a Legation and Kovno is a Legation.

And yet there is not three Legations but one Legation.

So also Riga is expensive, Tallinn is expensive and Kovno is expensive.

And yet there are not three salaries but one salary.

For like as we are compelled by the Private Secretaries to say there is one Legation and one Minister, so we are forbidden by the Chief Clerk to say that there are three salaries or three frais de representation.[1]

So likewise there should be one Secretary for Riga, one Secretary for Tallinn and one Secretary for Kovno.

And yet there are not three Secretaries but no Secretary.

No Secretary, not by reduction of the Chancery work into nothing, but by taking the Secretary to Moscow.

Absolutely none; by confusion of the Private Secretaries and not by desire of the Minister.

The Minister is made and created but forgotten.

The Secretary is neither made nor created, but proceeding to Moscow.

So there is one Minister, not three Ministers; one salary, not three salaries; no Secretary, not even one Secretary.

And in this Legation none is afore or after the other, although a good many people seem to be continually after the Minister.

The whole thing is most unequal and incomprehensible.

He therefore that would be saved, might sometimes think of HM Minister at Riga.

Such is the Baltic post – although any reasonable soul will find it hard to believe faithfully.

1. *frais de representation*: Expenses.

~

Algeria

'The Spanish Ambassador grabbed his suitcase and joined the rush'

RONALD BURROUGHS, HM AMBASSADOR TO THE
DEMOCRATIC AND POPULAR REPUBLIC OF ALGERIA,
OCTOBER 1971

Within diplomatic circles the 'Spanish Ambassador's Suitcase' despatch is by impute probably the greatest 'funny' of them all. Ronald Burroughs's peerless sketch of a night's entertainment in the Sahara Desert was not in fact a despatch – these were, strictly speaking, always addressed to the Foreign Secretary – but a letter. The recipient was Burroughs's colleague and fellow Arabist Sir James Craig, then head of the Near East and North Africa Department at the Foreign Office in Whitehall. Despite its irreverence and irrelevance to official business, the letter was given the honour of formal printing and circulation throughout the FCO in London and to posts abroad. Craig's own fine sense of style (see pp. 283–6) may have had something to do with the recognition accorded Burroughs.

A slightly sanitized version of Burroughs's tale has appeared in print before, in Sir John Ure's Diplomatic Bag.

As a piece of comic writing the despatch has aged well except for the tedious jokes about skin colour which sit oddly within the rest of the piece. Today one finds it hard to believe that worldly, highly educated diplomats would find jokes about black people being hard to see in the dark actually funny, even in 1971. But standards shift. Judged by modern standards, other despatches of the time from Africa and elsewhere occasionally strike the same flat note.

Burroughs wrote a second very readable letter from Algiers the same month, which follows on here. James Craig, to whom both letters were addressed, went on to become an ambassador, first to Syria and then to Saudi Arabia. His dazzling valedictories from Damascus and Dubai are in Parting Shots. *Readers may care to compare their responses with mine. I think the second ('Wallpaper') letter the finer, though uncelebrated: a bitter and disillusioned reflection on diplomatic life – for all its hilarity.*

CORPS – IN CONFIDENCE

Ref. No. NAA3/548/1   Departmental Series

NORTH AFRICAN DEPARTMENT
D.S. No. 1

Algiers: The Spanish Ambassador's suitcase
(Her Majesty's Ambassador at Algiers to Mr A J Craig)

BRITISH EMBASSY,
ALGIERS,
6 October 1971.

Dear James,

Having sent you in my previous letter an account of the Opening of the Judicial Year, I realise that I should have written to you somewhat earlier about the Affair of the Spanish Ambassador's Suitcase; an affair which has passed into local diplomatic legend.

It took place on the night of 19/20 June. The 19 June is a day which is always celebrated in Algeria as marking some event, which I have forgotten, in the Struggle for Independence. This year it was decided that against the background of the quarrel with the French Government over oil, the celebrations should most appropriately take place at Hassi Messaoud in the Sahara, where oil was first struck by the French. A pleasing note of additional insult would be given to the occasion by celebrating also the nationalisation of French oil interests on 24 February of this year.

For the purpose it was of course necessary to have all foreign Ambassadors present. I am never sure whether this insistence on our presence springs from a misplaced but delicate desire to give us pleasure, or whether it is an expression of Algerian xenophobia. The way these affairs are organised may be not the result of inefficiency but rather of fiendishly clever planning designed to torture the bloody foreigners. The previous year was, by all accounts, of such prolonged horror that it could only have been effected by design.

As 19 June approached the Corps began to speculate about what might lie in store for us. By the 17th nothing had been revealed. Protocole Department would only smile roguishly and say that it was to be a surprise. Indeed, when we were all informed of what had been arranged for our delectation it was a surprise; rather a pleasant one. It might have been another steelworks entailing a 5.00 a.m. start, and a return home at 3.00 a.m. on the following morning. Instead we were to be flown down to the desert at the civilized hour of 4.00 p.m., and beds were to be provided for the night.

As the special plane was due to start at 4.00 p.m., we were instructed to be at the airport at 3.00 for the traditional ceremony of standing on the tarmac for an hour or so in the blazing sun. We arrived variously equipped. Most Ambassadors brought brief cases containing a toothbrush, razor and pyjamas. A few brought rather elegant little dressing cases, and a certain Ambassador's case gave out the sound of clinking whisky bottles every time he put it on the ground.

The only exception was the Spanish Ambassador, who is a Lieutenant-General 'still on the active list my dear', as he assures everyone. He brought, not a brief case, but an enormous, splendid and expensive portmanteau, made of heavy leather with gold fastenings, and bound with elegant straps each with a heavy gold buckle. He arrived late, panting and sweating profusely as he deposited his case on the tarmac. Those of us who had got there earlier were standing under the shadow of the wings of our aircraft. There was no room for the Spanish Ambassador to join us, and he had to protect his bald head with a handkerchief knotted at the four corners, while the Greek Ambassador made remarks about fried brains being one of his favourite dishes.

Having stood around for an hour and a half the Chef de Protocole looked at his watch, asked Their Excellencies to group themselves before him, clapped his hands and said 'Prenez vos places dans l'avion. Vite, vite.' He urged us up the ladder at a gallop wringing his hands and saying, 'Nous sommes deja en retard, Excellences.'[1]

The Spanish Ambassador grabbed his suitcase and joined the rush. He got it half-way up the steps, fell over it and said something very rude in Spanish. With the Chef de Protocole yapping around the heels of the pack we pressed forward stepping over the suitcase and round the Spanish Ambassador who is of a shape that makes this operation difficult. Finally he was left alone on the gang-way ascending slowly backwards and dragging the suitcase up step by step.

He was installed in the rear, with his suitcase occupying the neighbouring seat. The doors closed and we took off. We were comforted by the announcement that as it was a day of National Celebration, this type of aircraft was being flown for the very first time by an all-Algerian crew. Some of us were more touched by this delicate attention than others.

Apart from one or two rather dashing tight turns designed to show off the burning flares at various oil well heads, we had nonetheless a comfortable and safe journey, punctuated by offers of bottles of Coca-Cola with the tops wrestled off by an air-hostess of quite remarkable plainness. There is much to be said for the wearing of the veil.

We landed at an airstrip in the desert, and the Spanish Ambassador had found the answer. It was easier this time to descend backwards sliding his suitcase towards him. Naturally, we had all been speculating about the contents. Some Ambassadors leaned to the view that it contained several gold-braided uniforms and loads and loads of medals. Others thought that he had brought a white tie and tails. The Greek however, believed that he had brought his wife 'en cas de besoin'.[2]

Standing on the sand, the Spanish Ambassador ran round and round his suitcase demanding to know where was the orderly who was to carry his baggage. He was ignored by the Chef de Protocole and the welcoming party. Rather we were told that our presence was urgently required in the salon d'honneur for a lecture on the oil-field and its operation. 'Where is the salon d'honneur?' we asked, 'Over there.' we were told, and a small hut in the far distance was indicated to us. 'Vite, vite Excellences.'

We trudged off through soft-sand for our lecture, with the Spanish Ambassador losing contact with the pack, and leaving a furrow behind him like a light plough. We heard our lecture. In Arabic, a language with which the speaker was himself not too familiar. Most of the Ambassadors identified it as Arabic simply because it wasn't either French or English.

As question time started, the Spanish Ambassador appeared through the door, clutching a couple of hernias acquired between the aircraft and the salon d'honneur.

For the next lecture, we had to move to another hut, mercifully quite near this time. Then into a bus to be conducted to our air-conditioned aluminium huts 'Pour une demi-heure de repos, Excellences. N'oubliez-pas vos baggages.'[3]

By this time it was black-dark with one or two oil-flares on the horizon. Our sleeping huts were scattered among oleander bushes in the artificial oasis created by the oil-engineers. They were numbered from 1 to 60 on what appeared to be a totally random plan, and each Ambassador was issued with a numbered ticket. As I stumbled between the bushes in the gloom I fell over an African Ambassador who affects a black Homburg hat, black clothes and shoes, and is only distinguishable in the dark when he smokes a startling white pipe.

As the most recently accredited Ambassador I was allocated Hut No. 60, which was the most distant and the most obscure. When I finally found it and opened the door it was already occupied by the Greek Ambassador, in the process of removing his trousers. I showed my ticket with the number 60 printed on it. He extricated his ticket from his trouser-pocket around his ankles, and it too bore the number 60. There ensued a diplomatic negotiation in which I made great play of the fact that since he had presented his credentials a full hour before me, I was obliged to yield him precedence. Plainly therefore he should be in Hut No. 59. Having satisfied himself that HM Government was a signatory of the revised Vienna Convention which reaffirms the rules of diplomatic precedence, the Greek Ambassador had no alternative but to pull up his trousers and depart into the Saharan darkness.

We had been instructed to parade at a certain spot among the oleander bushes at 8.30 p.m. The Chef de Protocole had insisted that we should be there 'exactement a l'heure prevue'.[4] He need not have bothered. We were full of impatience to see the Spanish Ambassador, and to learn what his suitcase contained. Would he be in full military uniform, or were the theories about the evening dress and the diamond studs and the insignia of many Spanish and Catholic orders to be confirmed? Perhaps he had been made a Field Marshal and would arrive with a little jewelled baton.

We assembled. The Chef de Protocole lined us up and counted us. We were two short. We didn't like to point out that one of the supposed absentees was the African Ambassador who affected a black costume, and who out of politeness had put away his white pipe.

A prolonged wait, while we considered who might be missing. It was the Spanish Ambassador. 'He 'ave great trouble with 'is corsets,' said the Bulgarian. 'No soldier to give the pull'. But he was wrong. At long last the Spanish Ambassador arrived through the bushes, and to confound us all, wearing the suit in which he had started out.

'Vite, vite,' said the Chef de Protocole, spotting the whites of the African Ambassador's eyes. 'We will now proceed to have un meshaoui.'

A meshaoui consists of a recently slaughtered sheep, impaled on a long pole and roasted slowly over charcoal. Its head, its hooves surmounted by short woolly socks, and what the Bible delicately describes as 'the appurtenances thereof' are all included in the dish. Having been escorted to a vast open tent in the desert where we passed between us convivial, family-sized bottles of Pepsi-Cola, and listened to numerous speeches, the meshaoui finally arrived.

The ration was one sheep to every three Ambassadors. I shared mine with two African Ambassadors. I had the head end and the horns kept catching my sleeve as I pulled pieces of hot meat away with my fingers. His Excellency at the rear end made a grab for the 'appurtenances' and rolled up the sleeves of his robe. He was nearly up to his shoulder in the interior of the animal, and kept saying 'Le gout de dedans est meilleur.'[5] As the meal progressed I became more and more alarmed. He showed every sign of disappearing up the rear end of the sheep, and I had visions of having to seize a pair of black ankles to recover His Excellency.

A nationalistic play was succeeded by hours of greatly entertaining music. Much of it consisted of three old nomads blowing down flutes which had been imperfectly constructed and which allowed air to escape from cracks in the side. The effect was rather peaceful and wistful. The bit I liked best however, was the appearance of a Western style orchestra. It was not the excellence of its rendition, but rather the fact that it contained a left-handed violinist. There is something satisfying about the concerted sweep of violin bows. But it is as nothing to the excitement of a row of violinists containing a Southpaw fiddle. The quick bits are the best, when his right-handed neighbour has to keep on ducking like a demented wood-pecker.

I will not trouble you with the rest of the night's entertainment, full though it was of delightful vignettes. We managed to get three hours sleep in our air-conditioned huts before reporting at our aircraft shortly after dawn.

The sun rose with its accustomed splendour over the desert horizon. The Spanish Ambassador made a parallel track in our wake through the sand with his suitcase.

The Saudi Arabian Ambassador watching him outlined against the reddening sky, twitched his worry beads and said to me 'Excellency, you know that His Excellency the Spanish Ambassador is a member of the S.S. twice over?'. 'No', I replied 'I know that he is a Lieutenant General. You mean that he resigned from the S.S. and rejoined it later?'.

'No Excellency,' our esteemed doyen replied, ''e is Self-Service Sahara Suitcase. I must tell the other Excellencies my little joke' he added departing. He has been in this post for eight years, and his amusements are few.

The Spanish Ambassador left immediately thereafter for leave in Spain. He has only returned within the last few days and no-one has seen his wife. Was the Greek Ambassador's theory perhaps right and has the Spanish Ambassador lost the keys of his expensive suitcase? It is clearly a highly-prized object, and it must have given him great pain to bore air-holes through that expensively grained leather.

Yours ever
R A Burroughs

1. *'Prenez vos places ... deja en retard, Excellences'*: 'Take your places on the aeroplane, quickly, quickly ... we are already late, Excellencies.'
2. *'en cas de besoin'*: 'In case he needed her.'
3. *'Pour une demi-heure ... N'oubliez-pas vos baggages'*: 'For half an hour's rest, Excellencies. Do not forget your luggage.'
4. *'exactement a l'heure prevue'*: 'Exactly on time.'
5. *'Le gout de dedans est meilleur'*: 'The taste is better on the inside.'

∼

'Algerians use Ambassadors as wall-paper'

RONALD BURROUGHS, HM AMBASSADOR TO
THE DEMOCRATIC AND POPULAR REPUBLIC OF
ALGERIA, OCTOBER 1971

CORPS – IN CONFIDENCE

BRITISH EMBASSY
ALGIERS
1 OCTOBER 1971

A J M Craig Esq
North African Department

Dear James,

In the belief that the Head of a Department should know his territories in depth I send you the following account of this afternoon's doings. It was nothing out of the ordinary, and this is just why I recount it to you.

The first of October is 'l'ouverture de l'année judiciaire'[1] whatever that may mean, but it is obviously something important. On these 'important' occasions the Algerians use Ambassadors as wall-paper, and we were all duly summoned by the Ministre de la Justice, Garde des Sceaux[2], to attend the Palais de Justice at 4.00 p.m.

This does not of course mean that one goes to the Palace of Justice at 4.00 p.m. On the contrary, we all drive in the opposite direction to be in the street outside the Ministry of Foreign Affairs at 3.15 p.m. There we get out of cars and gather in groups. The African Ambassadors form a small group on their own higher up the hill. Those of us who are anxious to demonstrate that we are not racists shake them all briefly by the hand and descend to the white men's group a little lower, where we are joined by the Russian Ambassador, the North Vietnamese and other unidentified Orientals, while the Chinese hang about in the middle. The Russian Ambassador, who speaks nothing but Russian, is always accompanied by one or other of his polyglot Secretaries. The Chinese Chargé d'Affaires speaks only Chinese and is always accompanied by two of his monoglot Secretaries with beautiful smiles.

We enquire anxiously about each other's health, and lead each other off by the button-hole to ask whether there is any confirmation of the rumour that M. Bouteflika[3] was so exhausted by his trip to China that he has been obliged to go off to the South of France to chase young girls and thus 'regagner ses forces'.[4] The Japanese Ambassador, who always keeps his ear very close to the gutter, is sure that this is the case. 'And Excellenssy' he adds, 'he has been seen wearing a very broad tie.' Unfortunately just as we feel we may receive some even more juicy revelations, a whistle blows and we run for our cars.

The Doyen, preceded by a squad of maniacal motor-cyclists, moves off. We all follow, and for the honour of our various sovereigns (or presidents) there is a jostle reminiscent of the first fence at a not very well considered Irish point-to-point. Through streets temporarily devoid of traffic we drive at 60 miles an hour. The crowds line the pavements to see the Ambassadorial cortege of 60 cars go by, to be followed in due course by the President who drives even faster in a black Citroen surrounded by motor-cyclists like blue-bottles around a piece of bad meat.

The Ambassadorial wall-paper is unrolled in the Palais de Justice. I find myself between the Moroccan Ambassador and the Jordanian Chargé d'Affaires. Officially all relations between Jordan and Algeria have been severed, but the Jordanian explains to me for the sixth or seventh time that this does not mean what it says. With courtly grace and in fractured English he always addresses me as 'Excellency the Ambassador of Great Britain and Ireland of the North'. I am at a loss for a suitable formula in reply, so with typical English courtesy I always say 'Er – hello.'

In front of me sits a Slav. The back of his head is so flat that were it not for a bunch of curls at the nape of his neck, his ears would stick out behind, like the fins on a 1950's American car. His neighbour is a Latin-American. Like many Latin-Americans exposed to the light of any Continent but their own, he looks yellow, faintly dirty and consumptive.

So far we are well ahead of schedule. Only 15 minutes' wait in the street outside the Ministry of Foreign Affaires. Par for the course before the President's arrival would normally be a further hour. I bet the Moroccan ten dinars that today it will only be half-an-hour. He is even more optimist than I, and wins his 10 dinars with about 30 seconds to spare.

The President and his Ministers file in. All the Ambassadors stand to crane rudely, trying to spot the errant Minister for Foreign Affairs. He is not there. 'Il aura beaucoup de force, quand il rentre,'[5] whispers the Argentine Ambassador who talks French like a zip-gun, spraying the room with his Spanish 'R's.

The speeches begin. In Arabic, which few of the listeners understand. The first speaker gives us a mercifully short allocution of 20 minutes by the Moroccan's watch. He pouches a second 10 dinar note from me as a result. He is followed by a stone-faced legal luminary, speaking a language I don't recognise. I ask the Moroccan what it is. 'C'est un Arabe très très pur.'[6]

'But what is he saying,' I enquire.

'Je n'ai aucune idée. Il a un très mauvais accent.'[7] We leave it at that, while the Slav in front of me explores his curls, his little round fingers moving like white piglets through the undergrowth.

The hands on the Moroccan's ostentatious gold watch creep round and round, until there is a splatter of applause. The President and his Ministers leave without greeting anyone. The Ambassadorial wall-paper is rolled up and we have another point-to-point start. A by-stander spits at the Egyptian Ambassador's car, but does not give enough forward lead, and hits the windscreen of a Scandinavian colleague.

As the cortège jostles homeward, urged faster and faster by frantic whistle-blowing police, we collide with the President's entourage. The meat-safe and the blue-bottles scream across our bows, as we leave much Governmental rubber on the road with our sudden halt.

We separate, none the wiser. Certainly I have no idea of what has happened except that the Judicial Year has commenced, which I suppose is a good thing.

Yours ever,
R A Burroughs

1. *'l'ouverture de l'année judiciaire'*: 'The opening of the judicial year'.
2. *Garde des Sceaux*: Keeper of the Seals.
3. *Bouteflika*: In 1971 Abdelaziz Bouteflika was Minister for Foreign Affairs. Today he is President of Algeria.
4. *'regagner ses forces'*: 'Regain his strength'.
5. *'Il aura beaucoup de force, quand il rentre'*: 'He will have much strength, when he returns.'
6. *'C'est un Arabe très très pur'*: 'It is a very very pure Arabic.'
7. *'Je n'ai aucune idée. Il a un très mauvais accent'*: 'I have no idea. He has a very bad accent.'

~

Haiti

'Tyranny, oppression, tortures, assassinations and palace intrigues'

EDWARD 'NICK' LARMOUR, HM AMBASSADOR TO THE
REPUBLIC OF HAITI, OCTOBER 1970

Dr François 'Papa Doc' Duvalier was one of recent history's more appalling dictators. Some 30,000–60,000 Haitians are thought to have perished during his fourteen-year rule at the hands of the Tonton Macoutes. The President-for-Life's straw-hatted personal paramilitary force, wearing blue denim shirts and mirror glasses, sometimes stoned or burned victims alive.

The personality cult Duvalier fostered around himself was enhanced by voodoo, the traditions of which he helped to revive, and which is still practised by huge numbers of Haitians today. Papa Doc claimed to be a houngan, *or voodoo priest, modelling himself on Baron Samedi, the spirit of death.*

Having presented his credentials as non-resident Ambassador to Haiti, Nick Larmour returned to Kingston, Jamaica, where he flew the flag as resident High Commissioner. I met him there (my father had been posted to Kingston by his company) as an undergraduate, and remember his amused intelligence at the dinner table. His genial lack of pomposity helped persuade me that a career as a diplomat might be for me. The minutes show Larmour's Papa Doc despatch was warmly received by officials in Whitehall for conveying admirably 'the atmosphere, both

comic and more than slightly sinister, of this particular cor-
ner of Graham Greeneland'.

Larmour was correct in his prediction that Duvalier's ill
health would soon bring about a change of leadership in
Haiti. Papa Doc's death came in fact just six months after
the ambassador's encounter with him. The long list of
potential successors to Papa Doc in Larmour's despatch
had, however, one key omission. François Duvalier was in
fact succeeded by his nineteen-year-old son, Jean-Claude,
a possibility which Larmour's first impressions failed
altogether to consider. 'Baby Doc' ruled until 1986, and,
after a long exile in France, returned to Haiti in 2011, seek-
ing power once again.

The brain drain caused by decades of violent misrule still
blights Haiti today, as it also struggles to rebuild from the
utter devastation caused by a tremendous earthquake in
January 2010.

CONFIDENTIAL

(HA 1/1)　　　　　　　　BRITISH EMBASSY TO HAITI,
C/O BRITISH HIGH COMMISSION, KINGSTON,
19 October, 1970.

Sir,

I have the honour to report that I have at last been able to
carry out the instructions contained in your Despatch
No. PF 21542 of the 30th of April and that on the 6th of
October, I presented my Letters of Credence, and the Let-
ters of Recall of my predecessor, to Dr. Francois Duvalier,
President-for-Life of the Republic of Haiti.

As you will observe, I have been kept waiting for an appointment for five months. I had made many attempts and had suggested various blocks of dates during this period but none of them had proved convenient. This is in part due to the unbelievable inefficiency of the Haitian Government machinery and in part to the fact that, as a Note from the Ministry of Foreign Affairs quaintly informed me, the President-for-Life 'had granted himself a well-earned leave during July and August' and had decided to undertake none but the most urgent tasks of Government . . .

The summons to Haiti came at two days' notice but the organisation surprisingly worked and the protocol was impeccable. Although everything was a bit behind the advertised time, I drove in a motorcade with motor cycle escort, was received with all due honours by a whole battalion of the Presidential Guard, whose band made a very creditable shot at 'God Save The Queen', and was passed through a succession of more and more elevated officials and Ministers until I was ushered into the Presidential Presence. His office, where the ceremony took place, is a modest enough little room. He sat behind a large and imposing desk on which I looked surreptitiously (but in vain) for the mummified head of one of his would-be assassins, which popular legend (and some recent publications) have alleged that he keeps permanently by him for Voodoo purposes.[1] A suite of Ministers and senior officials stood by whilst I presented my Letters, all dressed (like myself) in tropical white suits of varying degrees of cleanliness and all, except the cheerful Chief of Protocol, looking, I thought, distinctly unhappy and ill at ease. Papa Doc himself was beautifully turned out and received me with much dignity and some warmth. Although I had been told that there were to be no speeches and had therefore, putting my text aside, limited myself to some very brief politenesses, the President did in fact deliver a short speech; but in a voice so low and a delivery so mumbling that I had some difficulty in following it. He referred to 'clouds in our relationship in the past' which he hoped had now been dispelled and ended by wishing me a successful mission and sending his greetings and best wishes to The Queen. We then sat down tête-à-tête and I was able, at this shorter range, to hear a little more clearly what he had to say ... At the end of the interview I withdrew and received again in reverse order the courtesies with which I had been welcomed.

The whole business had a certain air of unreality. Apart from a curious sheen on his face like black parchment, which gives him a slightly ghostly appearance, Papa Doc looked exactly like anybody's family doctor or solicitor or retired diplomat. His incredibly low speaking voice, his hesitant delivery and his general air of mildness made it difficult to remember that I was shaking one of the most bloodstained hands in recent history. This was the man who had personally taken command of a firing squad which shot nineteen officers of the Presidential Guard, some of whom he suspected, probably with justice, of being his daughters' lovers, and who had ordered the execution out of hand of a whole family of seventeen for failing to report the arrival in their village of allegedly unfriendly agents. These are but two of a hundred examples that could be quoted of acts of similar ferocity ...

I had never before met Papa Doc ... [He has] suffered at least one heart attack on top of his chronic diabetes and my impression was of a man of eighty rather than the 63 years to which he admits ... [M]y Guyanese colleague, Mrs Gaskin, Mr Laister, my First Secretary (Information) who accompanied me, and I all shared the quite definite impression that he is a very sick man, that he has gone rapidly down hill in recent years, and that he is perhaps not likely to be with us too much longer.

I questioned my diplomatic colleagues about the likely succession and got, as one might expect, a variety of guesses. Some thought that the Minister of Finance, M.C.M. Desinor, was a likely candidate; but most agreed that, though able enough, he was unusually corrupt, even for a Haitian Finance Minister, and that he might, despite his present, perhaps ephemeral, popularity with the President-for-Life, before long be exiled or at least dismissed. Another name mentioned was that of the President of the National Bank ...The Commandant of the Presidential Guard, Colonel Gracia Jacques, an ex-Tonton Macoute thug who, as the President-for-Life's personal and apparently trusted bodyguard, in fact controls the instruments of power, might seize the imperial purple: but he has neither the brains nor the education for the job and if he were to try to stage a coup, seems more likely to meet the fate of Sejanus,[2] Prefect of the Praetorian Guard under Tiberius, who was so unwise as to make a premature bid for power. I slip thus into the Roman past because I have been lately reading the preface by Graham Greene to the recently published 'Haiti and its Dictator' by Bernard Diderich, in which he compares Haiti with the Rome of the late Empire. This is by no means inapt: besides the tyranny, oppression, tortures, assassinations and palace intrigues, Haiti has its counterpart to the Senate and the aristocracy in the mulattos, a lively and talented race who, powerful in the past, now however no longer, like their Roman precursors in their time, either play, or will be allowed to play, any part in the Government of the country. That is conducted in a corrupt and remarkably inefficient way by the President and his immediate advisers, mainly trusty blacks who might be compared with the freedmen who used to run the Imperial Roman machine and kept faithfully enough the <u>arcana imperii</u>.[3] Whoever succeeds, I imagine that the same quality and colour of Government will continue, though just possibly in a more merciful and more enlightened style. My noble and unhappy Italian colleague, whose wife lives permanently in Italy because she does not, as he sadly put it, like the heat or the germs, speculated about the succession and thought it not impossible that Madame Dominique, who is apparently indeed a formidable woman and the only person of whom the President is said to stand in awe, might in the event win power for herself and her husband after her father's disappearance from the scene. But, though dominated by his wife, Colonel Dominique loves the fleshpots, and will not easily be persuaded to quit Paris. A more likely possibility, in the short term is a combined Tonton Macoute/Army junta, such as has temporarily taken power in the past. But all bets are open: in Haiti anything can happen.

1. *mummified head ... for Voodoo purposes*: Larmour should have tried the closet. The head belonged to Blucher Philogenes, an army officer who led a failed coup attempt in 1963. Duvalier kept this gruesome souvenir in a cupboard, so the story goes, believing it could predict the future.
2. *fate of Sejanus*: Sejanus (20 BC–AD 31), a Roman soldier, used his

friendship with the Emperor to gain high political office, and became de facto ruler of the entire Roman Empire when the reclusive Tiberius left Rome for Capri in AD 26. Sejanus consolidated his power through bloody purges. His downfall five years later was swift; arrested on suspicion of conspiring against the Emperor, Sejanus was strangled and his body cast down on the Gemonian Stairs; a dishonourable death.
3. *arcana imperii*: State secrets.

~

Morocco

'5 hours and 11 minutes' notice'

RONALD BAILEY, HM AMBASSADOR TO THE KINGDOM OF
MOROCCO, APRIL 1972

Being kept waiting in Morocco has been the fate of mightier personages even than Mr Bailey. When Queen Elizabeth and her Royal entourage paid a goodwill visit to Morocco in 1980 her composure was strained by King Hassan II's eccentricities. After enduring a desert performance of 'falcons savaging live pigeons' she was kept waiting for three hours in ninety degree heat, while Hassan 'saw to arrangements' in his air-conditioned trailer. 'Going to Morocco is a bit like being kidnapped,' commented one of the Queen's associates.

Three months ago today I presented my Letters of Credence to His Majesty King Hassan II of Morocco and so ended 10 weeks' 'purdah'. The ceremony, although recently much simplified, still had the touch of the 'Arabian Nights' – the guard of honour in red and gold with flowing cloaks, the giant black-faced halberdiers lining the stairs and the King himself in the simple monk-like burnous that he and his Court affect on these occasions.

For the first two and a half months of my stay in Morocco it was made clear to me that I should make no calls on officials or foreign colleagues until His Majesty had accepted my credentials. Neither could I leave Rabat. I was regaled with stories of other Ambassadors who had dared to do so for even a day or so and who having failed to attend the unexpected and instant summons had to wait another three months. After a false alarm in December I received 5 hours and 11 minutes' notice of the presentation ceremony. I understand this is generous notice by Moroccan standards.

$\sim$

Jordan

'My washerwoman handed in her notice together with a segment of her behind'

GLENCAIRN BALFOUR PAUL, HM AMBASSADOR TO THE HASHEMITE KINGDOM OF JORDAN, FEBRUARY 1973

More from, and about, Balfour Paul can be found on pp. 277–83.

RESTRICTED

BRITISH EMBASSY
27 February 1973

The Right Honourable
Sir Alec Douglas-Home KT MP
etc etc etc

Sir,

THOUGHTS ON THE PROTECTION OF DIPLOMATIC AGENTS

No matter can be of more lively concern to an Ambassador, however marked the degree of Wisdom, Loyalty, Diligence and Circumspection he may exercise in other fields, than the security of his person. Nor is this concern peculiar to himself: the abduction, temporary or permanent, of an Ambassador by terrorists is almost bound to impose on your hardpressed administrative departments an unwelcome measure of overtime.

It was with these twin considerations in mind that I was prevailed upon, towards the end of 1972, to propose to the Department that they should furnish me, for my protection, with a Large Dog – the local breeds, as I argued, lacking both discipline and decorum. The response was generous and instantaneous. (It was also, I learned later, experimental.) And so it was that, just in time for the Christmas festivities, there arrived at Amman Airport in a moderate-sized lift-van – thoughtfully inscribed, in order to facilitate its passage through Customs and Immigration, 'This Side Up. Very Vicious' – the scion of a long line of Cruft's champions, Auslander of Druidswood (now abridged, to reflect the undertone of human sacrifice, as Druid).

In this despatch, and in response to an enquiry from Security Department, I have the honour to submit some observations on this experiment, which may be of value to those considering its wider application.

Druid was accompanied by a Guide to German Shepherd Dogs, published by the Pet Library Limited and movingly dedicated by its author, Madeleine Pickup, to 'All those Beloveds who have gone on Ahead to where Separation is Unknown'. It has proved an even more absorbing <u>vade mecum</u>[1] than Druid himself. My interest was quickly engaged by reading, in its historical chapter, how 'Rittmeister (cavalry captain) Max Emile Friedrich von Stephanitz, having recognised the potential beauty of the native sheep-herding breeds of Wurttenburg and Thuringia founded the Verein für Deutsche Schäferhunde'[2]; and how 'lack of sex character is strongly condemned by the Germans, and in America it is marked as a <u>serious</u> fault if the male is bitchy or the bitch doggy. No mention,' Miss Pickup continues, 'is made by the British.' (She was writing of course some years ago.) It was, however, less encouraging to turn to the chapter on Training and to discover that an Alsatian is 'made' in his first six months – less encouraging, since Druid was seven months old on arrival; and his 'making' seemed, at least to someone as cushioned from brute realities as a Head of Mission, to be distinctly incomplete.

For within a few days, despite my rigorous attention to Miss Pickup's injunctions and my continuing to share with him what is left of my bedroom, Druid had left his mark indelibly on most of my household furnishings and staff. My washerwoman handed in her notice together with a segment of her behind. Though quickly mastering sundry arts, such as opening locked doors with his teeth, Druid has proved unable to distinguish between lightly boiled cubes of red meat and other vaguely comestible objects, such as antique silver ash-trays, ladies' footwear or the toys of my Head of Chancery's baby daughter who happened to be lodging with me – the whole range of the latter, together with the whole range of my Social Secretary's nylon tights (at the average consumption rate of one every three days) having been successfully ingested. His louche proclivity for dancing unmonitored on the dining-room table, against which even Miss Pickup omits to recommend a specific, has enlivened its sober patina with baroque striations, has materially affected the complement of damask napkins on the Residence inventory, and has even reduced to scrap metal several of the silver napkin rings once lavished on my children by godparents at their baptism. Locked on one dramatic evening in my bedroom – for he is not yet sufficiently representational to accompany me to such occasions as the South Vietnamese National Day reception – he located in a chest of drawers and consumed a year's supply of vitamin powders, proceeded high-spiritedly to lay a paper chase of foam rubber mattressing round and round the Master Suite and to masticate the major part of the top blanket on the double-bed on which, after recovering from a bout of nausea on the carpet, he remained comfortably ensconced till my return, relieving himself in it at intervals.

It should be noted, when considering the postings of Guard Dogs, that the excreta of animals are regarded by Moslem domestics as <u>haram</u> (forbidden); but, as Miss Pickup might put it, an Ambassador enterprising enough to dispose strategically through his premises a supply of worn towelling and buckets of ready diluted Lysol (in the recommended proportions of 1:4) will soon adjust himself to his guardian's foibles and learn to manage their removal on his own.

This further observation from my experience may be in place. Whereas the general run of grocers' boys, by now at least twice shy, have learnt to park their bicycles by the gate, deposit their merchandise by agreement in a remote cache and pedal swiftly away, Druid is otherwise conspicuously courteous to unexpected visitors with whom he is unfamiliar, licking their extremities with great friendliness when he has opened the door for them. Only towards my domestic staff does he maintain an attitude of stern suspicion, resolutely protecting me from (at any rate) my Early Morning Tea.

Some early reluctance was shown at having to accompany me daily to my office, and particularly at having to ascend its several flights of marble stairs. However, this was soon overcome by stationing my Defence Attaché, whose trousers have long been impregnated with the necessary aroma, two or three steps higher up and thus, bit by bit and bite by bite, enticing my protector to make the ascent.

But it is not easy, even in a relaxed and freightless post like the Hashemite Kingdom, to accommodate the two or three hours training exercises for a Guard Dog recommended by Miss Pickup into an Ambassador's modest daily schedule.

A request for the addition to my staff of a Third Secretary (Dog Handling) has not found favour and would in any case be a breach of the essential dog/ambassador intimacy. Fortunately a continuous stream of political reporting is, in these post-Plowden[3] days, no longer imperative; and since the successful exploitation of my Defence Attaché's trousers on the stairs to my office, the number of human callers there has conveniently decreased. So within a year or two I hope to have moved on, during my idle moments, to Pickup page 157 and to have embarked on the more advanced lesson in which the pupil, after being gently scratched on belly and chest for some minutes, submits to the order 'Die for your country'! Meanwhile, I confess there are moments when I feel it might be more convenient for everyone if I simply did it myself.

I am sending a copy of this despatch to Her Majesty's Representative at Ulan Bator.

I have the honour to be Sir

Your obedient Servant
H. G. BALFOUR PAUL

1. *vade mecum*: Guidebook.
2. *Verein für Deutsche Schäferhunde*: Association for German Shepherd Dogs.
3. *post-Plowden*: The recommendations of the 1964 Plowden Committee on Representational Service Overseas led to a greater emphasis on the promotion of exports, and a reduction in ambassadors' traditional 'political' work.

~

Turkmenistan

'The free condom policy causes him alarm . . . His solution is to request manfully large numbers'

PAUL BRUMMELL, HM AMBASSADOR TO
TURKMENISTAN, APRIL 2002

When diplomats write letters of complaint to London, certain tropes tend to appear time and again. One is the bewilderment felt by ambassadors in countries very different *to the UK on receipt of blanket instructions issued by well-meaning officials in Whitehall. The National Salute to the Sultan of Muscat and Oman, the first despatch in this collection, is the finest example. The tele-letter (secure email) below is another, which adds a modern, politically incorrect twist.*

It was sent by our ambassador in Ashgabat to the Medical and Welfare team in Personnel Command, in response to an official circular instructing posts to start issuing free condoms to their staff. To British eyes this doubtless seemed like a responsible initiative designed to halt the spread of HIV. The trouble was that many of the staff on the receiving end were not British. UK embassies overseas are staffed at the lower levels by a considerable number of foreign nationals: 'locally-engaged' (LE) staff who draw a pay cheque from HMG but may be presumed to remain culturally attuned to their own country. And of course the sexual revolution that has transformed British society since the 1960s passed much of the developing world by.

When the FCO released Brummell's letter to us, they explained that 'its tone is light hearted and its circulation was limited to two people, who received it in that spirit'. We understand that the FCO COMCEN (Communication Centre) gave it a far wider distribution than that, however, and it was soon being forwarded and copied high and low throughout the Foreign Office and to posts overseas. Brummell wanted his despatch to make his colleagues think, as well as laugh, something the Foreign Office readily acknowledge: 'It does make some important points about the potential impact of limited prior consultation,' they told us, 'and the need to be culturally sensitive in promulgating a policy which applied to all FCO employees worldwide.' It's hard to believe the characters that Brummell so graphically describes were as hypothetical as claimed; one senses the Ambassador knew some of them quite well.

Jack Straw was Foreign Secretary at the time. In 2010 without naming names he told us of an ambassador to 'one of the "Stans"' whose despatches could bring 'tears of laughter to your eyes'. The humour was 'at the expense of the dictator where he was, and this kind of pantomime – but actually very serious pantomime – at which he has a ringside seat'. Straw recalled the Ambassador describing 'having to attend the national day banquet, and seeing this man who had gold statues all over the capital prance around in self glorification . . . It would have been good if he and his acolytes had read it. Because it might have made them realise just what lunatics they were.' Straw insisted every single one of this ambassador's despatches went into his ministerial box for personal reading. No prizes for guessing who wrote them (the regime also fits the bill – see pp. 46–53 for more on Turkmenistan).

Uzbekistan, Tajikistan, Kazakhstan, Kyrgyzstan . . . Could our embassies in the 'Stans' turn out to be a new goldmine of comic despatches, the successors to earlier hotspots like Vietnam and South America? Possibly. But these countries are also resource superpowers so the FCO is understandably careful about what it releases. The Foreign Office took the unusual step of refusing outright our FOI request for four First Impressions despatches from the region (including two from Brummell), saying that they contain sensitive political and commercial information which is exempt from disclosure.

FM ASHGABAT
TO TELELETTER FCO
TELELETTER 16
OF 101100Z APRIL 02

From: Paul Brummell, HMA
To: [name withheld]
And To: [name withheld]

SUBJECT: A CONDOM CONUNDRUM

Summary
1. New policy on condoms is welcome, but local implementation is not straightforward.

DETAIL
2. FCO Circular 104 of 3 April (some here wondered whether it was sent two days late) sets out new policy regarding the distribution of condoms to staff. This is welcome evidence of the Administration's willingness to respond to the public health concerns of all our staff, LE and UK-based. But implementation is not entirely straightforward. Consider the following hypothetical members of an Embassy:

– Young Miss T, of a deeply conservative family, has a new boyfriend. She has recently discovered that he once dabbled with injected drugs, and is worried that he may be HIV Positive. She is, in short, exactly the kind of member of staff the new policy is designed to help. But she is terrified that her work colleagues might discover that she is actually having sex. She would never place an order for condoms from her employer, and is nervous of taking condoms from a 'help yourself' basket in the ladies toilet as she believes her two female colleagues will quickly work out her secret.

– Vivacious Miss U has no regular boyfriend. She enjoys clubbing on a Friday night, and will occasionally end the evening with male company. The new FCO policy cannot, however, help her.

The local night clubs are frequently subject to police raids, with all customers searched. Under local practice, any unmarried women found in possession of condoms are liable to be arrested as prostitutes. Miss U therefore has to rely on a responsible attitude from her male partners.

– Pious Mrs V believes that all forms of contraception are a sin. She is angered by the new FCO policy, which she believes to be evidence of declining British moral values. When a basket of condoms appears in the ladies toilet, she flushes them all down the loo. The resulting blockage of the plumbing is resolved at a cost of fifty pounds to local budget.

– Corrupt Mr W is newly married. He and his wife are desperate to start a family. He has, in short, no need for condoms. But he is not one to look a gift horse in the mouth. He takes as many free condoms as he thinks he can get away with, which he then sells on to his brother, who runs a market stall.

– Pug-faced Mr X has many attributes. Unfortunately, none of them have brought him any success with women. Not his stamp collection, his heavy metal, his gurning. The free condom policy causes him alarm. He has no need for them, but certainly does not want his colleagues to know that. His solution is to request mannishly large numbers. They then lie in the back of his wardrobe where, at Her

Majesty's expense, they sit moving inexorably towards their three year expiry date.

– Raffish and experimental Mr Y (known to friends as Mr Y Not), would like to see more consumer choice, to include French ticklers and assorted fruit flavours.

– And well-endowed Mr Z is concerned at the FCO's apparent one size fits all policy.

3. Decisions regarding local implementation of the policy can address some of these problems; but no method seems to solve all. A requirement for staff to sign for condoms would for example help placate Mrs V, and thwart Mr W's crimes, but at the considerable cost of failing to help Miss T. Conversely, anonymous means of distribution, such as a free-vend machine in the toilets, may eventually come to be trusted by Miss T, would resolve Mr X's concerns, but would offend Mrs V and provide Mr W with a licence to print money. I fear this telegram must conclude lamely not with a solution but with a caution: this is a positive and welcome policy, but its implementation locally in the very different cultures in which FCO posts find ourselves is not nearly as straightforward as FCO Circular 104 implies.

Signed . . . . Paul Brummell

~

Mongolia

'The hotel's electric clocks were made to go, even if in some cases with only one hand'

SIR REGINALD HIBBERT, HM CHARGÉ D'AFFAIRES
IN ULAN BATOR, AUGUST 1965

The very name 'Outer Mongolia' is a byword for some-where impossibly remote and off the beaten track. Being sent as a junior diplomat to Mongolia might not have struck Reginald Hibbert as a great career move. But, the first British envoy in the modern era to be posted there, as Chargé d'Affaires in Ulan Bator Hibbert managed to turn the situation to his advantage.

Hibbert 'made his name', say some who read his des-patches the first time round, on the quality of his reports from what was then a Communist satellite state, a country about which most of his readers in the Foreign Office knew nothing.

After enduring two freezing years in Mongolia, Hibbert came in from the cold, rising rapidly through the ranks to become Political Director in Whitehall, a job at the very heart of great-power diplomacy. He ended his career on the Rue du Faubourg Saint-Honoré, in the most beautiful and lavish British Embassy in the world, as Ambassador to France.

CONFIDENTIAL

BRITISH EMBASSY,
ULAN BATOR.
27 August, 1965.

U.N. Seminar on the Participation of Women in Public Life

Sir,

Miss Sheila Harden, the United Kingdom observer at the recent seminar on the Participation of Women in Public Life which was arranged in Ulan Bator by the United Nations in cooperation with the Government of the Mongolian People's Republic will I think be submitting a report on the proceedings of the seminar. I have the honour to report on the significance of the seminar as an event in the diplomatic life of the M.P.R.

The seminar was the first international conference with delegates from non-communist countries ever to be held in Ulan Bator . . . The seminar, no doubt a minor event by U.N. standards, was an important new achievement in the M.P.R.'s policy of obtaining recognition on the world stage as a fully sovereign and independent state.

The Mongolian authorities made very careful preparations. The eight Mongolian English language students at Leeds University were not allowed to stay in England more than six months, so that they could be available in Ulan Bator as organisers and interpreters during the seminar. The sessions of the seminar were held in the hall and rooms of the Great People's Khural. The national ballet, opera and circus were re-opened in the middle of the holiday and provincial tour season to entertain the delegates.

All Foreign Ministry officials capable of speaking western languages were concentrated on servicing the seminar and its delegates. The Ulan Bator hotel was partly refurnished and extensively redecorated in the days preceding the seminar. The hotel lift was made to work for two weeks and the hotel's electric clocks were made to go, even if in some cases with only one hand. The menu improved gratifyingly and the service for residents deteriorated sadly as a result of the prodigious effort to feed and serve the delegates in their segregated dining-room in a manner which would not shock them. The picturesque but impoverished and shabby Sunday market was closed by the police for the duration. An east German woman who claims to be the only trained hairdresser in Mongolia and who usually does business privately with the ladies of the diplomatic corps was brow-beaten into becoming the official hotel hairdresser for a fortnight. The postal and telegraph services remained open for excessively long hours (but the service did not improve correspondingly because the girls spent most of the time contriving to have their hair done by the east German). A comically vain effort was made by the police to enforce good road drill among pedestrians in the neighbourhood of the hotel. Special and exceptional arrangements were made for most delegates to be entertained privately by some of the Mongolian women associated with the seminar.

All these efforts were concentrated on a dozen Asian ladies, three Asian men, three American observers, a British observer and a large contingent from the U.N. Secretariat. The operation was generally successful. The aim seemed to be to keep the seminar participants totally occupied and totally segregated in the company of a fixed staff of approved Mongols of both sexes . . . The Mongolian Government managed to have its cake and eat it, in the sense that the seminar went off successfully and the participants were overwhelmed with well-organised hospitality, while the chances of wrong thoughts being spread in simple Mongol minds by the presence of so many representatives of non-communist Asian states were reduced to a minimum.

Miss Harden will no doubt report on the effect of the Mongolian hospitality technique on the minds of the visitors. My own impression was that the delegates, thanks in large part to the robust and humorous leadership of Mrs Lakshmi Menon, and in the closing stages after her departure to that of Mrs Ambhorn Meesook of Thailand, were not deceived by it. Besides, the seminar lasted two weeks; and ten days is about as long as most people can remain blind to the real nature of the system here, deaf to the absurdity of the claims of perfection made for it in the name of Lenin, and insensible to the meagreness of such modern, material civilisation as exists in the M.P.R.

~

Unknown

'A changing world of challenging change'

UNKNOWN DIPLOMAT, APRIL 1994

Certain aspects of modern life seem almost deliberately designed to get up the noses of British diplomats. One, as previous despatches showed, is political correctness. Another is management-speak. Like much of the public sector over the past thirty years the Foreign Office has been subjected to wave after wave of efficiency reviews led by management consultants; and their misuse of the English language has reliably enraged even mild-mannered diplomats.

The backlash reached its apotheosis in a 2006 valedictory despatch by Sir Ivor Roberts, who was ending a distinguished diplomatic career as ambassador in Rome. 'Too much of the change management agenda,' wrote Sir Ivor, 'is written in Wall Street management-speak which is already tired and discredited by the time it is introduced. Synergies, vfm, best practice, benchmarking, silo-working, roll-out, stakeholder, empower, push-back and deliver the agenda, fit for purpose, are all prime candidates for a game of bullshit bingo, a substitute for clarity and succinctness.' The phrase 'bullshit bingo' unfortunately leaked, along with much else, into the Sunday papers – and thus (as we recount in Parting Shots) began the end of the valedictory despatch, which the then Foreign Secretary was persuaded by senior officials to ban forthwith.

What follows is proof that Roberts was tapping into a long-established vein of similar dyspepsia. Unlike other extracts in this collection the circular below is not genuine diplomatic traffic, however; rather, it was an April Fool's Day spoof. Nevertheless, it is said to have been carried, forwarded from terminal to terminal, in the same Foreign Office communication system that enabled real despatches to be read right across the Diplomatic Service.

The circular is deliberately stuffed with ghastly acronyms, not all of them fictitious: the PUS for instance is the Foreign Office's civil service chief, the Permanent Under-Secretary; the DUS and AUS are his deputy and assistant *under-secretaries. The Diplomatic Service career ladder is inverted so that the most senior staff are on pay grades 1–3 and under-secretaries are dozens of rungs above secretaries (who are by no means the same thing as private secretaries and who are now called personal assistants, anyway). DS10s are therefore at the bottom of the heap. The anonymous author of this circular would appear to sit somewhere in the middle.*

FOREIGN AND COMMONWEALTH OFFICE

CIRCULAR 1 /14 / SPOOF02

TARGET AUDIENCE: ALL STAFF, EVEN DS10S

If you are a secretary, please ask a friend to read this circular to you.

FOREIGN AND COMMONWEALTH OFFICE MANAGEMENT PRIORITIES AND OBJECTIVES ASSESSMENT PROGRAMME: MAKING THE CHANGE TO MEET THE CHALLENGE OF A CHANGING WORLD OF CHALLENGING CHANGE

Management is about change. Many changes are likely in the FCO as a result of the Whitehall-wide, ocean-deep, mountain-high, pencil-thin, thorough-going, wide-ranging, across-the-board, up the creek and underneath the arches Whitehall Review of Whitehall (WRW), recently conducted by the Management, Objectives and Operations Cabinet Office Working Group (MOOCOW).

Meeting the challenge of this change will be a challenge for all of us, requiring, as it will, change, and bringing with it, sometimes radical, challenge. This circular is to let you know how the FCO is meeting this changing challenge. The Board of Change Management and Challenge Assessment (BCMCA: chaired by the PUS, consisting of all DUSs and AUSs), has identified the following processes which must guide our approach to the challenge of change and the opportunity of options:

(a) <u>change management</u>: assessing which changes to manage,

(b) <u>managing change</u>: the process by which changes are first identified, then assessed, then managed;

(c) <u>the management of change</u>: where managers, having identified and assessed change, and assessed and identified how to manage it, set up a committee(s) to ensure that both the change management and managing change processes are managed in order to produce the desired managed change;

(d) <u>challenge management</u>: it is essential that we distinguish between change (see above) and challenge; a challenge is a change which, while being managed, changes, thus producing further change and the challenge of channelling the process of change in a direction which optimises our opportunities, while not prejudging our priorities for action, in the Post-Cold War, after-the-Berlin-wall, pre-EMU, run-up to the IGC world of the future.

<u>Challenging the change of future challenges</u>.
The main challenges which will need to be met by FCO senior management are the following:

<u>Senior Management Review</u>: the Senior Management Review (SMR) has challenged the FCO to assess what changes should be made to the FCO structure at Grades 1–3.

A Working Party (WP), meeting daily, chaired by the PUS and consisting of all Deputy and Assistant Under-Secretaries has begun an independent and wide-ranging review of the activities of Grades 1–3 (now known as the Senior Grade Cadre Management Group Stratum (SGCMGS)). Its work continues: it is scheduled to produce its report by 30 March 2007. But its initial, preliminary, indicative and firm initial, provisional conclusions are:

– that all staff in Grades 1–3 make a full and appropriate contribution to the FCO's work;

– that all staff in Grades 1–3 are at least satisfactorily loaded: for example, each DUS or AUS attends at least one meeting every day for consultations on important management issues with other members of the Senior Grade Cadre Management Group Stratum (SGCMGS);

– that structural inefficiencies in the FCO appear to be tightly concentrated in Grades 4–10. And S1, S2 and S2A. And Security Officers. And messengers. And those people who drive those vans.

– that the Senior Grade Cadre Management Group Stratum are paid much less than their equivalents in other professions (results of survey by independent management consultants Dimwit, Dolalley and Workshy covering senior management remuneration in the diamond-broking, narcotics trafficking and popular music production industries).

The Working Party's initial, preliminary and provisional final conclusions are:

– to establish a separate, independent Change Management Committee, or CMC (chaired by the PUS, consisting of all DUSs and AUSs) to oversee the production of a report on the likely implications of the Senior Management Review for staffing at Grades 4–10;

– that, separately, the Board of Management (BOM) should commission a paper from a new-entrant DS9 in Starting Pay Section, PSD on how best to adapt the FCO's entire personnel management system for Grades 4–10 in the light of the Change Management Committee's paper on managing the challenges of this change; this paper to be written by 3 April 1995, and to focus on the introduction of flexibly-graded, job-centred, objective-focussed, short-term contracted, exponentially-oscillating 'work bands' to replace the outmoded, outdated and overstretched grading structure: officers will be freely able to move within their core work band from operational function to operational function better to optimise our flexibility to reconfigure the spatial geography of our work resource environment and to minimise dislocation at the all-important human resources/financial perspectives interface; this paper to take note of the likely implications of the forthcoming Treasury Uplift and Regressive Downsizing Study (TURDS);

– that the Policy Management Board (PMB), and, separately, the Board of Policy Management (BPM) should reflect on the likely implications of the managed change process in the wider perspective of the FCO's overseas commitments;

– that we should not rush into the upcoming environment of managed change, changed management and planned challenge without a wholescale, hewn-from-the-solid, salt-of-the-earth review of the FCO's future policy priorities. The Policy Management Board have therefore commissioned Policy Planning Staff to produce a number of papers, for early discussion by the Board of Policy Management, to include the following:

(a) Is America a large country?

(b) Foreigners: why they aren't English;

(c) Germany after the Berlin wall: did it get bigger?

(d) Ethnic imperialism, tribal nationalism and loose big-power confederation in a globalising economy: implications for British consular policy;

(e) The Commonwealth: kindly aunt or sex-crazed stepmother?

(f) Japanese economic power: Pacific Rim or lavatory bowl?

(g) The challenge of China: opportunities for the British trouser press industry; (joint FCO/DTI paper);

(h) The Pope: is he really a Catholic?

The Board of Changing Management Challenges (BCMC) are confident that this process will result in a tighter, more focussed, objectively-objectivised, goal-oriented, target-chasing, foot-dragging Service better suited to meet the challenges of the post-national, pre-global 'wash and go' world of the future.

<u>Junior staff Expenditure-Saving Process (JESP).</u> The Junior staff Expenditure-Saving Process is a result of the King Charles St-wide Policy Review of Staffing Management Procedures. I know that the JESP has caused some worries among staff, who fear that it will result in jobs being cut simply to save money. That is not the JESP's intention. Rather, it will contribute to our ability to challenge the changes of future challenge by restructuring our expenditure on staffing levels at the middle, middling, junior and juniorish Grades by a gradual process (lasting, perhaps, many days) of re-assessing our job requirements in the light of diminishing real-terms resource availability. There is no intention that any staff will be dismissed, though the Policy Board of Managers' Management Board (PBMMB) is unable to rule out the possibility that, at some time in the future (perhaps 27 February 1995), structurally-enforced voluntary early career curtailment procedures may have to

be instituted in a very limited number of cases (probably affecting about 837 officers).

I know that there is apprehension in the Service about these changes. You should not be worried. The process of change offers new challenges for us to change to deal better with the challenges of a changing world of challenging change. I can assure you that the Policy Management Managers Policy Assessment Board has the interests of the Service as a whole as its highest priority . . .

A M Woodforthetrees
Chairman of the Board of Change Policy Management
The big office with the nice furniture and the view over
  Horseguards
King Charles' Street
1 April 1994

2. First Impressions

PART I: SOUTH-EAST ASIA

Indonesia

'Sour, hungry and hostile to foreigners'

SIR ALAN DONALD, HM AMBASSADOR TO THE
REPUBLIC OF INDONESIA, JULY 1984

BRITISH EMBASSY
JAKARTA
31 July 1984

The Rt Hon Sir Geoffrey Howe QC MP
LONDON

Sir

FIRST IMPRESSIONS OF INDONESIA

Although this is my first posting to Jakarta, I have visited
Indonesia before: for a week in 1959, three days in 1982 and
an unforgettable 24 hours in 1983.

My first experience of Jakarta 25 years ago was depressing. The public utilities were hopeless: nothing seemed to
work. The city seemed to be a patchwork of kampongs.
Some pretentious public buildings were linked by a few

main roads. One winced (as now) at the Soviet-inspired statues. It was the time of anti-imperialism, anti-colonialism and empty slogans. The people in the streets looked sour, hungry and hostile to foreigners. No-one had much good to say about the economy or the will of the people to work. I privately hoped that I would not have to set foot in Indonesia again.

The second (post-Sukarno) visit was quite different. As one of Lord Carrington's party on his official visit to Indonesia in January 1982, I had a completely new picture. I saw a bustling, thriving community in a capital which had already acquired some of the outward appearances and certainly the traffic of modern cities like Bangkok and Singapore. The organisation of the visit was excellent: the leaders we met were intelligent and confident – men who knew where they and their country were going.

The following year, in March 1983, I arrived 24 hours late (travelling on the national airline) only to be caught up in a riot which swept through the streets of Jakarta. The campaign for the presidential election had opened that afternoon with the burning of the platform on which the Government spokesman was addressing a large crowd. After my business at the Foreign Ministry, it took me nearly three hours to get through to the airport with a colonel and an armed military escort in an army jeep, weaving our way through burning motorcars and a mass of excited youths. I missed the plane, but I saw the problems of security and public order in a country where there is no trained civil police force and where the choice often lies between the absence of control and calling the army in with full force. To my astonishment, the Indonesian papers the next day made no mention of any disorder and the campaign was enthusiastically described as having got off to a good and quiet start.

Since I presented my Credentials 10 weeks ago, I have heard of a fire which destroyed a district in the north of Jakarta making 20,000 people homeless. It was said to have been started by a bunch of torchbearing tearaways on motorcycles acting on the instructions of a rich Chinese Indonesian businessman (alleged to have good contacts with the President) who wanted to acquire and develop the site as a commercial property. One of the arsonists was caught by the locals who cut off his hand. There has been no mention in the press of the incident. The bland way in which the street disorder in 1983 was treated and the cover up of the big fire illustrate quite well the difficulties of a foreign observer getting a true perspective on this complex country, which has the fifth largest population in the world and stretches in an archipelagic chain for 3,500 miles. By way of comparison this is the same distance roughly as from Paris to Ottawa or Peking to Moscow or Tokyo to Darwin. The people living on the over 6,000 habitable islands are drawn from over 300 ethnic groups and practice forms of all the world's major religions. Thus I cannot after only ten weeks make any reliable judgement of Indonesia . . .

∼

'Nothing is said directly'

SIR ROBIN CHRISTOPHER, HM AMBASSADOR TO THE
REPUBLIC OF INDONESIA, 1999

Consensus rules in Java. Nothing is said directly, explicit disagreement or criticism is culturally offensive and confrontation is almost unthinkable. At a personal level, as a new arrival I am constantly aware, in every conversation, of the search for underlying agreement – with a smile. When Soeharto showed Soekarno the door in 1966 he did so with the words 'Father, I always wished to respect you but you would not let me.' On my second day here I read a speech given by the Commander of the Armed Forces at the Military Academy on the dangers of 'egocentric assertiveness' during the forthcoming elections. Only at the end of the lecture did it occur to me what he meant: he was instructing his troops not to shoot on sight.

~

Malaysia

'First impressions here could be guaranteed to mislead'

DAVID GILLMORE, HM HIGH COMMISSIONER TO
MALAYSIA, DECEMBER 1983

The High Commission in Kuala Lumpur was a stepping stone for Gillmore, whose career was to take him on to higher things. In 1990 he became Permanent Under-Secretary of the FCO, the UK's most senior diplomat. He was elevated to the House of Lords in 1996, as Baron Gillmore of Thamesfield.

MALAYSIA: EARLY IMPRESSIONS

From my office window I look down on a bustling city sprouting skyscrapers, some of them elegant and original in design, where traffic moves smoothly on newly-built urban motorways between well-tended gardens. All in all, it does not look much like the third world. The Malaysian middle classes are sophisticated and well-to-do. A small but growing proportion of the bourgeoisie enjoying the new affluence is Malay; not long ago it was almost entirely Chinese. There are complaints about the bureaucracy; but by most third world standards, public administration is conducted with commendable efficiency.

To the casual visitor, therefore Kuala Lumpur, if not the rest of this country, offers a prospect reassuring in its Western-ness and stimulating in its apparent energy and dynamism. But it is not, I suspect, quite as simple as that. Beneath the surface of Malaysian society there are contradictions and tensions. It is for this reason that I have entitled this despatch 'Early Impressions'; I would guess that first impressions here could be guaranteed to mislead.

... Any generalisation about Malaysian society could probably be countered by its opposite. The considerable affluence of the Kuala Lumpur middle class can be set against the poverty of the kampongs; the sophistication of the bourgeoisie against the superstition and backwardness of the bumiputra peasant class; the Westernised manners of the educated classes against the Malaysianness (in its diverse racial forms) of the rest. These contradictions would be of little importance if they did not tug at the fabric of society itself. The contrast between wealth and poverty, sophistication and backwardness is mirrored in the contrast between what is visible on the surface or said in public and the reality beneath ...

Perhaps nowhere are double standards more visible than in the government's attitude to Islam. The government is clearly concerned that fundamentalist Islamic views are infiltrating among the young. In an effort to cut the ground from under the Islamic opposition, the government has made considerable efforts to convey an appearance of Islamic respectability. Malaysia now has an Islamic bank as well as an Islamic university. But when it comes to individuals the double standards are sometimes painfully apparent. A senior Malaysian official, in recent negotiations with the Australians over the RAAF base at Butterworth, insisted that messing for Malaysian and Australian officers should be separate since the former were obliged to eat meat which was not 'halal'. He brushed aside the fact that things had been this way for the last 20 years and had never caused a problem. But once the formal negotiations were over, he was quite unembarrassed to be seen in private consuming several large whiskies with his Australian counterpart. Public performance and private behaviour are no longer easy bedfellows.

~

Vietnam

'Analogies with the lower deck of the Royal Navy'

JOHN FAWCETT, HM AMBASSADOR AT HANOI, MAY 1974

All countries may be equal within the United Nations General Assembly, but as the setting for notable despatches, some stand taller than others. For our purposes, the hierarchy among countries is in fact the inverse of the usual world order. By and large, diplomats representing HMG in the capitals of superpowers and great trading nations wrote less remarkable despatches than those toiling away in obscure backwaters.

Having researched two volumes of these despatches we have learned that if it is striking description, droll national stereotyping and general eccentricity you're after, then the places to turn to are Africa, the (then) banana republics of South America and – looking east – to Vietnam. Indochina seems to have exerted a curious grip on the imaginations of those serving there.

As one of the despatches below by John Stewart attests, diplomats were rotated in and out of 'hardship' posts like Hanoi rather frequently. They were nevertheless still expected to write the customary First Impressions and Valedictory Despatch on arrival and departure. Each one was filed away in the Foreign Office archive, building up over time into a vivid record of what was obviously a challenging post (see also Daphne Park's remarkable valedictory on pp. 365–75). Robert Tesh, representing HMG in rat-infested Hanoi in the late 1970s, asserted simply that 'most foreigners in Vietnam, diplomats or not, are on the verge of insanity' (see Parting Shots, p. 320).

(CONFIDENTIAL) *Hanoi*

16 May, 1974.

Sir,

I have the honour to report that North Viet-Nam is a puzzling sort of place – particularly for someone who has never studied Marxism-Leninism nor lived in any other Communist country.

After a while, I began to cast about for something in my own experience which in any way resembled life under the system here; and to see analogies with the lower deck of the Royal Navy in the years 1947–49. There is the same minority who, for one reason or another, co-operate fully with the authorities; and the same majority who manage, most of the time, to stay out of trouble but whose object, now the war is over, is to get along as comfortably as they can. Other points of resemblance are overcrowding; low pay; a taste for beer and the cinema; 'fiddles' of every kind; readiness to do 'rabbit jobs' – *i.e.* private jobs in public time and with public materials; and the general feeling (amongst the unenthusiastic majority) that life is a long haul, things stay much the same and energy should be conserved.

The differences, however, are instructive. The Naval Discipline Act, as then interpreted, pales before the sanctions available to the authorities here: the prisons have a bad reputation, as do the labour camps, even though the object of the penal system is not so much punishment as re-education in dutiful Communist thought and behaviour. The definition of subversion is wide and the treatment it attracts is harsh. In the navy, there was always plenty to eat. Here, there is no starvation; but the rations are low, 'free-market' supplements to them are expensive and most people look rather under-fed. In the messdecks, overcrowding of men without their families didn't greatly matter. Here, the shortage of urban housing is a major source of misery – my houseboy and his wife and three children share one small room with ten other people now the police will no longer let him and his family live in our house. The lower deck was tolerant towards 'intellectuals'. Here, in a society with its full share of highly talented people, intellectuals must keep strictly to the party line.

Much though I like the North Viet-Namese, I should hate to live as one of them under their present system. It is not, I am told, as repressive as the Chinese one, let alone the North Korean. Nevertheless, in my book it is a tyranny, founded on class-hatred and maintained by indoctrination, propaganda, isolation, surveillance, fear and force . . .

I remain a *soi-disant*[1] Ambassador, prevented from presenting his credentials. I have considered putting up a brass plate reading 'H.E. (Hanoi) failed'. Such, however, is the courtesy of the Viet-Namese, and of my diplomatic colleagues, that the situation has for the most part proved more interesting than painful. We now hear that 'a decision has been taken in principle' – whatever that may portend.

Mr Barrington, in his Despatch 'First and Last Impressions of Hanoi', addressed to your predecessor, has given an admirable account of the sights and sounds and feel of this post. I like it here; and enjoy bicycling about (a privilege denied to my predecessors) and living in our oddly-shaped but quiet and airy house. We are also seeing as much as we can of the country, for example, by driving to Do Son, the former French beach resort outside Haiphong where Rule No. 6 (English version) reads 'Visitors will be advised not to drink too much until they are drunk'. The Viet-Namese themselves are interesting people to deal with; and the Diplomatic Corps is full of vitality and information, reliable and unreliable. I incline to place in the former category the view of the Egyptian Embassy that Ho Chi Minh has not been well embalmed.

1. *soi-disant*: Self-styled; 'so-called'.

~

'The worst climate in the world'

JOHN STEWART, HM CONSUL-GENERAL AT HANOI, MAY
1975

RESTRICTED

BRITISH EMBASSY,
1/1 HANOI,
26 May 1975

The Rt Hon James Callaghan
MP etc etc
Her Majesty's Principal Secretary of State for Foreign
and Commonwealth Affairs

Sir,

FIRST IMPRESSIONS OF HANOI

I have the honour to report that after three months in Hanoi
I am still baffled, infuriated and fascinated by these peculiar
people. Later in this despatch I shall try to expand on and
explain these reactions but I have opened with these words
because they, the Vietnamese, are so different from any
people I have encountered before and because my reactions
to them and their exoticism must permeate what I write.

Writing of one's first impressions of Hanoi and its people
has a difficulty peculiar to this place. The circumstances of
the post during the past 20 years have meant that there has
been a complete change of staff almost every twelve
months since 1954. I am, I believe, the 17th Head of Post to
occupy this seat in 20 years. As a result of this coming and

going, a first impressions despatch has landed on the desks in your Department with the inevitable regularity of an income tax demand. I have read the despatches of my distinguished predecessors and have been impressed and awed by the clarity and humour with which they have described so accurately and completely Hanoi and its people. The only trouble with this magnificent series is that they have left me very little to write about that is new or significant. I do however have one great advantage denied to my predecessors which will not be reflected here, but will I trust show up in later writing. Just one month after my arrival the Communists opened their blitzkrieg in the South and so I have had not only the interest of discovering a completely new country and people but also the fascination of following the last few days of a 30 years war. I shall be the first of H M Representatives here to see Vietnam at peace.

'Vivid, unstable, sensitive, imaginative, passionate, full of laughter, impulsive and unconcerned, malleable, deceitful, vain, generous and turbulent,' so wrote a Frenchman who had been closely associated with them for some 20 years. After less than 20 weeks here I agree completely with his epithets but I would add one further which is, I believe, a better encapsulation of the Vietnamese and Vietnam and better suited to give some understanding of their character and recent history: 'stubbornness'. It is this characteristic which has allowed them to prosecute the war for Communism against overwhelming odds and at a terrible cost in men, resources and standard of living. This national trait can be shown by two vignettes from the behaviour of my staff. My driver cannot accept a delay caused by the frequent traffic jams in this town. When he comes to a street completely jammed by vehicles, a jam furthermore which shows every indication of extending right to our destination, he will not wait for the jam to clear. He will try and wriggle his car through the jam; he will try and drive through spaces clearly too small for the car; he will back out and try another route. Until the block is cleared he will not cease his furious activity. If I tell him there is no hurry, that the block will clear in time and nothing he can do will speed our progress, he ignores me. He knows best! This too is a national characteristic. My domestic servants demonstrate everyday this extreme pigheadedness and arrogant assumption of superiority. I have a mild preference for drinks without ice; but when I told my steward this, he looked at me with pity and contempt and continued to put ice into everything I drank. When I sent him back to the kitchen to remove the ice, he argued that it was better for me to have ice, and in the end it took almost two months to impose my will over this ridiculous matter. To me this blind assertion of determination is the clue to the success of the North Vietnamese in achieving what logically was an impossible victory over the whole might of the United States and what was in many ways a stronger society in the South.

They are an egocentric people, filled with the knowledge that they are the torch-bearers of the revolutionary fight and that the centre of the world is at Hanoi. Their feelings towards the outside world mirror almost exactly what I have read of the way the Chinese received foreign traders and Ambassadors in the 18th and early 19th century. Yes, the barbarians from outside may have more modern toys than we, but it is here in Hanoi that the Holy Grail of truth is known and guarded . . .

Many of my predecessors here have noted that the Vietnamese are improvisers rather than innovators or organisers. I can only echo this. The waste of time due to too much bureaucracy and lack of management has to be seen to be believed. A perfect example of this occurred in the streets around the mission and my house at the end of April where a convoy of trucks loaded with goods for the relief of the South sat complete with their crews for three weeks before finally taking off. I have had a gang of electricians working in my house now for not quite two months. In these two months they have succeeded in rewiring 4 rooms and the hallway; a similar job on my house in England, which is slightly larger, took 5 days for the whole house.

Why are these people as they are? The clues must be sought and can be found in interdependent factors of geography, climate and history. The Vietnamese people, during the whole of their expansion into Indo-China, have been cut off from the rest of Asia by the still fearsome barrier of the Annamese chain of mountains. To the west of this chain the influences are almost solely Indian; to the east, Chinese. It is the Annamese chain too which determines the climate of the Red River delta, surely one of the worst climates in the world, which must have its effect on their character . . . All to the east of the chain is shut off under a damp, impermeable ceiling under which one is cold and wet in the winter or hot and very wet in the summer.

≈

Laos

'A unique pot pourri in the world of diplomacy'

JOHN LLOYD, HM AMBASSADOR TO THE KINGDOM OF
LAOS, AUGUST 1970

The neutralist flavour prevailing in Vientiane can always be readily tasted at diplomatic and Government receptions when there are assembled together representatives of the Royal Lao Government ... of the U.S.S.R., of China, of North Vietnam, of Poland and the representatives of Japan, South Vietnam, Cambodia, the Philippines, India, Burma and Indonesia, and of some of the Western powers including Canada. This may be quite a unique pot pourri in the world of diplomacy. Not all are on speaking terms with each other and the Chinese, who never say anything of political importance in conversation, can be rude to the point of literally turning their backs on the Americans, allowing their deeds to speak louder than words. The Pathet Lao representative sometimes gets animated in conversation and refers periodically to lackeys and running dogs; while the Soviet Military Attaché, who cannot stand any Chinese for reasons best known to himself, shuns his Chinese colleague – who holds the nominal rank of Colonel in the rankless People's Liberation Army and is a jovial character – as if he had the bubonic plague ('I <u>never</u> speak to 'im' he told me with pride as we walked past the Chinese Colonel on leaving the French Embassy Fourteenth of July Reception). Sometimes the Lao taste for neutrality takes on a humorous twist as, for example, when the Soviet Ambassador approached the Minister of Posts and Telecommunications last June to ask him to issue some Lenin anniversary stamps and to organise a Soviet stamp exhibition for the anniversary. The Minister did not feel inclined to organise an exhibition of Soviet stamps as the town of Saravane in the South had just been captured by Communist forces. But he agreed to issue some Lenin anniversary stamps, though he told the Ambassador that to keep the balance he would issue a stamp to commemorate Franklin D. Roosevelt at the same time. When the issues duly appeared shortly afterwards, Lenin had two stamps worth 30 and 70 kip respectively, but Roosevelt had one stamp worth 120 kip; a subtle Lao way of saying that one Roosevelt is worth more than two Lenin.

~

'Perhaps nearer to being omnivorous than any other people'

ALAN DAVIDSON, HM AMBASSADOR TO THE KINGDOM OF LAOS, NOVEMBER 1973

Before Laos, Alan Davidson was sent by the Foreign Office to Tunisia, where he took up an interest that was eventually to eclipse his diplomatic career: cookery-writing. Unable to find good fish dishes in Tunis, Davidson set about writing his own book of seafood recipes. In Laos the newly promoted ambassador juggled his duties representing HMG with writing three more cookbooks on the local cuisine, which were published in Britain to growing acclaim.

Davidson stood out in Vientiane, driving through the streets of the capital in an imported vintage Bentley, and attending official functions wearing a plumed helmet.

After Laos, Davidson took early retirement aged just fifty-one (his wife and daughters had jokingly warned that he would become 'insufferably pompous if he had another ambassadorial post'). Leaving diplomacy behind, Davidson made a huge success of his true calling, writing more than a dozen books including his 1999 opus, The Oxford Companion to Food, *which took him twenty years to complete.*

CONFIDENTIAL

FOREIGN AND COMMONWEALTH OFFICE
DIPLOMATIC REPORT NO. 511/73

FAL 1/7 *General Distribution*

LAOS

9 November, 1973

FIRST IMPRESSIONS OF LAOS

*Her Majesty's Ambassador at Vientiane to the
Secretary of State for Foreign and Commonwealth Affairs*

(CONFIDENTIAL) *Vientiane,
9 November, 1973*

Sir,

My first impressions of Laos were disconcerting. Standing on the Thai bank of the Mékong soon after dawn on 20 August I listened to a transistor crackling in a nearby café. Smiling informants told us the news: a military coup was taking place in Vientiane on the other bank. Shortly afterwards, half way across the Mékong, I crossed the frontier into Laos. The Phi, or spirits which influence events in this country, did not fail to mark the occasion. The engine of the little motor-boat failed and the seat on which I was perched in it collapsed backwards.

Thus my initial impression was one of being adrift, in an uncomfortable posture, in opaque and swirling cross-currents. The symbolism was apt for a new Ambassador with no previous experience of Laotian affairs. It was also instructive to discover how quickly an unpromising situation could take a turn for the better. The seat was righted, the motor started up again, we clambered up to be greeted on the muddy bank by the reception party; and soon after we arrived at the Embassy the attempted *coup* petered out.

Vientiane has a population of less than 200,000 but it takes up a lot of space, straggling along the Mékong for 10 kilometres. Most of the buildings, which range from traditional Lao wooden houses on stilts through French colonial architecture to modern concrete buildings, are lower than the trees. The general effect is shabby but quite pleasing. There is at present no public transport and motorcars are still so few that the town can function with hardly any traffic lights or parking regulations . . .

I met one American on the eve of his departure from Laos after several years here. He was an USAID man, although he had a CIA face and physique. He told me that he had wanted to write a book about Laos. But he had only written the title; it was to be called 'You Must Be Kidding'. All within ear-shot chuckled their assent; they were unanimous in feeling that what goes on in Laos strains credulity. This is so, in some ways; but the proposition needs analysis.

There is nothing intrinsically incredible about Laos or its people. There is plenty to astonish the newcomer, but that is a different matter. The eyes of the young British doctor working at Paksane widen when he enters the hospital and sees what the local sorcerer, crouched by a bed, is doing to one of his patients. The newly arrived wife starts back when she sees some of the creatures and concoctions offered for sale in the market; for the Lao are perhaps nearer to being omnivorous than any other people. The tourist blinks when, admiring the huge triumphal arch at the end of Vientiane's only wide street, he is told that this is what the Lao fashioned out of cement given to them for a new airport runway. Everyone who comes here is taken aback by some or many aspects of the country, just as everyone is attracted by the amiability of the Lao.

But the surprises are the sort of surprises which are to be expected in a remote and primitive country. What really is extraordinary is the impact on this little kingdom of contemporary great Power politics. The country is too small and too primitive to carry the traffic of international animosities and rivalries which have been discharged through it during the last two decades. Earlier this year, Laos was harbouring up to 80,000 North Viet-Namese troops, 30,000 Chinese troops and army road builders, 20,000 Thai irregulars and shrouded numbers of American para-military forces. On top of that a quarter of the population have become refugees; and the economy and the armed forces have been subjected to massive injections of aid, as though a mouse was being given shots designed for a water-buffalo. The effects of all this on a young and weak country and a simple people are indeed sometimes hard to credit . . .

Thanks to our little Beaver aircraft, I and members of my staff are able to travel widely . . . seeing the country in this way dispels some illusions. Laos is no longer 'the land of a million elephants', but the land of fewer than a thousand. Not many of the great beasts had remained wild; and most of these, disturbed by the gunfire and bombing, have now splashed their way across the Mekong into Thailand. Nor are the remoter parts of the country as untouched as one would suppose. It certainly looks wild enough towards the Burmese and Chinese frontiers; but little of the original rain-forest has survived the 'slash and burn' agriculture practised by the hill-tribes. The people too, in these parts, have lost their virginity to the 20th century. I met a USAID official in the north-west who had once met a man who had never seen a wheel. It is doubtful whether any such could be found now. Only the butterflies and orchids seem unchanged.

~

Burma

'A travesty of its former self'

TERENCE O'BRIEN, HM AMBASSADOR TO THE SOCIALIST REPUBLIC OF THE UNION OF BURMA, OCTOBER 1974

Shortly after arriving in Rangoon, Terence O'Brien wrote the Foreign Office an ordinary despatch in the traditional letter form. But these impressionistic notes, which were also sent back to London, make for better reading.

FIRST IMPRESSIONS OF BURMA

NOTES

A. <u>Appearances</u>

1. First reaction to Rangoon was one of deep physical shock.
2. I have seen and lived in far worse conditions elsewhere in Asia; what is different about Rangoon is the oppressive, brooding atmosphere, a sullen cheerless city.
3. The <u>Burmese</u> appear far cleaner, better fed, better clothed than their counterparts in any South Asian city; but what an unsmiling, silent and withdrawn people they appear.
4. The streets and public parks are models of hygiene and civic care after the insanitary squalor of those in India, Pakistan or Nepal; but they breathe no light or life, only a drab, tired dullness of a regulated Society that has sapped the animation out of its people's public behaviour.
5. Rangoon has no particular historic or cultural significance (Shwedagon Pagoda excepted). It was built by foreigners as a commercial capital, the hub of Asia's rice trade and the world centre of the teak business. Perhaps this is why the Burmese seem so indifferent toward Rangoon.
6. The architecture a bit unimaginative; but the solid imposing buildings bespeak the former mercantile wealth of an imperial British past and a once thriving shopping centre that vied with Singapore,

Penang and Colombo. Today the city is a travesty of its former self.

7. <u>The best buildings</u> have been taken over by the new public Corporations. The latter have improvised all manner of make-shift adaptations giving the buildings the sorry appearance of our war-time Rationing Centres. Other buildings have become workers' hostels and now look like requisitioned barrack accommodation. Others again have been half occupied by gimcrack private businesses, half unoccupied and now largely derelict.

8. The purely residential area around Inya Lake is in much better shape.

9. But beyond that, the <u>industrial belt</u> of Rangoon is an untidy, sprawling shanty-town world where decay and neglect seem the salient features.

10. <u>The water front</u> is an equally pitiable memorial to former days of bustling prosperity. The ferry Journey to Syriam across the river is an excursion through a graveyard of rotting unseaworthy hulks.

11. Admittedly Burma was not looking its best when I arrived. The monsoon was in full swing and the civilian population were still frightened by what had happened in early June and resentful of the Government's recourse to force.[1] Nevertheless part of their sullen apathy must stem from the depressed conditions that have been allowed to overtake Rangoon.

---

1. *early June . . . recourse to force*: The Burmese army shot and killed around a hundred people in June 1974, ending a nationwide strike which had brought government offices and factories to a standstill.

Part II: FAR EAST

Japan

'As different from others as dogs from cats'

SIR JOHN PILCHER, HM AMBASSADOR TO
JAPAN, FEBRUARY 1968

'The last of the scholar-diplomats' was how one of Sir John Pilcher's successors at the Tokyo Embassy, Hugh Cortazzi, described him. It's amusing to note that these meticulously considered thoughts were addressed to a drunken buffoon of a politician, George Brown. Pilcher's First Impressions takes the form of a learned, encyclopaedic treatise on the Japanese people, covering everything from their ancient imperial history to their metaphysics (the 'sadness of matter'). In Whitehall it was received with warmth and even veneration. 'The ambassador has painted his picture with a broad brush and in bright colours,' wrote James Murray, head of the Far Eastern Department. 'A detail here and there may perhaps as a result have been over-emphasised, but the result is a "first impressions" despatch of unusual interest and value,' meaning 'writes interestingly and well but eccentric in focus'.

Sir John's courtesy was legendary. He had a policy (says one commentator) of offering

champagne to anyone who called on him regardless of the hour of the day or night. He once visited a provincial [Japanese] town to be greeted with banners saying 'Welcome to the French Ambassador'. He was such a tactful, diplomatic *person – and so keen to avoid causing loss of face – that he proceeded to speak in English with a French accent and pretended throughout his day-long visit that he was the French Ambassador . . . spending the day praising the country to the north of his temporarily adopted one.*

True or not in its detail, the story gives a flavour of the Ambassador's reluctance to offend.

Not so Lady Pilcher. Sir John was accompanied to Japan by his equally formidable wife, an old-school ambassadress who could sometimes come across as rather superior. It was said in the Office that Lady Pilcher (who as a gracious Patroness of the Japanese Ikebana Society reputedly complained privately that the art form seemed to consist mostly in gravel and dried sticks) had remarked to her daughter, on hearing that she wanted to marry a young financier and live with him in Barnes Common: 'Barnes Common? Barnes Common? But if a gel wants to change her gloves in the middle of the day, she can't go all the way back to Barnes Common.'

Sir John notes elsewhere in this abridged despatch how the 'entire nation' had been hit by an 'insatiable thirst for consumer goods'. Today, we are accustomed to the neon sheen of Tokyo, and to the global success of Sony, Toyota and other capitalist icons – and latterly, perhaps, to the doldrums into which the great economic power has fallen in middle age. But in the 1960s consumerism was still something of a novelty for the Japanese. The Ambassador was much taken with the question of how long mere economic success would satisfy a people for whom militarism was a more familiar source and token of national pride.

In the final analysis it was not a return by Japan to military aggression that worried Pilcher, however. Rather, the

Ambassador feared 'the pull of China'. Japan's classless, ascetic society, he thought, could all too easily be turned Communist. The friendship extended by Britain, the United States and others since the Second World War has, indeed, been motivated in large part by the desire to keep Japan 'anchored in the West'. In the event Japan plumped firmly for the West, but the choice is still there, still as stark as Pilcher found it, and still troubling for Japanese foreign policymakers.

Pilcher's opinions on the Japanese hardened over the course of his posting. Departing Tokyo in 1972 the ambassador wrote a valedictory despatch calling them 'narrow-minded and egotistic, lacking an international outlook and barren of philosophy'. Pilcher also feared, quite wrongly, that they might secretly be building nuclear weapons.

To set into context the almost anthropological tone of Sir John's report – as from an explorer visiting a parallel world or another age – we append beneath this despatch another British diplomat's account from the same country, written almost a century to the day earlier: our then Second Secretary's description of the ceremony of hara-kiri.

CONFIDENTIAL

<u>THIS DOCUMENT IS THE PROPERTY OF
HER BRITANNIC MAJESTY'S GOVERNMENT</u>

FJ 1/6   *Foreign Office and Whitehall Distribution*

JAPAN
19 FEBRUARY, 1968
SECTION 1

IMPRESSIONS OF CONTEMPORARY JAPAN

Sir John Pilcher to Mr Brown. (Received 19 *February)*

(CONFIDENTIAL)   *Tokyo,*
                                                  12 February, 1968
Sir,

I have the honour to offer some reflections on contemporary Japan as I find it after an absence of some 30 years and four months in the country now.

The monk, painter and poet Basho, visiting the battlefield of Sekigahara, on which the fate of Japan for several vital centuries had been decided, felt moved to address to the empty, green plain the '*haiku*': 'Oh grass of summer, you are all that remains of the dreams of warriors!' Were he able to revisit his country now, after its recovery from the unprecedented devastation of the last war, and were he to take the famous Bullet train, the sight of the unending factories springing up all along the 300 miles from Tokyo to Osaka might well inspire in him the same reflection as the lush grass on that plain. Into this all too flourishing industrial development (with its lamentable hideosity) have gone the devotion to duty, the energy and the idealism of the '*kamikaze*' pilots. The dark, satanic mills seem to embody now the aspirations of a race of warriors. The question is for how long.

The Japanese in the course of their history have veered in different directions, always seemingly at the behest of their ruling family. Under Prince Shotoku in the seventh century they swallowed the civilisation and religion of T'ang China. The Emperor Meiji, after his restoration to the position his ancestors held in the remote past, appeared to sponsor the Westernisation of his country and its opening to the world exactly 100 years ago. It was the present Emperor, who, in the spirit of his reign title 'Showa' meaning 'radiant peace' (which had hitherto sounded so ironically in Japanese ears), brought the last war to an end by his heroic and dramatic broadcast. He thus in popular estimation saved his country and his people from total annihilation. For this he is accorded unending gratitude.

The Japanese of course, are as hypocritical as others have found us. They know well how to cloak their mundane ambitions in the full panoply of the highest moral obligations. In the 1930s the military – in line with long-established tradition – had got the Emperor, the theoretical source of all power, into their hands. They interpreted his will to be the aggrandisement of his empire ... When this 'mission' did not succeed and the very existence of the Japanese State was threatened, it was obvious to all that the military had not only failed to carry out their interpretation of the will of the Emperor, but also that they had misled him. Far from the prestige of the Emperor suffering from the great humiliation of the first national defeat known to Japanese history, by his courageous broadcast he emerged as the saviour of his country and as a man to whom the military had done a great wrong. To the awe his position traditionally inspires are therefore now added sympathy and affection.

It is to me of the greatest significance that the Emperor remains at the apex of the Japanese edifice. Without this keystone, the whole structure might well have collapsed (as indeed happened in China in 1911). Japanese morale is based on an excessive sense of nationalism, born of their geographical remoteness from the Asian mainland; they are situated 80 miles off Korea – as though we lay at the same distance off Norway. They tend to think of themselves as being as different from others as dogs from cats. To a dog presumably the highest living dog is The Supreme Dog. They emerged from the mists of the past grouped round their Emperor, whom they regarded as on a par with the divinities or heroes of rock, stream, waterfall or grove and with the historic or legendary figures of their past.

This abnormal cohesion was given a solid Confucian structure under the ascendancy of the Tokugawa Shoguns (which followed the battle of Sekigahara) and was further accentuated by the policy of isolation (1636–1868) imposed upon the country. No people has ever been so regimented probably as under the 'military government' of the Tokugawas. Every detail of life was prescribed, from the dress permitted to each age and profession, to the proportions of rooms. Frugality and austerity were enjoined on all: ostentation was the nadir of vulgarity. Loyalty was the supreme virtue, before which every other consideration had to give way. The sacrifice of self, wife, child and family to further the interests of the superior to whom loyalty was due is the very stuff of Japanese drama to this day . . .

The military in the 1930s exaggerated the pattern. Self-sacrifice became a fetish, to die for the Emperor an end in itself. 'Thought-control' saw to it that 'the heartless legalism of the West' and its enervating individualism were kept at bay. To be seen with a golf club meant censure for a man, while women with permanently waved hair were summoned to the police station for a severe talking to. In the end the excessive exclusivity inculcated defeated the purposes of the 'divine mission'. The Japanese soldier proved incapable of understanding the outlook of others or of treating them as comparable human beings. From this springs the cruelty that astonished and shocked the world . . .

Observing this from afar, I thought that defeat would teach the lesson to the Japanese that they are as other men are. This alone, together with the discomfiture of the military, I thought, should make the Japanese reasonably normal, without necessarily destroying their cohesive structure, upon which their successful national life depends. This has proved to be the case. Exclusivity has gone, even to the point of neutralism and voluntary dependence on others advocated by the Left of Centre. On the other hand, cohesion has become so rooted in the national psychology as to seem virtually indestructible; it has become part of Japanese physique. The individual Japanese never seems quite fully developed until ripe old age. Alone, he is all too often diffident, inconclusive and awkward; he finds fulfilment in the group. This cohesive, 'holistic' tendency of the Japanese means that the group is stronger than the sum of its members. From an individual, no startling decisions can be expected; a group may plan a Pearl Harbour or an economic miracle.

Again, the Japanese are not an intellectual race; they rely upon intuition and in a group upon the insensible friction of mind upon mind to find decisions almost instinctively (just as they prefer an object of art to appear to be 'born' rather than 'made'). In this they are vastly encouraged by the typically Japanese development of Zen Buddhism, which holds that enlightenment can never be attained by the intellect through reason, but only by a flash of intuitive perception. The military deduced from this that the reflex action of the warrior in severing a head with a sword, rather than risk pausing to reason with its owner, was morally justifiable. However admirable the effects of Zen on aesthetics, its anti-rational influence on the national psychology has been of questionable value . . .

In their world there is no barrier between man and the rest of creation. Man is a stone among stones, a bird among birds. Other animate and inanimate things have a greater intrinsic significance to them than to us. The fact that portions of the human personality regroup with others on the same plane of spiritual development and move up and down the scale of objects and beings means that for them a table or a plant is closer to the human being. Man is considered in his cosmic setting. He is viewed as a drop in a stream; a passing phenomenon, here one moment and gone the next. The transience of existence, the evanescence of all things and the 'sadness of matter' are the inevitable commonplace sighs of Japanese conversation and literature. Moreover the world is an illusion: the Calderon-like cry 'since I am convinced that reality is in no sense real, how can I admit that dreams are dreams?'[1] haunts their senses – and offers only a poetic escape.

Many assume that because they are modern, they must be 'Westernised'. This is far from the case. They were influenced by the post-Christian idealism and humanity shown by the American conquerors, but fundamentally they approach the 20th century in fact from different premises to our own. Loyalty and cohesion have stood them in immensely good stead. They are loyal to their ministry or firm with almost the fervour of religion. Once they enter an organisation, they offer themselves to it for life. The web of obligations sees to it that their superiors – theoretically, but usually – look after them for life. Yearly increments of salary are paid to all. Housing is commonly provided. Even wives or husbands might be found by the employers, if requested. Education is often completed by them. Habit demands that civil servants should retire early (just as Emperors in the past retired to a Buddhist retreat, where as monks they ruled the country from behind the 'screens'). They move into industry, while retaining their sense of loyalty to their former ministry. Hence the ease with which the Government can influence or even direct industry through a vastly extended 'old boy net'.

Their holistic tendencies fit well into the bureaucratic life of the age. They present baffling problems to foreigners. Under their system nothing can be done in a hurry. Prior notice must be given of a point, which will then be studied endlessly by the relevant group, before any decision can be reached. Moreover, generally, the foreigner must himself show an awareness of the principles of loyalty, if he is to make headway. Once the Japanese are 'engaged' their sense of loyalty comes into play; they are therefore unwilling to engage themselves, unless they are sure of the other side. It becomes almost a question of making friends, before successful business deals on any scale can be achieved. This is time-consuming and entails frequent visits to Japan, and great patience is required . . .

The Japanese are an awkward mixture of Prussian respect for order, combined with an Italian sensibility (but without the Italian genius for improvisation). They have been nurtured and sustained on ideals. The war turned many of their ideals into shattered illusions. They have in consequence been content to adopt a low posture, to turn in on themselves, to set their house in order and to seek economic prosperity . . .

They need a greater trading space. A kind of common market with China is the obvious answer, but the shape and compatibility of the China to come are not yet visible and may not become so for a very long time ... These problems, which obsess every thinking Japanese, clearly admit of no militaristic solution. The temptation in the long run for Japan will rather be to make common cause with China. Whether they succumb to that or not will depend on how China shapes and how firmly they are anchored in the West. Let us not forget, however, that between the Confucian ideal of achieving harmony here and now in this world and the Communist hopes of building a Utopian, classless society, the difference is relatively small. Apart from the national institution of the Imperial Family, Japan is now virtually a classless society. Land reform has eliminated any territorial wealth. 'Fun' is exclusively on expense accounts. In my opinion, based on so short a view of contemporary Japan, future danger may well lie in the pull of China.

For the time-being, however, I think Basho, were he living, would have been right to conclude that the teeming factories have canalised and made constructive the aftermath of the dreams of the warriors, who led Japan so terribly astray only 30 years ago and whose teachings and antics in Japan and China remain so vividly present to my mind ...

I have, &c.
J. PILCHER.

---

1. *Calderon-like cry 'since . . . dreams are dreams?'*: *Life is a Dream*, by the Spanish playwright Pedro Calderón de la Barca (1600–1681). 'What

is life? An illusion, / A shadow, a fiction, / . . . / For all of life is a dream, / And dreams, are nothing but dreams.'

∼

'A dead silence followed . . . it was horrible'

BERTIE MITFORD, SECOND SECRETARY AT
HM LEGATION TOKYO, MARCH 1868

Mitford, later created Lord Redesdale and the grand-father of the famous Mitford sisters, penned the following account for the FO to satisfy British curiosity about the infamous hara-kiri ritual. During an incident in the civil war of 1868, some foreign representatives were fired on by one of the warring factions. The officer responsible was sentenced to die by hara-kiri, a sort of hybrid of suicide and beheading, though the relief granted by a swift decapitation is somewhat diluted by the disembowelling which precedes it. Mitford, who does not spare the details, seems satisfied that the rigid formality with which the execution is conducted renders it a noble, just punishment.

I was last night sent officially to witness the execution by harakiri (harakiri from hara the belly and kiri root form of kiru to cut) (self-immolation through disembowelling) of Taki Zenzaburo, the officer of the Prince of Bizen. He it was who gave the order to fire upon the foreign settlement at Hyōgo on the 4th of last month (February) . . . As the harakiri is one of the customs of this country which has excited the greatest curiosity in Europe, although owing to the fact that it had never hitherto been witnessed by foreigners it has seemed little better than a matter of fable, I will tell you what occurred.

The ceremony, which was ordered by the Mikado him-self, took place at 10:30 at night in the temple of Seifukuji . . . A witness was sent from each of the foreign legations. We were seven foreigners in all.

After an interval of a few moments of anxious suspense, Taki Zenzaburo, a stalwart man 32 years of age, with a noble air, walked into the hall, attired in his dress of ceremony with the peculiar hempen cloth wings which are worn on great occasions. He was accompanied by a kaishaku and three officers who wore the jimbaori or war-surcoat with gold tissue facings. The word kaishaku, it should be observed, is one to which our word executioner is no equivalent term. The office is that of a gentleman; in many cases it is performed by a kinsman or friend of the con-demned, and the relation between them is rather that of principal and second than that of victim and executioner. In this instance the kaishaku was a pupil of Taki Zenzaburo, and was selected by the friends of the latter from among their own number for his skill in swordsmanship.

With the kaishaku on his left hand, Taki Zenzaburo ad-vanced slowly towards the Japanese witnesses and the two bowed before them; then drawing near to the foreigners they saluted in the same way – perhaps even with more deference. In each case the salutation was ceremoniously returned. Slowly and with great dignity the condemned man mounted on to the raised floor, prostrated himself before the high altar twice and seated himself on the felt carpet with his back to the high altar, the kaishaku crouch-ing on his left-hand side. One of the attendant officers came forward bearing a stand of the kind used in temples for offerings, on which wrapped in paper lay the waki-zashi, the short sword or dirk of the Japanese, nine inches and a half in length, with a point and an edge as sharp as a razor's. This he handed, prostrating himself, to the condemned man who received it reverently, raised it to his head with both hands, and placed it in front of himself.

After another profound obeisance, Taki Zenzaburo, in a voice which betrayed just so much emotion and hesitation as might be expected from a man who is making a painful confession, but with no sign of either in his face or manner, spoke as follows:

'I, and I alone, unwarrantably gave the order to fire on the foreigners at Kobe, and again as they tried to escape, on the 11th of last month (4th February 1868). For this crime I disembowel myself, and I beg you who are present to do me the honour of witnessing the act.'

Bowing once more, the speaker allowed his upper garments to slip down to his girdle, and remained naked to the waist. Carefully, according to custom, he tucked his sleeves under his knees to prevent himself from falling backwards; for a noble Japanese gentleman should die falling forwards. Deliberately, with a steady hand, he took the dirk that lay before him – he looked at it wistfully, almost affectionately – for a moment he seemed to collect his thoughts for the last time, and then stabbing himself deeply below the waist on the left-hand side, he drew the dirk slowly across to the right side, and, turning it in the wound, gave a slight cut upwards: during this sickeningly painful operation he never moved a muscle of his face. When he drew out the dirk, he leaned forward and stretched out his neck – an expression of pain for the first time crossed his face, but he uttered no sound. At that moment the kaishaku, who, still crouching by his side, had been keenly watching his every movement, sprang to his feet, poised his sword for a second in the air – there was a flash – a heavy, ugly thud, a crashing fall – with one blow the head had been severed from the body.

A dead silence followed – broken only by the hideous noise of the blood throbbing out of the inert heap before us which but a moment before had been a brave and chivalrous man. It was horrible.

The kaishaku made a low bow, wiped his sword with a piece of rice paper which he had ready for the purpose, and retired from the raised floor, and the stained dirk was solemnly borne away, a bloody proof of the execution.

The two representatives of the Mikado then left their places and crossing over to where the foreign witnesses sat called us to witness that the sentence of death upon Taki Zenzaburo had been faithfully carried out. The ceremony being at an end we left the temple. The ceremony, to which the place and the hour gave an additional solemnity, was characterized throughout by that extreme dignity and punctiliousness which are the distinctive marks of the proceedings of Japanese gentlemen of rank; and it is important to note this fact, because it carries with it the conviction that the dead man was indeed the officer who had committed the crime, and no substitute. While profoundly impressed by the terrible scene it was impossible at the same time not to be filled with admiration of the firm and manly bearing of the sufferer, and of the nerve with which the kaishaku performed his last duty to his master . . .

~

Korea

'Little more than a jerry-built slum'

IAN MACKENZIE, HM AMBASSADOR TO THE REPUBLIC OF
KOREA, AUGUST 1967

(No. 15. Confidential and Guard)   *Seoul,*
25 July, 1967

Sir,

After pacifist, neutral, affluent, Socialist, birth-controlled
Sweden, Korea presents an extreme contrast. Magpies are
about the only thing the two countries have in common.
By comparison with Stockholm, Seoul, three-quarters destroyed during the war, is little better than a jerry-built
slum full of jeeps and Japanese-built cars jostling with
buses and army trucks to jump the queue. I find it pleasant
enough to live in nevertheless.

Coming to Korea is like entering a war camp, with the
whiff of a police state to boot. A curfew is enforced for
four hours every night. Military and school uniforms
abound. A Central Intelligence Agency actively rounds up
alleged spies, and militias are being got ready to deal with
the threat of guerrillas. An anti-Communist law circum-
scribes the activities of writers and Opposition politicians
alike. Far from wanting the Viet-Nam War to end, the South
Koreans would be near bankruptcy tomorrow if it did.
With memories of their own war against Communism,
kept alive by frequent incidents along the Armistice Line,
most of them believe in armed resistance to the Communists anywhere.

PART III: AMERICAS

United States

'They need a friend'

SIR OLIVER WRIGHT, HM AMBASSADOR TO THE UNITED
STATES OF AMERICA, SEPTEMBER 1982

BRITISH EMBASSY,
WASHINGTON D.C. 20008,
TELEPHONE: (202) 462-1340,
30 September 1982

FROM THE AMBASSADOR

The Right Honourable
Francis Pym MC MP

Dear Secretary of State,

THE SPECIAL RELATIONSHIP

Now that I have completed my first calls here – at the White House, on the Administration and up the Hill – I thought you might like to know how I have found things before the complexities of daily business confuse the general picture. The overwhelming impression is one of great friendliness: Britain's reputation here ... is high: and her Majesty's Government, despite steel[1] and pipeline,[2] is in very good standing.

The Evidence. The President, in his speech of reply when I presented my credentials, himself mentioned 'the special relationship'. Subsequent experience so far everywhere in Washington has convinced me that it represents the declared attitude of the present US Administration to Britain and its Government ...

Blessed with a condign quantity of professional scepticism, I have naturally asked myself whether all this was just flattery for a newcomer; and whether this is what they may be saying to the other boys. I do not think so. On the contrary, I believe that the Reagan Administration wishes to have a special relationship with us . . . And I think it wishes to have it for a number of different but interlocking reasons.

First, I think the Administration wants it for reasons which are no less valid for being clichés of many years standing: a common language, common thought processes, common values, common heritage and a variety of shared interests. More particularly, they consider the philosophies of our two governments to be compatible . . . We do not go out of our way to be awkward when our interests diverge and indeed, tend to apply our minds to overcome problems when inevitably they arise.

But the most important reason, in my view, is that the Americans experience keenly the loneliness of being the Western super power. They need a friend whose opinions they value and whom they can trust. They accept our commitment to Europe but think, as we do, that, this should reinforce not weaken the trans-Atlantic relationship . . .

They value the cross check we can provide on their own analyses and the second opinion on their own policies. They need, in short, someone to talk to, and find in us someone worth talking to. They may not always take our advice, but they will take it into consideration when, as is their prerogative, they make up their own minds.

1. *despite steel*: The EC–US steel dispute was a bitter trade war. In 1982 US steel producers filed more than one hundred anti-dumping complaints against their competitors in Europe.
2. *pipeline*: At the height of the Cold War, the participation of European

companies in the construction of a massive gas pipeline across the USSR provoked a major transatlantic tiff. A 1980 US embargo on exported materials designed to halt the 2,800-mile Trans-Siberian project was dismissed by Lord Cockfield, the UK's Secretary of State for Trade, as 'repugnant in international law'. Realizing he was beaten, Reagan told his cabinet 'they can have their damned pipeline'.

~

Canada

'The result this time could well be yes to secession'

SIR ANTHONY GOODENOUGH, HM HIGH COMMISSIONER
TO CANADA, JULY 1996

For much of the 1990s, Canada appeared to be on the edge of break-up. Demands by the French-speaking eastern province of Quebec for greater autonomy culminated in a 1995 referendum, and the closeness of the result stunned the world. The federalists, led by the Prime Minister, Jean Chrétien, carried the day with 50.6 per cent of the votes, against 49.4 per cent wanting independence.

Quebec had opted to remain part of Canada. And yet, the tide towards independence was still strong. So strong that just nine months later, Britain's newly appointed High Commissioner in Ottawa was cabling London with a fresh warning about secession. The Canadian federation, feared Anthony Goodenough, might not even last out the decade.

In fact, what Goodenough was seeing was the high-water mark of the Québécois sovereignty movement (the high-water mark so far, that is to say – we do not want to be caught out making any unnecessary predictions of our own).

In 2003 the same electorate who in 1995 nearly cast Quebec asunder from Canada ejected the pro-independence Parti Québécois from the provincial government, voting in to office the centre-right Liberal party instead, on a federalist platform. A poll taken in Quebec in April 2011 showed support for independence had sunk to 41 per cent, with 59 per cent supporting the status quo.

It is interesting to speculate on what foreign ambassadors posted to London today are reporting on Scotland's debate about independence; and to note that, at least in the case of Quebec, it can be a mistake to assume that a trend in one direction will never turn.

Canada is faced with three significant internal political problems of which one, the Quebec issue, threatens Canada's survival as a nation. The other two, the growing alienation of the Western provinces and the aboriginal issue, are less serious ... In a nutshell, the threat of Quebec's secession remains real. Opinion among the hundreds of Canadians with whom I have discussed the question here and in London is divided pretty equally between those who believe a united Canada will continue somehow to muddle through and those who fear the worst.

M. Chrétien is an optimist. He told you in May that he expects an eventual solution. He does not believe the majority of Quebecois really want to separate, but to negotiate a better deal for themselves. He has made clear that he will not accept a UDI.[1] If the separatists win a referendum, Quebec will have to negotiate its independence with Ottawa.

Many Canadians believe Chrétien is over optimistic and criticise the Federal Government for inactivity. I share their concern. I see a risk that M. Bouchard, Premier of Quebec, will call a provincial election unexpectedly early, win and use the momentum to hold a referendum in which the result this time could well be yes to secession. Events could still go either way. But we should not exclude the possibility of secession. This could happen before 2000.

Western alienation is not an immediate threat to Canadian unity. But, both in Alberta and British Columbia, I encountered resentment against Quebec and frustration with the Federal Government for its failure to deal firmly with Quebec and its alleged insensitivity to Western concerns. Calgary has a distinctly American feel about its admirable enthusiasm for free enterprise and individual initiative. And the strong Chinese immigrant influence in British Columbia, where for example half the primary school children in the Vancouver area are said to have English as their second rather than their mother tongue, is weakening its links with Canada East of the Rockies . . .

Many Canadians I meet worry that they lack a recognisable national identity and that this too, along with the Quebec issue, Western alienation and aboriginal dissatisfaction, will weaken the ties that bind the nation together. So much is heard about the Canadian mosaic of peoples (compared with the American melting pot) that I had expected to find greater identity differences between the Canadians I have met in my travels across the country. Instead I find that even Canadians of widely differing ethnic origins share common characteristics: civic mindedness, tolerance, lack of stridency, seriousness of purpose.

1. *UDI*: Unilateral Declaration of Independence.

∾

Brazil

'Like the United States . . . if the South had won the Civil War'

SIR JOHN RUSSELL, HM AMBASSADOR TO THE FEDERATIVE
REPUBLIC OF BRAZIL, MAY 1967

In 1967, senior clerks gave Sir John Russell's First Impressions from Brazil wide distribution, labelling it 'very long, but magnificent'.

Correspondence alongside it in the archives shows just how seriously diplomats took their amateur literary efforts. After the Office had his despatch formally printed, Russell had a subordinate write from Rio to point out a spelling mistake. The word 'tartarugan' – meaning 'shaped like a turtle-shell', which the ambassador used to describe the theatre in Brasilia – was rendered incorrectly. An inquiry traced the error to 'misplaced erudition' by a clerk in the Stationery Office, who late on a Saturday night consulted five dictionaries before deciding the ambassador must have meant the Miltonian 'tartarean', meaning the 'lower levels of hell'.

There are two more despatches from Russell on pp. 64–71 and 71–82.

<u>THIS DOCUMENT IS THE PROPERTY OF</u>
<u>HER BRITANNIC MAJESTY'S GOVERNMENT</u>

AB 1\9   *Foreign Office and Whitehall Distribution*

BRAZIL

23 MAY, 1967

SECTION 1

FIRST IMPRESSIONS OF BRAZIL

Sir John Russell to Mr Brown. (Received 23 May)

(No 21. Confidential and Guard)   *Rio de Janeiro,*
18 May 1967

Sir,

My first impressions of Rio de Janeiro are overdue: and mixed.

The startling natural beauty of the city's setting is soon eclipsed for the struggling resident by the heat, the humidity, the noise and the abysmal incommodity of the town. Rio is ill-designed and overcrowded; it is provincial, badly run, uncomfortable and shabby. Its architecture is of an unexampled mediocrity. Like the surface of the moon Rio is short of water, covered in dust and pocked with deep holes. Rio's telephones do not work and its light regularly goes off without warning: its murderous traffic serves only to winnow the quick from the dead: whilst its domestic servants are, hands down, the worst in the world. Its weather is vile for six months of the year: and the torrential summer rains, which fall regularly every Christmas, as regularly put the improvident city clean out of action. Its administration is capable of improvement in almost every respect. Rio in fact is a far cry from the tourist paradise that it has so long been cracked up to be. 'The Paris of Latin America' indeed! No lotus-land this: and its demystification is long overdue.

Brazil to-day makes you speculate rather on what the United States would have been like if the South had won the Civil War. And the comparison is not all that unfair when you reflect that Colombus only discovered America eight years before Cabral stumbled upon Brazil. What explains the enormous difference? The Portuguese character, I suppose, allied to a tropical climate and 300 years of slavery . . .

If my *introduction*, Sir, smacks a trifle sour, it is that it reflects the appalling frustrations of daily life here, the time and nerve-eroding struggle against the active hostility of allegedly inanimate objects. But the Bay of Rio is one of the great sights of nature and when it emerges through the steam-heat you cannot fail to be enchanted. The people too are gay and friendly.

Meanwhile I owe the Department this conventional despatch. After six months the native hue of first impression is already a little sicklied o'er with the pale cast of thought. So, for better or for worse, to paper: otherwise this despatch will no longer be what the title professes – an essentially subjective account of how the country first strikes the writer, in my case a happily virgin newcomer to the subcontinent.

Brazilian society, it appears, has changed greatly in the last 25 years, turning progressively inwards upon itself; and you must on arrival dismiss your preconceived ideas of a sophisticated European sort of world. To-day it is a very local breed educated in Brazil, essentially Latin American: mainly monoglot, increasingly self-sufficient, and rather parochial ... Assimilation is a single-generation process here: and Brazil has the gastric juices of a python.

The first Portuguese settlers came to Brazil with a powerful strain of Moorish (and Jewish) blood already running in their veins. (The northern frontier of Africa is in effect the Pyrenees.) They lived by slave labour: and did much of their colonising in bed. The result is a pleasant enough race of an equable temperament and a rich burnt-honey colour. Brazilians say proudly that they have no *colour bar*: but I have yet to see a black general, a black Minister, Senator, Deputy, Ambassador or professor. As Sammy Davis, Jr., said of his recent visit: 'Sure I saw niggers riding in Cadillacs in Brazil: and they were all chauffeurs.' Of course there is a colour bar: money, education, hence opportunity – all these are denied to the blacks ...

The people of Brazil cover a wide range. At one extreme you have the predominating Portuguese, Italian, German and Scandinavian stock: the prosperous Asiatics, mainly Lebanese and Japanese: then the poor whites and up-country Portuguese/Indian 'caboclos': then the great bulk of Portuguese-negro mestizo, which infuses every stratum of society: and at the other extreme the plain West African negro, the shiny blue-black descendant of slaves emancipated a bare 80 years ago. A 'pure' African is almost as rare in Brazil to-day as a 'pure' Portuguese. But all are Brazilian: most are Catholic: all are integrated: most are happy.

And the Indian? Lo, the poor Indian, he left little behind him in Brazil – no art, no architecture, no written language, nothing of Aztec or Inca glory. But he has two kindly and innocent inventions to his credit, the hammock and the bouncing rubber ball.

Abhorring all forms of violence, relaxed, easy-going and fatalistically cheerful the Brazilians are, on the debit side, feckless and inconstant, not very truthful, not very forceful, undisciplined and sadly lacking in sustained endeavour. Punctuality is a solecism, exactitude a reproach, contracts are unburdened by sanctity, intrigue is a substitute for organisation. It is a race agreeably lacking the ferocious moral rectitude of the Angry-Saxon . . .

The national character is nowhere so intensively displayed as right here in *Rio de Janeiro* which, for my prime purpose, is Brazil. (Like the Derby of 1769: 'Eclipse first, the rest nowhere.') Rio is a city of over 4 million people, a few of whom live in extravagant luxury, many in equally extravagant poverty, all of them under a provincial administration of quite staggering mediocrity. The clue to their apparently limitless docility lies, I suggest, in three elements, three safety-valves.

First – the beaches. Imagine, Sir, a great warm blue ocean pounding on white sand from Euston to Shepherd's Bush, and the inhabitants of Bloomsbury and Marylebone and Paddington and Notting Hill wandering happily down through the streets in their bathing-suits under a blazing sun to their daily swim. Then you have something of the permanent holiday atmosphere which goes so far to make the discomforts of this city tolerable to its swarming population. The beaches are the main substitute for revolution. (They also drown a lot of people daily.)

Then football. Even the bold, blasphemous Beatles might feel a salutary qualm of humility before the continental renown of a black god like Pelé. For the masses 'futébol' has replaced religion. It is a national obsession. And I am daily grateful that it was not we who put Brazil out of the World Cup.

Then carnival. And the greatest of these is carnival. It is the mass escape, open for four delirious days of every year. But I have already dealt with carnival in a recent despatch: so no more of it here.

I also dealt there with that terrible but essential element of this city, the element in which carnival has its roots – the 'favelas', the shanty-towns that hang precariously on the steep face of the hills which hem Rio in against the sea. Here three-quarters of a million blacks eke out voodoo-ridden lives of poverty, filth, disease and crime unrivalled in any bidonville of Africa. Without carnival they could hardly fail to erupt.

Behind these three safety-valves there is another even stronger force of conservatism and restraint – the family. Affection, pride, community of welfare, mutual protection, pooled earnings – all these make of the Brazilian family the country's strongest bastion against despair.

Of the rest of the country, so far I can speak at first hand of four other cities only.

São Paulo is Milan to Rio's Rome, Dusseldorf or Manchester to Rio's Marseilles. São Paulo is the cigarette skyline of downtown New York superimposed overnight on Welwyn Garden City – rich, hard, pushful and undisciplined, the centre of Brazil's booming industry, a city of over 5 million expanding by 250,000 every year; brash, self-sufficient and self-centred, painfully plain: a vulgar city-come-lately still in its shirtsleeves. You have to see São Paulo to understand the material growth of this country and its new economic chauvinism. Its automobile industry produced 200,000 vehicles last year; and this year they say they are going to double it. Everything you can do, São Paulo can do better.

Brasilia. A spiky fringe of green glass skyscrapers cuts up from the virgin green crust of the scrub-savannah to lay bare a red murram soil like that of Tanganyika. 'Cité de l'espoir' André Malraux[1] called it. And there it sits – or rather there it springs! – the embryo of the Pure City. Founded on the three pillars of Legislature, Judicature and Executive; soon to house all the Federal Ministries: already boasting a university, a subterranean Crown-of-Thorns cathedral and a huge, blind, tartarean theatre: the supporting cast deliberately limited to half a million souls. Divorced from the pressures of Rio – from its slums, its commerce, its international high life, its appalling communications, all its old chaos and corrupting charm – this new federal abstraction rises Phoenix-like from the clean, high bush-veld, the dream of Oscar Niemeyer and Lucio Costa:[2] a city without a traffic light or a factory chimney. Like Jerusalem in the psalm, Brasilia is built as a city that is at unity with itself.

Petropolis. Ah, Petropolis, if only in parenthesis; and our charming old summer Embassy up there. The little forlorn villas: the florid Garibaldian statuary in the Jardim Publico: the imperial palms, the flamboyants, the plumbago and the cannas; all heavy with the homely but ill-requited benevolence of Dom Pedro II.[3] Something of Boudin's Trouville,[4] something of Homburg under King Edward VII,[5] something of Leamington Spa in early Betjeman: all the slow, green charm of a late empire ville d'eau.

And, fourthly, *Bahia*. Two hundred of the best baroque churches anywhere: an upper town of fine Portuguese colonial streets wide, tree-lined, commodious: a lower town, down in the harbour, full of a Moby Dick romance – negroes and sailors, and brothels and bars and chapels, the bows of the ships leaning in over the market stalls. A city of prostitutes and painters and priests, and writers and sea captains. Huge trees and wonderful beaches. The whole perfumed with that intoxicating blend of sweat and salt, and tar and timber, and drains and donkeys, frangipani and frankincense.

This great rambling disparate country, the size of Europe, is presently governed by a *revolutionary regime*, which came in three years ago and which, by Latin American standards, is good. Arbitrary, yes: but not oppressive: disciplined, responsible, devoted to a rather humourless ideal of administrative improvement . . .

Above all, the revolutionary regime is trying to bring some semblance of honesty to the Administration of a country by tradition extravagantly and entirely corrupt. The last Persian Ambassador here, a jolly rogue by the name of Abdy Hamzavi, said to me in London last summer – 'My dear boy, after a few weeks in Brazil you will realise that in the arts of corruption, deceit and fraudulent bankruptcy we Persians are in our infancy.' In the interest of a resumption, one day, of British business in this country I hope to be able in due course to convince the Department that this sufism no longer holds good . . .

This brings me directly to the question of the *British material interest in Brazil*. In the 19th century we owned this country in all but name; and Brazil was effectively a British mercantile colony. We monopolised the country's trade; then we built its ports and roads and railways. In the 20th century we sold out, to pay for two world wars: or were taken over. Now we are a pale shadow of our former self. Can we recover any of our old position? Do we in fact want to? . . .

The Brazilians, I believe, want us back. They are hurt by our apparent indifference of recent years. They find it hard to believe that it is the harsh economic facts of modern life in a small island which alone can have turned away from them the face of the power which so recently dominated the South Atlantic – the England of Nelson and of Maitland, of Castlereagh, Cochrane and Canning, the England that brought the Portuguese Royal Family to Brazil, that beat Napoleon and ghosted the Monroe Doctrine and abolished the slave trade and won the Battle of the River Plate. They want us back, if only to save them from the suffocating embrace of their North American benefactors.

The dear, good, kind, quixotic *Americans* – here somehow they manage to appear overwhelming, crude, carpet-bagging and proprietary. Throughout the sub-continent the Alliance for Progress yields a terrifying harvest of corn-fed ingratitude. But under the plastic horror of the 'American way of life' the Brazilian has yet preserved a shame-faced nostalgia for the vanished dignity and independence of his European heritage. The mind boggles at the charity–unpopularity ratio which the Americans have achieved. Last fall I even found the Brazilians wanly celebrating Thanksgiving: now why? Could they not have been spared at least that indignity?

Reading back through this enormous despatch I find that I have still missed so many of the really important things – early morning on Copacabana beach: the flamboyants and the orchids and the huge butterflies in their gaudy club colours: my *chers* but invisible colleagues: the liberal reforming Church: the ill-chanced Governor of Guanabara State ('Avec moi le deluge'): the tumbling rocks and condemned apartment houses: Rio's third-rate 'international' airport: the Brazilian Foreign Service, supposedly a model of its kind to South America: the vast unexplored interior of the country which has swallowed up Colonel Fawcett[6] and Martin Bormann[7] and Che Guevara:[8] the startling political amorality of ex-Governor Lacerda: this great handsome fake of an Embassy, much admired by all Brazilians: the extreme elegance of the ladies: Peter Fleming's fountain: the oddities of the vernacular (– Brazil's secret weapon 'uisque nacional': girls in 'décotés' drinking 'cotels' in a 'lanchanet' and listening to 'os Bitles'; the 'futébolista nocauteado' – how sad, for he was the 'lider' of his 'tim'!): then Avenida Haddock Lobo (now who on earth was he? and who Enrique Dodsworth?): Russel Square, honouring my (almost) namesake who built Rio's first (and actual) sewers nearly a century ago: the great Cristo lit up at night on the Corcovado 2,000 feet above us: the voodoo drums beating nightly in our 'favela': the few old Portuguese houses still surviving like stumps of decayed teeth in the rows of concrete skyscrapers: the twilit British nostalgia of Rio Cricket Club slowly dying across the Bay in Niteroi: and in the Maracanã Stadium a football crowd of 200,000 packed in like some great windblown herbaceous border: the little constant cups of coffee, black and sweet as sin: the nightly flowers and candles set out along the beaches to the distant gods of Dahomey and the Slave Coast: the rich oriental smells, the blacks and the pretty girls, the football on the beaches: the leisure, the poverty, the gaiety – all this is Rio.

But to wind up my cyclorama: and to my *Conclusion*.

The Brazilians say that their country grows at night whilst the Government is asleep. Brazil is a young country, of enormous size: such animals mature slowly and Brazil's present failings are the failings of immaturity. But in the long run, united by a single language, a crucible of blending cultures, her chequered, intelligent population expanding at startling speed, endowed with every gift known to nature, how can Brazil reasonably fail the call to greatness?

I have, &c.
JOHN RUSSELL.

1. *André Malraux*: French author and statesman. 'Cité de l'espoir' means 'city of hope'.
2. *Oscar Niemeyer and Lucio Costa*: Architects. Costa designed Brasilia's urban plan, while Niemeyer was responsible for many of its buildings. Both were great believers in the aesthetic appeal of concrete.
3. *Dom Pedro II*: Emperor of Brazil, 1831–89.
4. *Boudin's Trouville*: Eugène Boudin was a major influence on the Impressionists who followed him; his 1864 beach scene is much admired for its use of colour.
5. *Homburg under King Edward VII*: In the nineteenth century Homburg, near Frankfurt, was a fashionable spa and gambling resort. The half-German King Edward VII visited no fewer than thirty-two times.
6. *Colonel Fawcett*: The inspiration for the Indiana Jones stories, in 1925 Percy Fawcett disappeared in the Brazilian jungle while searching for a lost city known only as 'Z'. Over the years 100 people from thirteen separate expeditions are said to have perished trying to retrace Fawcett's steps and discover his fate.
7. *Martin Bormann*: Around the time Russell wrote this despatch, the Nazi-hunter Simon Wiesenthal believed Bormann was hiding in the South American jungle. A Lord Lucan figure, Bormann was

Hitler's top lieutenant at the end of the Second World War. Having disappeared, he was tried *in absentia* at Nuremberg. The mystery was solved in 1972 when human remains found in a Berlin railway yard were identified as Bormann's.

8. *Che Guevara*: Russell was getting carried away here; Che had little to do with Brazil. He died in the Bolivian jungle, and his famous motorcycle journey took in almost everywhere in the South American continent but Brazil.

~

Panama

'A marvellous mechanical achievement and a sad human failure'

DUGALD MALCOLM, HM AMBASSADOR TO THE REPUBLIC OF PANAMA, MARCH 1971

(CONFIDENTIAL)   *Panama City,*
                                  25 March, 1971
Sir,

To place in proper perspective my first impressions of this post, I must record the – so to say – advance impressions which I received in London while preparing to come here. I quote from the post report ' . . . walking is not agreeable (or, particularly for female staff, safe) . . . there are attractive beaches . . . but it takes two hours to get to them . . . Sharks are a hazard and it is as well to keep within one's depth . . . Humidity, average 89.2 per cent . . . termites . . . Ladies' teas'; from the personal security report ' . . . The Residence is a large rambling house with many entrances. I cannot see what can be done to protect it'; from the front page of the inventory supplied by the Department of the

Environment ' . . . Items on pages 35–37 should be deleted as they were destroyed on the orders of the municipal health authorities following the death of the occupant from purulent meningitis'; and more in the same vein from conversations and letters. Against this background first impressions were almost bound to be favourable, and so indeed they were.

The city is an agglomeration of tumbledown wooden relics of canal-building days, with a bustling market and commercial area spreading out into a modern section of fine American-style office and hotel buildings and large areas of pleasant villas each in a colourful garden. There is a great air of activity and development . . .

What now of the Canal, which is the mainspring of the country, and of the Zone which encloses it? As I pass from the town to the Zone – from a seething tenement area across a six-lane highway and through an 8-foot wire barrier – I have a slightly James Bond feeling of passing from a human untidy world into an almost unreal Dr. No territory, where everything is done electrically and hygienically by switches, and controlled by very large guards dressed like 'The Lone Ranger'. It is all a marvellous mechanical achievement and a sad human failure. Panamanians are bound to recognise that a large proportion of their wealth comes directly or indirectly from the Canal, but they would be superhuman if they did not feel a fierce resentment towards the Zone. This resentment is all too evident. Whatever the original Treaty[1] or President Roosevelt may have said the Zone is plainly a colony. Apart from the troops necessary for local defence there are installations which in other countries would be the subject of military base agreements. There are shops, banks and places of entertainment which, in Panamanian eyes should be contributing to their economy, and there are civilian inhabitants, including Panamanian nationals who pay taxes to neither Government. There is also much unused space. The Zone itself is pressed so close up against the limits of the two main cities, Panama and Colon, that both are denied their natural areas of expansion, so that both are investigating highly costly schemes of reclaiming land out to sea.

1. *Treaty*: Under the terms of a 1904 Treaty, the United States paid Panama $10 million to purchase six miles of land along each bank of the Panama Canal. Later treaties reversed the arrangement, with Panama regaining the Canal Zone land in 1979, and the waterway itself on 31 December 1999.

~

Mexico

'Latin American David to the Gringo Goliath'

JOHN GALSWORTHY, HM AMBASSADOR TO MEXICO,
NOVEMBER 1972

The Mexicans have an almost pathetic yearning for economic independence and, though most of them realise in their hearts that this is a chimera, their public utterances on the theme of foreigners and super Powers are apt to sound somewhat shrill in non-Mexican ears.

But it is really all meant for Big Brother north of the Rio Grande. A newcomer is struck by the fact that it is the Americans who are foreigners here, not the Europeans or the Japanese. This is especially, but by no means exclusively, true with the younger generation of Mexicans. I was disbelieving when my German colleague warned me that outside places like Mexico City, Acapulco or the other main tourist centres, it was wiser to be heard talking in a foreign tongue which could not be mistaken for American. But I now know what he meant: the attitude changes instantaneously when you identify yourself as an Englishman or other European.

Whose fault is it? I award (this *is* a first impressions despatch) eight points of blame to the Americans and two to the Mexicans. The latter for their excessive vanity and their irrepressible relish for playing Latin American David to the Gringo Goliath up north, regardless of the basic facts of their economic life: 70 per cent of Mexican foreign trade is with the US, the heavy tourist income which helps to correct the imbalance in their current account is overwhelmingly American and the US is by far the largest source of foreign capital. But having said that, the American profile here strikes a newcomer (and certainly one conditioned by 10 years in Western Europe) as provocative to say the least. For the Americans Mexico is their backyard, and that is just the way a large proportion of them behave here. They patronise to an alarming degree. I had my first taste of it when I flew in here from New York. A young American businessman (admittedly after four double brandies and several dry Martinis) was talking to an older Mexican sitting beside him in the 'plane: 'Why don't you just treat us like normal friends and pay a little attention to our weaknesses and characteristics?' asked the Mexican. He got the reply: 'We don't need to: we are rich and powerful.'

≈

Bolivia

'Any excuse for a party'

RONALD BAILEY, HM AMBASSADOR TO THE
REPUBLIC OF BOLIVIA, OCTOBER 1967

The Indians believe in any excuse for a party. Once upon a time it must have been provided by the Inca gods. Now each locally favoured Saint on his or her day of the calendar provides the occasion. A German supplier of aspirin has shrewdly produced elaborate illustrated Saints calendars, to be seen in village shops throughout the country. On feast days the people dress up in the most elaborate, embroidered costumes hired for the occasion. The Archangel Gabriel in shining silver and armed with his short broadsword keeps order among the vast crowd of masked devils and bears. Often there will be a hundred or more at a time dancing the same monotonous rhythms to the sound of a brass band. Most of the substance of the poorer classes is spent in this way. A gardener or a peasant will spend a whole month's income for this brief day of glory. Both men and women drink chicha. This is made by the older women who spit partly masticated millet into a pot. When water is added it quickly brews a heady alcoholic gruel and with this good cheer inside, they dance late into the night. A friend of ours asked her maid who was the father of her child. She said she could not see his face, but he was such a handsome 'devil'! I should have added that included in the hire of the costume are the services of a boy to put the hirer to bed when he is too inebriated to continue dancing and take the costume back in good order to the owner!

~

'Twice enslaved'

JOHN TAHOURDIN, HM AMBASSADOR TO THE
REPUBLIC OF BOLIVIA, MARCH 1972

Just occasionally a reader familiar with a country described in these despatches will feel the ambassador has completely missed the point or the spirit of a place. There is nothing wrong with Mr Tahourdin's first impressions of Bolivia – all the criticisms are fair – except for what they miss. If you don't see the magic of this high Andean fastness, if you don't feel what's addictive about its sharp light, bleached plains, glittering lakes and awesome peaks, and if you don't soften at all towards its impassive, wary, stoical native people with their blank expressions and amazing capacity to endure, then what's left is admittedly frustrating and tiresome. But Tahourdin's despatch is worth reading for its joke (told by Bolivians against themselves) alone. As for the rest – he should have got out more. The potential immigrants who never (as he points out) got as far as Bolivia, are the losers: and so is he.

We also include (on pp. 250–53) Tahourdin's despatch from Senegal: an account which makes only the most cursory (and imperceptive) references to the landscape, the indigenous people or the atmosphere outside French-influenced high society.

La Paz,
30 *March, 1972.*

Sir,

I have the honour to submit some first impressions of Bolivia.

The first view of La Paz – particularly on arrival by train at night – is spectacular. An immense cluster of lights in a huge bowl. By day the mighty Andes, with peaks over 21,000 ft. high encircling the city in a majestic embrace, produce a scenic effect of such splendour beside which the Swiss Alps resemble a toy model.

The Bolivians, who possess a disarming capacity for self-criticism, are fond of telling the story that when the Almighty at the Creation was apportioning the world's riches, someone intervened to say that what was one day to be Bolivia was being unduly favoured. This objection was swept aside with the retort: 'Wait until you see the kind of people I am going to put there.' The human material could indeed hardly have been more unpromising: a nation part Spanish, part Indian. From Spain she inherited characteristics which include so strong a streak of personal ambition, self-seeking acquisitiveness and violence, alternating with indolence. The other half, consisting in part of a race twice enslaved (once by the Incas and once by the Spaniards), was cowed, ignorant, with a physique enfeebled by centuries of living in almost unendurably hard climatic conditions.

Following independence from Spain, Bolivia had a territory which made it the third largest country in Latin America . . . as a result of a series of disastrous wars, Bolivia proceeded to lose to her neighbours one-half of her territory, including her entire Pacific coastline. She is, however, still fifth in the league.

Things might not have been so bad if the Spanish/ Indian combination had been leavened over the years, as in Brazil, Argentina or Chile, with a vigorous stream of subsequent immigration from Europe – Italians, Germans and British. But the facts of geography worked against this. With Bolivia deprived of her sea ports and faced with the consequent difficulty of access – until the advent of the jet – the would-be immigrants turned elsewhere.

~

Uruguay

'Strangely-named terrorists'

SIR GEOFFREY JACKSON, HM AMBASSADOR TO
URUGUAY, SEPTEMBER 1969

'Set piece reports from Montevideo at the commencement and termination of Ambassadorial missions tend to follow a predictable pattern,' a senior clerk in the American Department minuted on this despatch, 'and Mr Jackson's First Impressions is no exception.'

This rather jaded response was prompted by the extended metaphor of Uruguay as an ageing beauty queen which the ambassador used to frame his despatch. Sir Geoffrey Jackson's tone is certainly rather whimsical.

Living in Montevideo rekindled the ambassador's passion for Uruguay. But this love affair was to end very badly. A year after penning his first impressions Jackson was kidnapped by the Tupamaros, a violent band of urban guerrillas. For eight months the ambassador was held captive underground in a cage made from chicken wire, guarded by trigger-happy revolutionaries.

As the despatch shows, with kidnappings a common occurrence at the time in South America, Jackson was aware of the threat from the outset. He later described the feeling:

> . . . [E]arly in 1970 . . . I began to sense that accumulation of recurrently anomalous situations which the late Ian Fleming defined so neatly. His James Bond says somewhere that 'Once is happenstance, twice is coincidence, and three times is enemy action.' When, after a relatively quiet life, nocturnal telephone-calls begin to proliferate; when one's hitherto pleasantly solitary walks along beaches and sand-dunes and in pine-forests begin to bristle with horizon-marching silhouettes and sudden encounters with the courting young in unlikely trio formation . . . when for the third time one's path is crossed by professional violence literally on one's doorstep – by this time the least perceptive of mortals begins to grasp that, however much the world around him may be changing, his own private life is changing still more.

Early on in Montevideo the ambassador had made contingency plans, instructing his wife, Evelyn, that in the event of his capture there should be no ransom paid, nor any negotiations or publicity. Jackson owed his release in September 1971 to Edward Heath, the Prime Minister, who overrode the ambassador's wishes and arranged for a ransom payment of £42,000.

Jackson was knighted on his release and retired from the Diplomatic Service two years later. We append an extract from his later account of the kidnapping in his book People's Prison *(1973): a passage in which, though Sir Geoffrey was not quite a García Márquez, its author shows (as does so much diplomatic writing) some of the signs of the novelist manqué.*

After democracy was restored to Uruguay in 1985 the Tupamaros began a slow march into the political main-stream. As part of the Broad Front coalition, the political wing of the Tupamaros won the 2009 parliamentary elec-tions, and in 2010 one of their number – a former armed guerrilla, José Mujica – became President of Uruguay.

This First Impressions is worth reading not least for the irony of what was to follow.

(CONFIDENTIAL)   *Montevideo,*
                                         17 September, 1969.
Sir,

To meet a childhood sweetheart again after much of a life-time can, by all accounts, come as quite a jolt. Admittedly my own long-standing fondness for Uruguay had been essentially a courtship by correspondence and proxy, from the Latin American desk of the then Foreign Office, and later from Assembly Delegations at the United Nations. Even so, I felt on my arrival last July that the photographs the lady had sent me had perhaps been somewhat over-taken by the years.

Her Administration – and her capital – were in evident need of a face-lift. Her economy has lost its figure, though laudably she has taken of late to remedial exercises. Politically she is not sure whether she prefers the ostrich feather boas of her Edwardian 'belle époque' or the miniskirt of today; neither really suits her style, and the combination of both even less. But she retains the ruins of a lovely face, and her heart is still in the right place; so I needed only briefly to compose my expression, and was not really disappointed. And after these few weeks I have concluded that the pretty girl of long ago still survives inside a somewhat weathered *fausse jeune*, who has also perhaps gained in personality what she has lost in glamour.

Even with dethroned beauty queens vital statistics remain a point of reference. Uruguay's exports and imports are £64 million and £58 million, and her population 2,590,158 . . .

[I]t is hard – though nowadays possible – to starve in Uruguay. She produces a superabundance of good food – beef, lamb, game, fish, vegetables, salads, fruits, wines – in the valediction of Henry King, 'all the human frame requires'. Lest even so 'her wretched trade expires' is President Pacheco's present concern . . . The social unease provoked by such paradoxes is reflected in incessant strikes . . . And lurking behind, though legally unmentionable, are the mysterious and no longer preposterous 'Tupamaros'. These strangely-named terrorists – most inappropriately so in a land with no admitted Indian heritage – have lost their political innocence since their first overt murder last August, and yet more so since the United States Ambassador to Brazil was kidnapped by comparable, and doubtless allied, forces in that neighbouring country. Since starting this despatch they have kidnapped a key employers' negotiator in the bank strike, who is still missing and unheard of.

Yet nothing is ever hopeless in this paradoxical country ... It is therefore possible, even probable, that the Uruguayan back is at last against the wall, that her people see, with final authentic fear, the true jeopardy to their three good meals a day, to their increasingly shabby empire-style mansions, parks, public buildings, hospitals and monuments, to their scratch fleet of miraculously-preserved vintage private motor cars, to their whole economic box of well-saved combings ...

I – like many predecessors – must draw attention to a continuing and major invisible British asset in this country, itself conversely an enduring asset to Uruguay's own democracy. A few days ago, at the annual Caledonian Ball in Montevideo, I watched 450 participants, mainly all-Uruguayan, and young Uruguayan at that, battle till dawn for space to perform, with competence and evident enthusiasm, everything from an eightsome reel to the Dashing White Sargeant. The idol of all the girls was a statuesquely handsome and impeccably kilted pipe-major of pure Italian extraction, to my joy quite authentically named Macucci. In the gallery were numerous – and influential – admiring parents, and several tables had been commandeered by the Government and municipality. The reflection occurred to me that there are in Montevideo several Missions whose Governments would pay – and by all accounts do pay – many millions of dollars a year to achieve the very position of confidence and acceptance which Britain has no need to buy, but needs only to maintain and preserve ...

To revert to my initial image, Britain's fidelity to Uruguay's once endearing young charms is staunchly reciprocated, and at a time when Britain's, too, might to many seem faded. Small attentions can ensure the persistence of this regard while Uruguay's house and estate are put in order. And she may be a rich widow yet, and platonically appreciative of enduring friendships – even though she could one day of course marry one of the gentlemen next door.

But the relations of Uruguay with the Argentine and Brazil are another, and less predictable, story.

I am sending copies of this despatch to Her Majesty's Ambassadors in Washington, Buenos Aires and Rio de Janeiro.

I have, &c.
G. H. S. JACKSON.

From People's Prison (1973) *by Geoffrey Jackson*

As always, I was relieved when we turned in from the open corniche into the narrow and crowded side-streets leading to my office, and I was joking with my driver as we edged slowly along the single lane left by the vehicles parked on either side. We were at a point where virtually every day we had to wait for delivery-trucks to finish unloading at one or other of the wayside stores, so I did not pay especial attention to a large red van – certainly of three, possibly of five tons – until it edged out from the curb as we drew level. There was little room for my driver to swerve, but ample time for the truck-driver to realize and correct his mistake. I knew however that frequently they did not do so until after impact, and was not really surprised when, despite my driver's signals, he bored relentlessly into our left wing. With a philosophical shrug, and obvious resignation to a coachwork job and some ineffectual insurance activity, Hugo opened his door to climb out and take particulars.

Instead, as the cab-door opened and the truck-driver leapt down, a young man stepped out from nowhere and struck Hugo savagely over the head. Simultaneously there was a violent rattle of automatic weapons which continued for what to me seemed an endless time; one of its main constituents originated from a sub-machine-gun concealed in a basket of fruit carried by an apparently innocuous bystander – my captors were very proud of this refinement, of which I was told repeatedly afterwards.

The driver of the truck climbed into my chauffeur's seat, and opened the opposite door for a second young man. A third put his arm around the door-pillar and expertly unlocked the back door from the inside . . . My attackers were not masked – the last human faces I was to see for a long time. They were thoroughly conversant with the idiosyncrasies of the Daimler – its gear-shift, with some rather exotic characteristics from Montevideo; the door-locks; and the power steering; I found my mind formulating the many circumstances in which this familiarity could have been acquired.

Our driver, whom I could see clearly in the mirror, was, as I have said, a face I had met recently. He had blunt features, a moustache half-way Zapata-style and, again, this rictus of tension, concentration or – I would not blame them – sheer fright. Three of the four I would recognize again instantly, were I to live to be a centenarian . . .

PART IV: EUROPE

France

'Images of Britain as a Victorian sweatshop economy and haven for Islamic terrorists die hard'

SIR JOHN HOLMES, HM AMBASSADOR TO THE
FRENCH REPUBLIC, OCTOBER 2001

FM PARIS
TO PRIORITY FCO

SUBJECT: FRANCE: FIRST/SECOND IMPRESSIONS

A couple of months in Paris is as good a time as any to attempt a few impressions – second more than first in my case since I spent four years in Paris in the mid-1980s ... My strongest impression this time is one of continuity. The place feels the same, as does the administration/bureaucracy. France seems to have changed less than its big European neighbours, particularly Britain. The main political contenders for the forthcoming Presidential election were at the top of politics 15 years ago too. The shift of generation evident in Britain, Germany, Italy, Spain and elsewhere has not so far operated here. This frustrates the younger politicians, insofar as any of stature have been allowed to develop, and bores the voters ...

The political/intellectual climate has not apparently changed much either. Much of it is still dominated by a peculiarly French view of the world, where shades of anti-capitalism, anti-Americanism and anti-globalisation remain fashionable, or at least politically correct . . .

Not an original insight, maybe, but I am still struck by how conservative France remains. The attitude of what you have, you protect remains fundamental for many. Keeping existing jobs has greater priority than creating new ones. Acquired rights are almost sacred. Innovation is to be resisted, not embraced. The attachment to la France profonde continues to give French farmers clout far beyond their economic weight . . .

We wonder why the French don't seem to suffer more for apparently flouting today's economic rules. Maybe one day they will. The 35-hour week's[1] daftness is bound to show through sometime. It may be that the French only get away with present policies now because of the country's other advantages, including hugely improved infrastructure and a formidably clever and effective administrative (as opposed to political) class – and because the rigidity of the country's labour and tax laws is matched only by the ingenuity of companies in getting round them . . .

Meanwhile the big change I do notice is in attitudes to Britain. Rivalry and stereotyping have not gone away. Images of Britain as a Victorian sweatshop economy and haven for Islamic terrorists die hard. Infrastructure and health service comparisons favourable to France are two a penny. Snide comments sprinkle the pages. (Nothing as vitriolic as the British press about the French of course.)

1. *35-hour week*: A novel labour law introduced by Prime Minister Lionel Jospin in 2000. Limiting the working week to thirty-five hours was supposed to reduce unemployment by forcing firms to hire more

workers to make up for the lost hours, while improving the work–life balance of existing employees. The French parliament has twice since watered it down, allowing more overtime.

~

Denmark

'An oasis of sanity in a stupid world'

SIR OLIVER WRIGHT, HM AMBASSADOR TO THE KINGDOM OF DENMARK, JANUARY 1967

Sir Oliver Wright found little to dislike in the Danish system. Of course it would be a mistake to assume that Denmark is not a very different country from Sweden, but his despatch makes for an interesting comparison with one that Sir Jeffrey Petersen wrote thirteen years later upon departing Stockholm (see pp. 352–5). Where Wright saw Scandinavian social democracy as a kind of utopia, Petersen saw 'The Swedish Model' as essentially broken.

CONFIDENTIAL   *British Embassy,*
(1011/5)   *Copenhagen,*
<u>Despatch No. 5</u>   *9 January, 1967.*

Sir,

Arriving in Denmark after six months of commuting between London and Salisbury, I was struck by a local concern about the Rhodesian problem, quite disproportionate to the extent of any Danish interests involved. The reason for this concern, given to me by the editor of Copenhagen's leading morning newspaper, will serve as my text for the customary despatch on first impressions. 'There is,' he said, 'no poverty or injustice in Denmark today, so that there is little for us to quarrel about at home. But human beings must have an outlet for their idealism; and since we have very few interests at stake there, Africa provides as safe an outlet as any' . . .

In the countryside, as in the towns, there is order, comfort, well-being, without ostentation or waste. The streets are filled with small and family-sized cars; sports models and limousines alike drive infrequently past. The pavements are thronged with citizens attractively but modestly suited, shod and shampooed: boys with ringlets down to their shoulders and women over-expensively furred and perfumed are alike comparatively rare. The shops are filled with well-made merchandise and with shoppers with well-lined pockets, but Strøget is no Bond Street. Policemen are seldom needed and therefore seldom seen, since it would be wasteful to spend good money on what is not necessary; the most hostile looks and words are reserved for those, generally foreigners, who cross the street against the lights . . . Even weekend picnickers take their litter home to their own dust-bins. The Danes, descendants of the Viking conquerors of Britain a thousand years ago, have thoroughly domesticated Nature and disciplined their own natures . . .

Puritans may object that my editor friend's words are cynical and shocking. They may well be both; but there is also a refreshing honesty about them. If the heroic virtues are at a discount in Denmark, so are hypocrisy and cant. The way Danish society is organised may well provide too little scope for men's aggressive instincts, although the

Socialist People's Party provides a vehicle for political, and suicide an outlet for social protest; but there is compensation in the clear-eyed candour about what makes human beings tick, in the tolerant respect for the other man's view and interest, and in the unashamed delight in material pleasures which informs the whole Danish attitude to life. The ease and naturalness of everyday relations between men and women in Denmark are the most attractive I have so far encountered in twenty-one years of globe-trotting at the tax payer's expense.

It seems to me, therefore, that, by and large, Danish hearts are in the right place, although they might perhaps, with advantage, beat a little faster; and that Danish heads are screwed on the right way, although they might perhaps, with advantage, calculate a little less furiously. This is a satisfied – even, the envious would say – a self-satisfied society; but, given the experience of the human race over the past few thousand years, one ought not to turn up one's nose at the achievement of a polity in which practically the only legitimate complaint is that there is nothing to complain about... Like the Hippo Valley Estates in the Rhodesian low veldt, Denmark seems like an oasis of sanity in a stupid world. It will be interesting to see what I feel like when the time comes for me to write my valedictory despatch, when I know the place properly, and when the spectacles of the new arrival have lost their rubescence.

I am sending a copy of this despatch to Her Majesty's Ambassadors in Stockholm, Oslo and Helsinki; to the United Kingdom Mission at Geneva, and to the United Kingdom Delegation to the European Economic Community at Brussels.

I have the honour to be, Sir,

With the highest respect,

Your obedient Servant,
Oliver Wright

~

Austria

'Hitler could hardly have been anything but an Austrian'

SIR ANTHONY RUMBOLD, HM AMBASSADOR TO THE
REPUBLIC OF AUSTRIA, MAY 1968

Among diplomats of the old school, and when it came to making incredibly offensive sweeping generalizations about foreigners, Sir Anthony Rumbold was in a class of his own. He arrived in Vienna in 1968 on something of a roll in this regard, having signed off from Bangkok the previous year with an uproarious valedictory despatch. 'The average intelligence of the Thais is rather low,' he wrote, before venturing that 'licentiousness was the main pleasure' among leading Thais, and suggesting that the country's Foreign Minister might be insane.

Compared with what he made of Austria, below, we can only conclude that Rumbold actually rather liked Thailand. While venting his spleen about Vienna the ambassador did however manage to get at least one thing significantly wrong in terms of predicting the future. The Austrian capital, which Rumbold thought had not the 'remotest possibility' of becoming 'the headquarters of any kind of

*international grouping, whether political or economic',
is today home to several of the world's biggest non-
governmental organizations, including the oil producers'
cartel OPEC and the International Atomic Energy Agency.*

CONFIDENTIAL

THIS DOCUMENT IS THE PROPERTY OF HER BRITANNIC MAJESTY'S GOVERNMENT

CA 1/12   *Foreign Office and Whitehall Distribution*

AUSTRIA
20 May, 1968
Section 1

A VIEW OF AUSTRIA

Sir Anthony Rumbold to Mr. Stewart (Received 20 May)

(CONFIDENTIAL)   *Vienna,*
                                          14 May, 1968
Sir,

No European can be entirely objective about a European
country (least of all about his own). His views are influenced by his upbringing, his circumstances and his age-
group. My children think of Austria as an agreeable place
in which to go ski-ing. Music-lovers or those with musical
pretensions think of it in terms of the Salzburg festivals
and the Vienna Opera. My own view of Austria is coloured
by my recollection of the prominent and enthusiastic part

played by so many Austrians in the Nazi movement. Moreover the few months I have now been professionally engaged in Vienna have not weakened my loyalty to the school which I joined in early youth and which regards Austrians as 'wet Germans' (the 'best' Germans according to this school being the Berliners). The Austrian writer Ferdinand Kürnberger uses the following untranslate-able words to express this about the character of his country-men: 'Feig ist es, schlaff, schrottig, waschlappig, mattherzig, schwachmütig, kraftlos, nervlos, energielos, widerstand-los'.[1] There are some who trace this back to the experiences of the counter-Reformation, particularly in Vienna, when the Protestant and libertarian mass movement was thoroughly defeated, leaving behind a thick sediment of cynicism and opportunism. But whatever the reason it seems to me that Hitler could hardly have been anything but an Austrian and that A. J. P. Taylor, the only English historian to have unravelled the fall of the Empire, is right in considering Hitler to have been Austria's revenge for Königgrätz.[2] I think it as well to declare my prejudice at the outset.

Austria is a small country in terms of population, area and 'gross national product'. But it is as complex as it is small. Clemenceau[3] defined Austria within its pres-ent boundaries as *le reste*, in other words what was left after the non-German parts of the old Empire had been taken away. The inhabitants of this rump all speak German of a kind (with the exception of some insignificant Slo-vene and Hungarian minorities) but they are not united by their common language. They are divided by historical, geographical and human factors ... A typical self-conscious Tyrolese is about as attached to Inner Austria as a modern Scottish Nationalist is to England ... [T]here are fewer organic connections between Vienna now and other parts of modern Austria than there are between London and other parts of England (let alone Scotland). Austrians from the western provinces rarely come to Vienna. They do their business at home, they spend their holidays among their own mountains or, if they can afford it, on the Mediterranean, and if they want bright lights they go to Munich. Salzburg was an independent archbishopric until 1803. It is now the playground of would-be sophisticates of all nations and lives on the sound of music. Burgenland was Hungarian until 1921 and it looks as if it still were. There is nothing in common between the Burgenland paprika-grower who gazes eastwards across the great plain and the prosperous Vorarlberg watchmaker whose father wanted in 1919 to join Switzerland from whose inhabitants he was indistinguishable as regards both race and outlook ...

The impression of aimlessness is particularly strong among the Viennese, whose city is only a capital in a formal sense. Between the wars, although too big to be the capital of such a small country, there was still a touch of universalism about Vienna which gave it some sort of point. Ten or fifteen per cent of the population were Jews; it was still possible to think about a Danubian federation of which it might be the centre, and it was a prize for the possession of which the rival ideologies thought it worth fighting. Now the Jews have nearly all disappeared, mostly murdered by the Nazis; there is not the remotest possibility of its becoming the headquarters of any kind of international grouping, whether political or economic; and its place in the new ideological or Great Power contest was fixed once and for all by the settlement of 1955[4] which, short of a cataclysm, is not likely to be upset or questioned by anybody. There is therefore no longer much *raison d'être* about Vienna, particularly since the rest of Austria cares so little about what goes on in it. To the small extent that it still exhibits a smiling countenance it is, as Hofmannsthal[5] said, because it no longer has any muscles in its face. There has indeed always been something feminine about Vienna, perhaps because of the strong Slav elements in its population, and the combination of aimlessness and femininity has unfortunate results. It makes it a sad and rather mean town. The people seem to lack charity towards each other. They rather enjoy denouncing each other for minor breaches of the regulations. They give vent to explosions of rage when inconvenienced in small ways. They cling to what they think of as their old traditions, treacly and anaemic though these were for the most part. Cheerful modern trends are disapproved of. The unhappy young go away when they can, mostly to Germany where they can make money and enjoy themselves. Nearly half the population draws some sort of pension. The dowdy clothes, the grim municipal tenement buildings and the general grubbiness make Vienna at certain times of the year look more like an Iron-curtain town than one which belongs to the West. Indeed the inhabitants of Prague and of Budapest seem to me to walk with a jauntier step than do the Viennese. There is certainly no more depressing sight than that of the self-conscious crowds of businessmen and their ladies at the famous opera ball, supposedly the glittering climax of a brilliant carnival season. Austria has the highest published suicide-rate of any country in the world and Vienna makes a disproportionate contribution to this record . . .

If they think about such things at all, the Austrians ought to be eternally grateful for the miracle by which they recovered their independence in 1955, except for the fact that they have always regarded themselves as entitled to specially generous allowances of good luck. If the Russians had not decided to make Austria neutral in the hope of Germany following suit, the country would presumably still have been divided and most of the population would have been materially much worse off. As it is they are both free and prosperous, at least relatively to what most of them have ever been before. Even for the Viennese it is a novel experience to be able to lead their private lives without pressure from external insecurity. It is true that the Austrians are far down the list in all the European economic league tables and that their standards of housing and hygiene are low. But they have plenty of money in their pockets to spend on what they enjoy, chiefly food and drink. There are no starvelings or 'criminals of want' to be seen among the bourgeois-looking May-day demonstrators. There are no extremists in modern Austria. Not even the students show signs of much restiveness. So long as conditions in the rest of Europe remain more or less stable we are not going to have any trouble from the Austrians. But they do not have reliable characters and are not to be counted upon in time of danger.

I have, &c.
A. RUMBOLD.

---

1. *'Feig ist es . . . widerstandlos'*: An Austrian friend suggests the following as helpful approximations: *feig ist es*, 'it's cowardly'; *schlaff*, 'flaccid'; *schrottig*, 'trashy'; *waschlappig*, 'loserish' (as in useless, idiot,

worthless person); *mattherzig*, literally, 'matte of heart' (i.e., dull-spirited); *schwachmütig* and *kraftlos*, 'weak'; *nervlos*, 'corwardly'; *energielos*, 'lacks energy/spirit'; and *widerstandlos*, 'unable to fight'.

2. *Königgrätz*: The Battle of Königgrätz in 1866 was the decisive battle in the Austro-Prussian War. Prussia won.

3. *Clemenceau*: Georges Clemenceau, Prime Minister of France 1906–9 and 1917–20. Nicknamed 'Le Tigre' for his harsh line against the defeated powers after the First World War, Clemenceau was a major influence on the Treaty of Versailles, which saw the Austro-Hungarian Empire dismantled.

4. *the settlement of 1955*: After the Second World War, Austria, like Germany, was divided into British, French, American and Soviet zones. In 1955 the country was given back its independence on condition of 'permanent neutrality'.

5. *Hofmannsthal:* Hugo von Hofmannsthal, 1874–1929, Austrian novelist and essayist.

~

Cyprus

'A wonderful island . . . Warts and all'

DONALD GORDON, HM HIGH COMMISSIONER TO
CYPRUS, DECEMBER 1975

The Southern European Department wrote a note of thanks to Donald Gordon upon receiving his report, which they considered an exemplar of 'the classic impressionistic first despatch style'.

'The political and historical complexities are indeed legion,' the note continued, 'but much also depends on the three leading personalities, Makarios, Clerides and Denktash, their actions, reactions and interactions. You have painted a vivid picture of them.'

Nicosia,
4 December, 1975.

Sir,

I doubt that further first-hand acquaintance with the complexities of the Cyprus situation is going to make the picture clearer: it may indeed well have the opposite effect. I propose therefore, Sir, to offer you my first impressions while these are still fresh.

The location of the High Commission offices serves to demonstrate that even-handedness as between the two communities which we strive to achieve. They are literally on the Green Line, in no-man's land. There is free access from the Greek Cypriot side and every day as I drive to the Office, past the battered houses that suffered in last year's fighting, the soldiers of the National Guard at their checkpoint give me a smart salute, or sometimes an amiable wave. They are not, to the casual observer, a smartly turned out or highly disciplined force: but some units fought with gallantry last year against heavy odds. There is no direct exit on the other side through the Turkish Cypriot front line some 150 yards away, but looking from our windows over the now deserted golf course, we see men of the Turkish Cypriot Fighters, who man the Nicosia sector of the Line, shouldering their muskets and going about other soldierly pursuits: and through my window come 'gung-ho' noises (to use an Americanism once fashionable in South Viet-Nam) as they take part in lusty martial singing. In this, as in other respects, the Turkish Army is somewhat reminiscent of the old Wehrmacht: full marks for toughness and fortitude, but a bit short on independent thinking.

From my window too I can see the hills of the Kyrenia Range silhouetted against the sky, a constant reminder of the small British colony (200–300 people) on the other side whose pleasant retirement in the sun was rudely disrupted by the Turkish invasion last year. They have shown courage in standing their ground, but they are worried about the future and understandably edgy about their position. We are in regular contact and they are always glad to see me and other visitors from this High Commission; but as they on their side lift their eyes to the hills, they are not always persuaded that the promise of the psalmist has been entirely borne out.

On my first day in Nicosia, the Director-General of the Ministry of Foreign Affairs, having flinched from sending a representative to meet my wife and myself on our arrival at Limassol at 7 o'clock in the morning, called on me instead of awaiting my call on him in order to make it clear that no discourtesy was intended. He told me with honesty that I could expect to be shown much kindness by Turkish Cypriots and Greek Cypriots alike. He was right. Unfortunately an ability to speak without bias is comparatively rare in Cyprus. Both parties to the dispute sorely exasperate their friends by their readiness to rake over the past and score facile debating points. They are quick to blame anyone – the other community in the island, the UN, the British – other than themselves for their present plight and show an unhappy ability to rock a boat which, in all conscience, is unstable enough already.

The essential problem is easy enough to identify. The earliest settlers in Cyprus, the Mycenaean Greeks and the Phoenicians, eventually blended to form the basic stock of the present inhabitants. Subsequent arrivals – Assyrians, Persians, Macedonians, Romans, Crusaders, Venetians, Turks and British – came and governed, but with the exception of the Turks, eventually left when their period of rule came to an end. The Turks, however, left behind a minority on the island who do not appear susceptible of assimilation but are too numerous to be ejected or dominated. They have lived for years in fear of a continuing Greek Cypriot attempt to do just that, and now that they hold most, if not all, of the cards, have every intention of ensuring that this will never happen again.

If both sides accept the realities of the situation, a workable arrangement is not inconceivable. Partition has since the days of Solomon represented the ultimate resort, and if Greeks and Turks cannot live together then they may have to live apart – not in separate sovereign States, for this would raise a whole crop of new problems, but under some bi-zonal arrangement. Both sides will have to accept that this is the best they are going to get. But the Turkish Cypriots doubt whether the other side really admit that Cyprus will have to be a Greco-Turk island and the Greek Cypriots hesitate to concede publicly bi-zonalism with all the sacrifices it must imply. One almost suspects at times that they have lived with tragedy so long – and it is in their tradition – that it has become for them a condition of mind to which they have formed a perverse attachment. There is also a body of opinion which believes that it might be better to soldier on rather than accept an unsatisfactory settlement . . .

Three figures stand out against the Cyprus scene: Archbishop Makarios, President of the Republic; Clerides, President of the House of Representatives and the Greek Cypriot negotiator in the inter-communal talks; and Denktash, Vice-President of the Republic, President of the so-called Turkish Federated State of Cyprus, and the Turkish Cypriot negotiator.

1. 'In these dark days man tends to look for little shafts of light that spill from heaven.' Alexander Cadogan, Permanent Under-Secretary of the FCO (*right*), entering the Potsdam Conference in July 1945. In the centre, Sir Archibald Clark Kerr, Ambassador in Moscow, author of the infamously vulgar telegram (p. 46).

2. Proof that the great man of Turkish diplomacy really did exist. His calling card, left at the British Embassy in Moscow, now resides in a scrapbook belonging to the former BBC foreign correspondent Douglas Stuart.

Mustafa Kunt
Secrétaire de l'Ambassade de Turquie

3. Sir Hughe Knatchbull-Hugessen (p. 90) with his wife in Shanghai, 1937. China was one of his many foreign postings. The ambassador was invalided home after his car was machine-gunned by a Japanese fighter aircraft.

4. Sir Eric Phipps, in dress uniform, with Hitler. The penultimate British Ambassador to Germany before the Second World War hated the Nazis and opposed appeasement.

5. Hermann Göring in hunting garb. The head of the Luftwaffe liked to show off at his country estate in the Schorfheide. Phipps described 'the almost pathetic naïveté of General Göring, who showed us his toys like a big, fat, spoilt child' (p. 89).

6. A family portrait. Sultan Said bin Taimur (*top*) ruled Oman for nearly forty years until deposed by his son in a 1970 coup. Qaboos (*bottom*) has reigned over Oman ever since.

7. John Phillips, the British Consul-General in Muscat (*in white shirt on left*), with other European expats, *c*.1960. The elder Sultan is in the centre foreground. Phillips's despatch is on p. 33.

8. A President in his prime: President Bongo of Gabon practises t'ai chi in Paris, 1970. 'In everything but stature he is larger than life,' observed the British ambassador, Anthony Golds (p. 261).

9. Sir John Russell, British Ambassador to Brazil, 1966–9. Russell built a reputation in the Foreign Office on his epic, comic despatches from Rio (pp. 64, 71 and 179).

10./11. Alan Davidson, British Ambassador to Laos, in official mode in Vientiane – the Bentley was Davidson's own – and at leisure in his garden in 1974. Talented eccentrics have long found a home in the Diplomatic Service but Davidson left the FCO the following year, and became a famous cookery writer (p. 152).

12. Papa Doc, with rifle. In 1970 the incoming British ambassador thought President Duvalier looked 'exactly like anybody's family doctor or solicitor . . . his general air of mildness made it difficult to remember that I was shaking one of the most bloodstained hands in recent history' (p. 111).

13./14. A curio of empire. The New Hebrides had a unique Condominium government with British and French Residents exercising joint control. The tiny Pacific archipelago was burdened with two legal systems, two currencies and two different police uniforms (p. 332).

15. Peter Penfold with Zainab Bangura, a Sierra Leone government minister. In 1997 Britain's High Commissioner backed a plan to ship arms to Sierra Leone, against a UN embargo. The official report criticized Penfold – but on his return to Freetown he was hailed as a hero (p. 59).

16./17. (Baroness) Daphne Park, pictured here as a young woman in wartime, and later in life, was a senior controller in MI6. She worked as a diplomat as cover. Her remarkable valedictory from Hanoi is on pp. 365–75.

18./19. Maksat. John Major's birthday horse had to be sprung from the clutches of the Moscow railway in the midst of a constitutional crisis. He has since found a happy home in Carmarthenshire, and is a champion endurance racer (p.47).

20. The Turkmenbashi. A screwball dictator, Saparmurat Niyazov held brutal sway over Turkmenistan from 1990 to 2006. This twelve-metre-high gold statue of the President rotated every twenty-four hours so as to always face the sun.

Makarios is the present manifestation of the long associ-ation of the Orthodox Church in Cyprus with the political life of the Greek Cypriots, a small neat figure in his azure vestments with a thousand years of Byzantine sophistry in his bland smile. A highly experienced tactician, he has shown great skill in trimming his sails in the prevailing political winds so as to ensure his continuing tenure of office. Whether he regards this as essential to the protection of Greek Cypriot interests as he sees them, or as an end in itself, is debatable. There must be a question mark over his qualities as a statesman. His failure to effect a settlement with the Turkish Cypriots over the 14 years when he held nearly all the cards is in large measure responsible for the present unhappy plight of the island. To the Turkish Cypriots 'His Byzantine Beatitude' as Denktash refers to him, is anathema and it is difficult to see a solution so long as he remains President. But, equally, it is difficult to see a solution without him, and he is quite capable of unobtrusively sabotaging a prospective settlement if it involves his giving up office.

Clerides has to cope not only with Denktash but with the Archbishop, and in this has shown both flexibility and real-ism. He looks like a prosperous lawyer with a taste for good living. It may therefore be relevant to recall that he baled out over Germany, escaped from a prisoner of war camp at the third attempt and made his way across the country to join up eventually with Tito's partisans. He has put his political future as leader of the Centre-Right at stake, knowing that Makarios will sell him out without hesitation if it suits his purposes and that there are political groupings, of the ex-treme Right and extreme Left, who have no wish to see a settlement in Cyprus and may try to take pre-emptive ac-tion if one appears a real possibility.

Denktash, an amiable extrovert, is a less subtle figure than Clerides. Where Clerides looks over his shoulder at Makarios, Denktash looks to the Turkish Army and Ankara who wield the real power. But although he often chooses to act the *enfant terrible*, it would be a mistake to underestimate his political skills.

My Turkish colleague, with some feeling, maintains that Turkish Cypriots and Greek Cypriots are incapable of ever reaching a settlement on their own, but are like children squabbling on the street who need a grown-up to come along and tell them to stop it. Mr Inhan is in no position to be sanctimonious, but he is right in that it will certainly take a concerted effort to achieve and enforce any settlement. Apart from anything else, the two parties on the island will have to learn that it is possible to have a dividing line without living in a continuous state of eyeball-to-eyeball confrontation . . .

People keep assuring me, nostalgically, that 'before the trouble' this was a wonderful island. It is arguable that the seeds of its destruction are sown in its own past history. But the Cypriots have a remarkable capacity for survival, born of considerable past experience – if only they can be induced to draw the right lessons. I hope they do. Warts and all, it is still an island of much charm.

I am copying this despatch to Her Majesty's Ambassadors at Ankara, Athens, Washington, the UK Delegation to NATO and the UK Mission, New York; to the UK Representative, Brussels and to CBFNE.

I have, etc.,
D. McD. GORDON.

PART V: NORTH AFRICA

Morocco

'The shadow for the substance . . . the word for the deed'

THOMAS SHAW, HM AMBASSADOR TO THE
KINGDOM OF MOROCCO, MARCH 1970

If it is clear that Morocco today must be counted an Arab country, it is a relief to find that, like Austrians and Germans, Moroccans are Arabs *mit mildernden Umständen*.[1] Geographical position, the population mixture, the incidents of history and a definite sense of Moroccan personality, all lead them to differ in mode from their Eastern Arab brothers . . . The opening towards the Arab world is not matched by any similar movement towards Africa south of the Sahara . . . [T]he natural attitude of the Moroccan towards the black African is little short of contempt. As Houphouet-Boigny[2] remarked to my Ivoirian colleague recently: *'Ils nous traitent toujours d'esclaves.'*[3] Nevertheless there are so many habits and attitudes of mind in Morocco which ring a familiar West African bell that I cannot help wondering whether the connections are not stronger than a Moroccan would admit. The disregard of time is probably too general to point anywhere in particular; but the ability to take the shadow for the substance or the word for the deed, stem as easily from Africa as from the Arab world; the tendency to treat foreign Ambassadors like a troupe of performing monkeys is reminiscent of ex-President Apithy, or indeed of the Kings of Abomey[4] before him; the sacred pools and trees, even the style of drumming, have much in common with black Africa; and it is a fact that only here and in the Ivory Coast has my household depended on me to change an electric light bulb . . .

Twenty-five years of absence elsewhere have confirmed one early conclusion in a field which, alas, impinges particularly on the likes of us: that Moroccan servants are as bad as any in my wide experience. It took me some months . . . to discover that my Moroccan servant had throughout his employment with me and for at least some of his employment with my predecessor combined his domestic functions and wages with the duties and wage of a point-duty policeman. I sacked him finally when I found him using my toothbrush.

1. *mit mildernden Umständen*: With mitigating circumstances.
2. *Houphouet-Boigny*: Félix Houphouët-Boigny, President of Côte d'Ivoire, 1960–93.
3. *'Ils nous traitent toujours d'esclaves'*: 'They always treat us as slaves.'
4. *Ex-President Apithy . . . Kings of Abomey*: Sourou-Migan Apithy, President of Dahomey (today Benin), 1964–5. Abomey was the capital of Dahomey.

~

Libya (The Libyan Arab Jamahiriya)

'Big Brother is watching'

PETER TRIPP, HM AMBASSADOR TO
LIBYA, MARCH 1971

Two reports here from British ambassadors in Libya, spanning the first decade of Colonel Qadhafi's rule after the 1969 coup which brought him to power. Reading these despatches the striking thing is how little the essential nature of the dictatorship seems to have changed from those early days right up until the revolution and subsequent NATO campaign that toppled Qadhafi from power in 2011.

The fault lines under the regime seem equally ancient. Peter Tripp's prediction in 1971 that the eastern half of the country around Benghazi had an independent streak 'which could yet cause Libya's present rulers trouble' of course came true, in the end.

The 1977 report from Tripp's successor-but-one, Anthony Williams, hit the nail on the head too, in its analysis of Qadhafi himself. The file shows that Williams's Head of Department, C. D. Powell, considered this despatch 'a shrewd and amusing piece, which strips down Libya and its leader to their bare essentials. The latter are more attractive when spread out on Mr Williams' groundsheet than when assembled into their unappealing whole.'

'Incidentally,' continues the memo, 'the experts say the Libyans were not always cheats, at least of each other, and probably learned it from Western carpet-baggers!'

(CONFIDENTIAL)   *Tripoli,*
                                                 2 March, 1971.

Sir,

The Post Report said one should not imagine Tripoli and Benghazi to be Mediterranean towns like Nice and Monte Carlo! The author of that advice must himself have had a very fertile (or over-worked) imagination. To most people Tripoli must seem a dump and Benghazi like limbo. The vastness and variety of Libya comes as a surprise. Driving to Benghazi – ten hours and 650 miles away – brings home to one the distance separating Tripoli from Cyrenaica, and illustrates the problem of maintaining cohesion between the two parts of the Embassy in those two places. The further drive to Cyrene, Apollonia, Beida, Derna and on to Tobruk presents a different vista and another climate: green hills, deep gorges, waterfalls, Scotch mists. I have not yet seen the Fezzan and the sand seas, another 8–12 hours' drive to the south and south-west.

Libya could never have been effectively one country – but it suited the convenience of its former transitory rulers to pretend that it was. The ruins of Sabratha, Leptis Magna, Apollonia and Cyrene testify to the attempts by former governors to establish centres of power from which to dominate and exploit the region. The present rulers by centralising the 'action' (and Government institutions) in Tripoli have effectively given to Tripoli a new predominance in a unified Libya. There is still, however, an independence about Cyrenaica which could yet cause Libya's present rulers trouble.

As a capital – as a town even – Tripoli is a mess. Despite its 450,000 inhabitants, only the main streets are paved, and many of those are increasingly potholed. Side streets are festooned with electric cables; drains scarcely cope with winter rain-water, and vacant lots are flanked by half-completed buildings. Tatty, revolutionary posters, surmounted by mis-shapen eagles, offend the eye at every turn: 'UNITY: SOCIALISM: FREEDOM' they proclaim. Double bills of the Leader with his latest foreign guest succeed each other on dilapidated walls. (Frequent official visits heralded by a military band in saffron tunics thumping out 'Daisy, Daisy . . .' are recurrent and tedious chores for the corps, called to wait for hours at the airport.) The police, in their Bulgarian-bought RAF-blue uniforms are everywhere – lounging ineffectually at street corners, outside Embassies, or miserably huddling in the slashing rain of January against walls and in doorways . . .

Old-established Embassies continue to occupy imposing residences. My own house is a barracks of a place (originally built for an Italian admiral) with erratic electricity, intermittent water and an aura of The Great Eastern Hotel about to go into liquidation. Before coming here I could not have known that within a fortnight I should be emulating Batman, climbing after dark up the sheer side of the house in a Force 8 gale to investigate and remedy an interruption in our water supply. The expulsion of the Italians removed almost all competent artisans and one must be able to turn one's hand to anything. Our very tenure of the residence seems insecure: a Municipal bulldozer recently breached our garden wall and was advancing on the tennis court before I drove it back. The Municipality had apparently expropriated part of the garden for a new road. We are now engaged in seeking a compromise which would leave us undisturbed. Meanwhile, the wall has been repaired – without prejudice.

What of the people? The inhabitants of Tripoli seem crushed and frightened: silent and suspicious. They are surprised if one greets them and slow to respond. Shopkeepers are reluctant to sell and will only grudgingly admit to having what one asks for. Women (of whom few are seen about) are generally shrouded in their coarse off-white 'barakans' – a length of cloth wound round the figure leaving one eye and a pair of (usually red) football stockings exposed. Foreign women and girls in Tripoli are stared at. Young girls are likely to have their bottoms pinched by young Libyans – an Italian legacy? Television, education and the Press are all of such an abysmally low standard that change is likely to be slow. The best hope lies in a leaven of foreign-educated students. The family, usually a powerful influence in Arab countries, is unlikely to provide much impetus for change, as the women are so confined. Libyan women tend not to go out. Husbands are afraid: Big Brother is watching.

~

'There are, I think, three Qadhafis inside one skin'

SIR ANTHONY WILLIAMS, HM AMBASSADOR TO THE
GREAT SOCIALIST PEOPLE'S LIBYAN ARAB
JAMAHIRIYA, JULY 1977

CONFIDENTIAL

FOREIGN AND COMMONWEALTH OFFICE
DIPLOMA REPORT NO. 245/77

NFB 014/4 *General / Economic (Q) Distribution*

LIBYA,
5 July, 1977

THE LIBYAN ARAB <u>WHAT</u>?: LIVING WITH
QADHAFI'S <u>JAMAHIRIYA</u>

Her Majesty's Ambassador at Tripoli to the
Secretary of State for Foreign and Commonwealth Affairs

(CONFIDENTIAL) *Tripoli,*
5 July, 1977.

Sir,

After six months and many thousand miles, it may seem late to record first impressions of Qadhafi's Libya. In a more straightforward country it would indeed be tardy. But here genuine and valid impressions – above the level of the travelogue – come few and far between. There would be little difficulty in dilating once again on the splendidness of Libya's Roman and Greek ruins or the awfulness of its hotels; but to form an impression on one's own – disregarding equally a catch phrase like 'maverick' and the self-perpetuating myths dispensed by old Tripoli hands – to attempt a critical yet sympathetic understanding of this angular and abrasive country, with its angular and abrasive leader, requires, as I have myself discovered, a lot of torn-up drafts.

One difficulty in such an attempt is the almost total inaccessibility of Qadhafi and his camarilla, not only to diplomats of whatever colour, but even to his own officials ... When the Prime Minister has so little access, diplomats can scarcely complain of having less: though for them the barrier to communication goes surprisingly far down the line. This must surely be the only country where not only are credentials presented no higher than to the Minister (now Secretary) of Foreign Affairs, but where even to do this may involve a delay of several months. While Ministers and Heads of Mission wait long hours to hear Qadhafi's (consistently wildly unpunctual) speeches, they are kept carefully apart and never, never mix. Nor, for diplomats, are there favourites exempted from this quarantine. It is at least some consolation for us ex-Imperialists to observe the hurt astonishment of brother Arabs, fellow members of the oppressed Third

World – and even our Soviet colleague and his associates – when they first come up against this contemptuous blank wall . . .

Meanwhile, the *Jamahiriya*[1]-watcher fares ill compared with his equivalents in Moscow and Peking, where lack of personal access is to some extent compensated by a mass of deliberately or unintentionally revealing literature. After nearly eight years of power, Qadhafi has published no more than the first chapter of his *pensées*; a promised second chapter to this 'Green Book' is more than a year overdue. The two officially authorised dailies contain exceptionally little worth reading, either on or between the lines. Speeches we have galore, but when they are not by Qadhafi himself, they are rarely more than ritual mouth noises, safe for the speaker but uninformative for anyone else. What we do have, of course, is Qadhafi's own speeches, rambling, discursive, sometimes Hitlerian; but spontaneous thinkings-aloud, which do throw occasional beams of light on the workings of a strange and complex, not unimpressive mind – always thinking, thinking inside its own closed cage of ignorance, prejudice and distorted information.

To begin to understand, even more to attempt explaining, the workings of that mind, as they have become manifest in its brainchild, the Libyan *Jamahiriya*, one must first go back to the origins from which it came. The Libyans, I have come to conclude, are not only very peculiar people, but even peculiar Arabs. Although they share some apparently recurrent Arab characteristics – the totally un-European lack of sympathy for artefacts or materials which makes them congenital false screwers and their shop stocks all shop-soiled; the pessimism over good being returned by good which leads them to get in the first cheat when they can; the resigned fatalism which accepts the results of incompetence as the will of God – yet they do not fall into established patterns. The Senussi were not, as became sadly apparent, another kind of Hashemites, nor are the un-nomadic Tripolitanians at all like the un-nomadic Egyptian fellahin. While, I understand, France has left a whole cultural imprint over Tunisia, Morocco and Algiers, and there is much still identifiably British in Egypt or the Gulf, all that Mussolini seems to have left in Libya are, in the bureaucracy, an Italian reluctance to take responsibility, in petty officials like the customs, a quasi-fascist arbitrariness, and among the sheep one finds tethered in side streets, a surprising willingness to live off left-over macaroni.

To identify the Libyanness of the Libyans, one must, I think, begin further back with their predecessors – in Tripolitania and along the coast, the Barbary Corsairs; behind and beyond them the great desert caravaners of ivory and ostrich plumes and, above all, black slaves. The peculiarity of that culture, from which the modern Libyans derive, was that it was essentially managerial and profit-taking, rather than creative or profit making. And those managed – the people who rowed the ships, tended the date palms, plied the trades, ornamented the mosques and palaces – were slaves, white as well as black, but probably more white than black. The source of white slaves was the merchant shipping of those Mediterranean powers not strong enough to protect their own – Spain, Sicily, Genoa, the Papacy and even, into the 19th century, the US. The source of the blacks was just those areas beyond the arid hell of the Sahara crossing, where Qadhafi now seeks clients and cheap labour: what are now Chad, Niger and the Central African Empire.

A thin time, of course, followed the great days of this slave-based society, but the Italian attempt, between 1911 and 1942, to reverse the roles was singularly unsuccessful. Now oil wealth can summon foreign white labour with even less trouble than was previously needed to capture it, and the Libyans have, it seems to me, fallen back very easily and naturally into the master's role. Even if unconsciously, the European outside his own continent tends to expect at least the remnants of that consideration to which the mere colour of his skin used to entitle him. One must accept that, to a large extent, this does not even occur to a modern Libyan of the managerial class. What is more, he has the – not exclusively Arab – characteristic of those who can hire skills without having to master them; that he has little respect for them or understanding of their difficulties and limitations. If concrete does not dry in time for the new (earlier) deadline, then one must bully the engineer.

Another factor which separates many Libyans, not only from Europeans but even from other Arabs, is their religious background. In summary and for a variety of reasons, there is a patriarchal element here – to which Qadhafi's family in particular belongs – which is not just Moslem, but holier-than-thou Moslem. Whether he practises it with genuine devotion or whether he has to be shovelled blind drunk off any aircraft that takes him temporarily abroad, the average Libyan, in fact, is convinced of the superiority of his religion over that of others (Moslem or non-Moslem). He claims the right, moreover, to be actively critical of those who decline to subscribe to it. The practice of Christianity in Libya is scarcely tolerated above the level to which there is toleration in the UK of homosexuality between consenting adults.

This religious certitude is another aspect of what I believe to be the Libyan's peculiar self-confidence. It is the accepted truism that brashness comes from an underlying lack of self-confidence. On the whole, I do not think this is generally true here, but rather that the average Libyan's total self-assurance makes a solid base for that typically rather didactic and even censorious air of superiority which (while no more than faintly bizarre for the European) is so indescribably irritating to fellow Arabs.

It is, perhaps, another product of this underlying self-confidence that the Libyans are, meanwhile, so difficult to move, so pawky, so unanxious to please; compared with the generous and mercurial Egyptians, the Libyans seem extraordinarily curmudgeonly. They do not like bargaining and rarely show any great interest even in effecting a sale. Their street accidents are low-voiced and totally undramatised. I have never yet attended a public speech, even by Qadhafi (and I have attended many) where the crowd was not smaller at the end than at the beginning; beyond the compact, spot-lighted cheer-gangs, the audience listens impassively and then drifts away . . .

A bare 15 years ago the first significant oil revenues began to come in . . . The material transformation which has resulted is, of course, flabbergasting. Roads and universities, hospitals, granaries, apartment blocks, generating stations, petro-chemical plants have appeared in inchoate clusters. Much of this effort is ill-co-ordinated or, indeed ill-conceived, based on a simplistic confusion between autarky and self-sufficiency. But, even so, the gap between then and now is enormous. And the psychological transformation has certainly been much greater – or should have been, were it not that, for the peculiar reasons I have set out, the

Libyans have taken it all so comparatively calmly, so much as their inherent due.

They were not unconscious, of course, that they themselves lacked the human resources either to exploit this new-found but temporary wealth on their own, or to convert it into the machinery of more permanent prosperity. But they have shown no hesitation about their own ability, not only to hire and fire, but to keep a master's choleric eye on, those who could be summoned to do the job for them. What is indeed above all notable – even in the time of King Idris, but much more since those young and apparently inexperienced officers round Qadhafi seized power in September 1969 – is the percipience and effrontery with which the Libyans have judged to a nicety the extent of harrying penalisation and general 'heads-I-win-tails-you-lose' to which oil companies and foreign contractors can be subjected, without driving them into packing their carpet bags and going.

In fact Qadhafi, Jalud and the other Revolutionary officers won their spurs by demanding, within weeks of achieving power, far more of the Americans, British and Italians than their elderly predecessors had ever dared – and getting away with it. The lesson of this experience and the kudos it earned have never been forgotten. There are little more than two million Libyans altogether, and the proportion of those who have any education, expertise or public spirit is minute. It is a tribute to the sheer dominance of personality among that quite small elite, which has now been raised to a supervisory role over the foreign oilmen, bankers, engineers and administrators who animate Libyan economic development, that few if any among the latter (even in their cups) admit to cutting corners with the Libyans. There are quite a number who ruefully admit that the Libyans have outmanoeuvred them . . .

There is about Qadhafi an element of that ruthless singleness of purpose, that blind disregard of obstacle or objection, which marks exceptional men. But, behind this, there lies the strength of the self-confidence, the self-righteousness, the lack of either awe or a desire to ingratiate which he inherits from his own people. There lies there also the weakness which derives from a stand-offishness, a failure to absorb the common Mediterranean and twentieth century cultures, a lack of intellectual interplay (or, of course, any glimmer of humour) which are just as typically Libyan.

In fact there are, I think, three Qadhafis inside one skin, only the first of whom is this strangely intuitive idealist of Notting Hill,[2] this emperor in new clothes which even his subjects half believe in. The second, not wholly unattractive either, is a kind of well-heeled Don Quixote, who insists that his revolution is 'international and humanitarian' and proclaims the rightness of Libya devoting her new oil wealth not just to her own betterment but to the betterment of all who are still struggling against odds up the path to development. Unfortunately this second character is even more bedevilled by illusions than the Knight of La Mancha; and moreover he is too busy a meddler, too eager a self-appointed lecturer on the lessons of mislearnt history, to escape easily from his own illusions. Starting over-confidently in the belief that all ill can be ascribed to imperialism and irreligion, that all good would flow from more Islam and more national liberation, it is only now, after years of misguided intervention, that he is perhaps beginning to learn that it is all more complicated than he thought – that the IRA are not liberating the Irish, that 'progressives' and Moslems are not necessarily on the same side.

Alas, behind both these ingenuous and muddleheaded originals, there lies another and more sinister character who bides his time and calculates his strike with unfailing tactical skill, who believes men can be bought and that he has the money to buy them – or buy their elimination; a shrewd, secretive, spiteful, sharp-clawed creature less reminiscent of Quixote than of the Thane of Cawdor, acknowledging no claim on himself of loyalty or gratitude, demanding nothing less than unquestioning compliance from others.

1. *Jamahiriya*: The year before Williams arrived in Tripoli, Qadhafi rechristened his country as the Great Socialist People's Libyan Arab Jamahiriya. Loosely translated as 'state of the masses', Jamahiriya was a system of (supposedly) direct democracy, based around tribal identities, and without political parties. To worldly diplomats familiar with the usual political flora and fauna, it was as if a new species had been discovered.

2. *Notting Hill*: We've had to make substantial cuts to what is a long despatch, and this refers to an earlier passage about the 'Green Book', Qadhafi's 1975 political tract. Williams actually held Qadhafi rather highly as a political philosopher. By making the concept of 'direct people power' central to his theory of government (however much he traduced that concept in practice) Qadhafi was in step with the prevailing political theory of the 1970s, the ambassador thought. 'The idea that a small pastoralist's son, sitting in a tent (and not bothering, for instance, to read anything very much), could conceivably have discovered the answer to problems which have baffled political theorists for three thousand years may seem difficult for us to accept. But that, while being so ill-informed, he yet anticipated a current trend of thought is still, surely, remarkable.' The Notting Hill reference is probably a nod to G. K. Chesterton's 1904 debut novel, *The Napoleon of Notting Hill*.

∽

Algeria

'The torturable classes'

JOHN ROBINSON, HM AMBASSADOR TO THE
DEMOCRATIC AND POPULAR REPUBLIC OF
ALGERIA, NOVEMBER 1974

Robinson achieved notoriety in the Foreign Office for recommending the closure of the embassy in Algiers – rather a risky move, as it was his first post as ambassador.

The new Ambassador made a down-payment on this strategy after surveying the Algerian scene in a First Impressions despatch notable for its pessimism. Having judged there was little chance of advancing British interests in the country, Robinson decided entirely on his own initiative to cut his headcount at the embassy, and sent some of his staff home. This was a remarkable thing to do, given that most ambassadors make constant pleas to London for more resources, not fewer.

CONFIDENTIAL

BRITISH EMBASSY,
ALGIERS,
1 November 1974

THE RIGHT HONOURABLE
JAMES CALLAGHAN, MP
Etc., etc., etc

Sir,

'This bloody country' (my Egyptian colleague). 'A people organised for theft' (my Ghanaian colleague). I have not lived in an Arab country before, and it is twenty-two years since I worked in a developing country. So I feared my own first impressions of Algeria would be too severe and too superficial. I did not report them. My second impressions, after eight months in this post, are little better. But they are at least based on more facts and more reflection, and may help to qualify the bullish tone about Algeria's prospects which I found in London before I came out here . . .

[T]here is no Algerian nation, as the first nationalists had to admit. There is a common religion but no common language, and little feeling of national unity. There were more Algerians fighting for the French than against them in Algeria, even at the end of the war for independence; and probably as many, perhaps more, Algerians tortured and mutilated and killed by the F.L.N.,[1] as by the French. The bulk of the people, well over half of whom are still illiterate, were, and are, apolitical: the 'torturable class', or as the Algerian Foreign Minister recently described 'the people' to a televised audience of trade union leaders, 'human dough' . . .

Fear and secrecy are the most apparent characteristics, with an aggressive inferiority complex. Fear of assassination or ablation if you are at the top; fear of arbitrary authority if you belong to the torturable class. I shall not forget Boumediène's[2] uneasy glance at a folded envelope which remained in my hand when I gave him my Credentials; nor (he has since been dismissed) the Secretary General's face when his office window blew open at a clap of thunder. Whether at or away from work the tradition of clandestinity is deep-rooted. It weighs heavily on the Algerians' own efficiency, on the ability of foreign firms and advisers to help them, and on the normal operations of every diplomatic mission here . . .

Algeria's Industrial Revolution is in the first year of its third plan. Targets have been raised sharply since the increase in oil prices a year ago . . . Algeria has no hope of realising her current plan . . . [There are] obstacles: shortage and poor quality of management and suspicion of imported management advice; the state of the ports and internal communications, which already show signs of strain; the poor quality and rigidity of the bureaucracy; the belief that you have achieved something if you have decreed it . . . Machinery deteriorating in the docks; customs settling a score with the oil monopoly by detaining an urgently required computer for eight weeks or blocking the entry of a Soviet gift of much-needed welding goggles for over a year; scarce (and poor quality) draughtsmen drawing screws to scale because the floor workers are half-literate or less. Examples could be multiplied. 'Quality' in local Arabic is a French word . . . And over all, the physical waste and the feeling that it is not worth an effort; your pay will look no different, and you'll get on if you're well-connected, not otherwise . . .

Algerian agriculture is in a bad way . . . The last four-year plan aimed to increase production by 5%–6% a year, but growth was zero . . . My former Bulgarian colleague, who had worked with Bulgaria's economic planning for some years, told me: 'They are making all the mistakes we made from an even lower starting point.' And my North Vietnamese colleague tells me that there is far more profit incentive for collective farmers in his country.

But there is more involved here than the charge of importing and the dissatisfaction of the consumer. There are land-owners who stand to lose influence as well as land, as the revolution proceeds. There are all the implications of a situation in which the government is seen to take over ultimate responsibility for agricultural production. And there is, still on the horizon, the prospect that once the peasants have been made politically conscious, which is a main object of the revolution, the 'human dough' will begin to rise . . .

No one knows how many people live in Algeria. The figure given by the Algerians to the IMF is 14.6 millions . . . But ordinary Algerians do not like to declare more daughters than they have sons, and many more live undeclared, for tax or other reasons, in the big cities . . . [T]he population will probably reach 25-millions in ten years' time and over 40-millions by the end of the century. Over half the population is thought to be under 19, and they breed young. Every difficulty which Algeria faces, and they are legion, is made more acute by the growth of population . . .

If I were paid to write history, I could be kinder to the Algerians: history has not been kind to them. But we have to deal with them as they are, and on the basis of what they are likely to become. In assessing their prospects, I am conscious that in comparison with some other developing countries Algeria's future may look more hopeful. Some aspects of Algeria today recall Southern Italy immediately after the war. But Southern Italy had Northern Italy, Algeria separated from her economic North in 1962. She is now engaged in a race against time (a phrase heard constantly in Algeria), to industrialise while oil reserves last and the oil price holds; while foreign confidence lasts;

before the pressures of population and consumption become critical; while the régime lasts. My Saudi colleague remarked that the Algerians had yet to learn that building was more difficult than destroying. (Algerians 'debaptise' French street names, where others would 'rebaptise'.) . . . An Egyptian doctor who worked in the maquis for the FLN during the Algerian war and stayed on in enthusiasm afterwards has described to me how utterly changed the atmosphere here is today, and how disillusioned he has become. The fire seems to have gone out, despite the strained efforts to rekindle it with calls for more struggle and more revolution.

('We can't eat Palestine.') Those who are able to reinsure abroad do so, and lethargy seems widespread. I do not see Algeria winning her race.

I have the honour to be Sir

Your obedient Servant
John Robinson

1. *F.L.N.*: The National Liberation Front fought a bloody eight-year guerrilla war with France (1954–62). Seven hundred thousand Algerians died to secure their independence, along with 30,000 French soldiers.
2. *Boumediène*: Houari Boumediène seized power in a 1965 coup and ruled Algeria as President and head of the military-backed Revolutionary Council until his death in 1978.

PART VI: SUB-SAHARAN AFRICA

South Africa

'Violence, escalating and uncontrollable'

SIR ANTHONY REEVE, HM AMBASSADOR TO THE
REPUBLIC OF SOUTH AFRICA, NOVEMBER 1991

Diplomats crave interesting postings, and few would have been more so than Pretoria in 1991. Nelson Mandela had already been released from jail when Sir Anthony Reeve took up his role as British Ambassador, but the Nationalist government was still firmly in power. Apartheid was clearly doomed, although still the political dispensation; only whites could vote in a referendum the following year as to whether the government should proceed in negotiations with the ANC.

The direction of those negotiations was, at the time, clouded in uncertainty. Many, like Reeve, were resigned to a protracted process, and saw risks on all sides. In the event, the talks were wrapped up quickly. The Multiparty Negotiating Forum, involving all of the main political groups, agreed the outlines of an interim constitution in November 1993.

Reeve was right to worry, however, that violence had the potential to knock the process off course. The momentum behind the initial CODESA (Convention for a Democratic South Africa) negotiations ran into the bloody sand of the Boipatong massacre in 1992, which saw forty-six dead. And the final talks at Kempton Park near Johannesburg

succeeded despite the dramatic intervention in June 1993
of an armoured car crashing through the glass windows of
the World Trade Centre, followed by some 3,000 right-
wing Afrikaner paramilitaries who stormed the venue in a
last-gasp protest against inevitable change.

Those incidents aside, the largely peaceful transition of
power from minority white to majority black rule in South
Africa was one of the greatest achievements in twentieth-
century politics. Nelson Mandela won the country's first
universal elections in April 1994 with 62 per cent of the
vote. The same year South Africa rejoined the Common-
wealth after three decades of self-imposed exile, and in
1996 Sir Anthony Reeve left Pretoria not as ambassador
but as High Commissioner.

BRITISH EMBASSY PRETORIA
1 November 1991

THE RT HON DOUGLAS HURD MP

Foreign & Commonwealth Office London SW1

SOUTH AFRICA: FIRST IMPRESSIONS

Sir,

In a country as large and diverse as South Africa, anyone's
first impressions are bound to be rather arbitrary. I have
travelled a lot in the past four months, visited all the main
cities, and far more townships and squatter camps than
most white South Africans. I have lunched in a score of

board-rooms, taken tea in pathetic shacks pervaded by the stench of raw sewage, opened classrooms and science labs, listened to countless children's choirs, attended the Currie Cup Final (Rugby being the white religion) and explored a diamond mine. I hope I have also developed a working relationship with the politicians, both major and minor: de Klerk and his Ministers, Mandela, Buthelezi and other non-'independent' homeland leaders, the high priests of the PAC[1] and AZAPO,[2] die-hards of the Communist Party (among them Joe Slovo), right-wing fanatics and left-wing lunatics. This indigestible mish-mash has of course left me confused, but some tentative conclusions have begun to crystallise.

I am surprised, first of all, not to have actually seen any corpses during my travels, though there was no shortage of pock-marked buildings, spent cartridges and burnt-out vehicles. I mention this only because any newcomer to South Africa cannot fail to be struck by the violence of this society. The political violence is a small part of the total. Last year there were nearly 18,000 murders of which more than 15,000 had no connection with politics. Most of the victims were black, killed by other blacks. Violence, and the fear of it, pervades South African society at all levels and the media (even the supposedly quality newspapers) revel in the details. The carrying and use of guns is commonplace. One bizarre example: a (white) doctor is trapped in his burning car after a collision. A (white) passer-by steps forward, borrows a gun from an onlooker, and shoots the doctor through the head, 'to put him out of his misery', as he afterwards tells the police. And another: a white farmer, in dispute with a black worker, welds the man to a metal table by his ankles and wrists and then sets him alight with petrol. The farmer has just escaped a gaol sentence by paying compensation of R40,000 (£8,000) to the worker (who survived). These two cases are unusual. Most of the violence is more mundane: seemingly endless shootings, stabbings, batterings of wives, children, husbands.

It is fashionable to argue that the violence is a by-product of apartheid, and to some extent this must be true. But violence in South Africa has a far longer history than apartheid. Shaka, the first Zulu king (who ruled in the first half of the nineteenth century when population levels were far lower than now) is said to have been directly or indirectly responsible for the deaths of two million people. Violence, escalating and uncontrollable, must still pose the greatest threat to the political transition that lies ahead.

The squalor of the life lived by most blacks remains the most vivid impression of my first four months here. In some ways it is a pity that there is so much international focus on Soweto which, by black standards, is a respectable address: a huge community, pretty seedy for the most part, but also provided with essential services, such as electricity and water-borne sewerage. It is home for many successful black businessmen, and for religious and political leaders. Their houses are not often palatial but they are comfortable. A short distance away, in the squatter camps of Phola Park or Orange Farm, living conditions are much more typical: no sanitation, no electricity, a stand-pipe in the street serving dozens of families. All over South Africa the picture is the same, in the formal townships it is not uncommon to find four or five families squatting in the backyard of each house and paying rent for the privilege. Most disturbing of all is the speed at which these urban squatter shacks are increasing . . .

What are the prospects for negotiated political change? I find myself oscillating, on an almost daily basis, between optimism and pessimism. At one level, the three main protagonists (Government, ANC and Inkatha) have declared their readiness to begin early negotiations; and the hitherto wide differences between them over mechanics and procedures seem to have narrowed significantly. At another level, the objectives of the government and the ANC seem quite difficult to reconcile. De Klerk has made it quite clear that he has no intention of surrendering power but is willing to share it. The ANC's position is much less clear-cut: the moderates among them may settle for power-sharing though most of them probably expect to win sufficient support in an election to make power-sharing unnecessary. A more radical faction within the ANC leadership tend to regard negotiation as a device for building up the pressure on de Klerk, in the hope that he himself might be forced to offer more and more concessions or that he might eventually be replaced by a hard-liner against whom a confrontation would be easier to justify. It is this faction, I believe, which is also responsible for the hard line on economic policy: seeking to maintain sanctions and attempting to block new loans to South Africa as a means of further weakening de Klerk's position. It will not be easy for the ANC to fudge such a fundamental internal difference . . .

Of course, blacks blame the Government for their plight but they are also expecting their own leaders to produce results. Mamphela Ramphele, the mother of Steve Biko's[3] child and now Deputy Vice-Chancellor of Cape Town

University, quotes the township lady who said 'Nelson Mandela has been out for six months now. Where is my house?' It may be self-evident to outsiders that the repeal of the Apartheid laws and the onset of negotiations will not of themselves improve the conditions in which most black South Africans have to live, but many blacks hope otherwise . . .

Over this ramshackle organisation, Nelson Mandela presides rather uneasily. He looks and sounds like a statesman though his increasing criticism of de Klerk (over his failure to deal with the violence) seems strident and incomprehensible to many whites, for whom the killing of blacks by other blacks in the distant townships is not an immediate concern. The pressures on him are great – far greater, as he admitted to me, than they were on Robben Island. There he led an orderly life, rising at dawn and dividing his day between study, physical exercise and discussion. He was usually in bed by seven. Now, in Soweto, he finds himself constantly badgered by his supporters wanting help, protection, food . . .

[W]e will need to monitor the shifts of political power and ensure that we are abreast of them. The re-distribution of power will be complicated and could happen quite slowly (for example through a lengthy phase of interim government). We will need to guard against the temptation of clinging too long to the old regime or equally, of moving too hastily in the direction of the new. It could be very damaging to our interests to miscalculate on this score. At the same time we should not make assumptions about the outcome. A betting man would probably put most of his money on the ANC but in our case, the race-course is best avoided . . .

Whatever some blacks may say to the contrary, the changes which President de Klerk has introduced cannot be reversed. And the need for a further election under the existing tri-cameral constitution by (at the very latest) early 1995 effectively imposes a deadline by which date we should know who is to rule the new South Africa. The unpalatable alternative for de Klerk is to call a further election before then, which he might lose (to the Conservative Party), and which could precipitate an all-out confrontation with the non-enfranchised blacks. The constitutional negotiations which lie ahead will inevitably be protracted and difficult since the prize is power. If the moderates on all sides can retain control, there is reason for some optimism about the outcome, but that is a sizeable if. Compromises by all concerned are likely to be portrayed by the extremists in their constituencies as betrayal: and the extremists in this country are well-armed. My own belief is that an agreement will be reached, though it may prove only the first stage of a more far-reaching transition. I am nevertheless relieved that a First Impressions despatch does not require me to make hard-and-fast predictions.

I am sending copies of this despatch to HM Representatives in Washington, New York and neighbouring posts.

I am, Sir,

Yours faithfully
ANTHONY REEVE

1. *PAC*: The Pan Africanist Congress split off from the African National Congress (ANC) in 1959 and continues to play a minor role as a political party in South Africa today.
2. *AZAPO*: The Azanian People's Organization was formed in 1978 as

a campaigning organization against apartheid. Rejecting the concept of South African statehood under white rule, black groups called their country Azania instead.

3. *Steve Biko*: Activist and founder of the Black Consciousness Movement. Biko became a martyr to many in the anti-apartheid struggle after he died violently in 1977 while in police custody.

~

Liberia

'Christianity and ju-ju'

SIR JOHN CURLE, HM AMBASSADOR TO THE
REPUBLIC OF LIBERIA, NOVEMBER 1967

(NO. 10. CONFIDENTIAL)   *Monrovia,*
21 November, 1967

Sir,

I have the honour to convey to you my first impressions of Liberia, the odd man out whenever African States are divided into categories, being americophone and in the dollar zone. The American influence and presence immediately strikes the new arrival: military and police uniforms, letter boxes and street signs are copies of those in the United States, Cadillacs carry rich Liberians about, whilst the personnel of the large American Embassy, the United States Aid Mission and Military Mission and the Peace Corps are to be seen everywhere ... There is also an older and pervasive American influence of a different kind dating from the circumstances of the foundation of the country a century and a half ago by liberated slaves and other free persons of colour from the United States. The effect of this early settlement was much as though some epidemic had wiped out the white population of, say, ante-bellum South Carolina, leaving the negroes to take over their houses and habits. From that time date a few charming red brick porticoed houses which would not be out of place in Charleston, formal habits of dress, inflated oratory, a lethargy which probably owes as much to the Southern States as to West Africa and a feeling that law, politics and religion are the most suitable occupations for gentlemen.

That rulers and ruled are the same colour disguises the fact that in essentials Liberia is still a colonial regime (albeit with no metropolitan power). As the freed slaves extended their sway from the coastal settlement over the tribes of the interior, they introduced forced labour not far removed from slavery and were eventually in trouble with the League of Nations over this and similar practices. It is less than 40 years since the last tribal revolt was suppressed . . .There has been a good deal of intermarriage between the tribes and the Americo-Liberians (a description no longer permitted in public): the latter, who scarcely thought of themselves as Africans, are now encouraged to emphasise their African identity. On suitable occasions, some of the wives of the Honourables exchange their Dior dresses for even more becoming lappas and head-kerchiefs, whilst President Tubman has become, perhaps no less surprisingly than Emperor Haile Selassie, a respected elder statesman of the Organisation of African Unity.

On his first Sunday here the new arrival is struck by the fact that the Americo-Liberians are a church-going people. This again is the effect of their history. Protestant Christianity on American lines was as much a sign of the 'civilised' Americo-Liberian as a top hat, and for high office in the Government it is almost as important to belong to one of the Protestant denominations as to be a Freemason . . . It would be presumptuous to speculate whether belief has even less effect on conduct here than in other Christian communities, but where honesty and chastity are concerned they do seem to have particular difficulties. Corruption is part of the way of life. President Tubman himself has peopled the country with bastard children and is said to hold the view, evidently shared by his compatriots, that monogamy is not suitable for Africans. Christian observances co-exist with ju-ju among the tribal Liberians. In the past three months there have been in Monrovia itself at least three ju-ju murders (parts of bodies being necessary for some of the ritual) and the practice continues of trial by the ordeal of drinking a poisonous concoction which only the innocent are supposed to be capable of vomiting or voiding. President Tubman denounces such things, but it is sometimes suspected that Christianity and ju-ju not only co-exist but overlap. Last year, the Hon. Clarence Simpson, a former Vice-President and Ambassador to the Court of St. James's and a pillar of the Episcopal cathedral, was publicly accused of procuring the murder of a woman in order to use her eyes and scalp for 'big political ju-ju'. It was generally accepted that the accusation had a political motive, but there seems to have been no feeling that the story was so wildly impossible as to be laughed out of court.

≈

Senegal

'Much more French than France'

JOHN TAHOURDIN, HM AMBASSADOR TO THE
REPUBLIC OF SENEGAL, FEBRUARY 1967

CONFIDENTIAL

<u>THIS DOCUMENT IS THE PROPERTY OF</u> <u>HER BRITANNIC MAJESTY'S GOVERNMENT</u>

JE 1/3   *Foreign Office and Whitehall Distribution*

SENEGAL
21 February, 1967
Section 1

Mr. TAHOURDIN'S FIRST IMPRESSIONS
Mr. Tahourdin to Mr. Brown. (Received 21 February)

(No. 5. CONFIDENTIAL)   *Dakar,*
17 February, 1967

Sir,

Now that I have been at this post for three months the time has come to set down, as is customary, my first impressions of Senegal which I have the honour to submit herewith.

Having had some slight experience of French colonial policy and practice in former French Indo-China, both before and after the Second World War, and having read something of Senegal before arrival, my first impressions of Dakar included few surprises. A French provincial town of the more elegant variety, neatly planned complete with tree-lined avenues, smart shops, and restaurants; white blocks of flats and villas set in attractive gardens; French housewives in their 'deux chevaux'[1] going about their daily shopping; Frenchmen sipping their aperitifs at pavement cafes. There are Africans too, but somehow they seem to merge naturally, and not too obtrusively, into the dominant French background.

Here one needs to add a significant qualification. Dakar is a French town, but there is an oddness which eludes one until one realises that it is a museum piece of provincial France of the Third Republic, untouched by the war and inhabited by a French community still 25,000 strong with an outlook mainly rooted in the past, both politically and economically, and oblivious of the enormous changes which have meanwhile taken place in the homeland of today. This explains why in Dakar one tends to find only French things. French cars, hoardings still proudly displaying only French merchandise. One searches in vain for the Italian delicacies or German gadgets now part of the normal stock-in-trade of the metropolitan French *supermarché*. Here it is all much more French than France . . .

This sense of artificiality is heightened the moment one leaves Dakar. With the exception of St. Louis, the former capital, with its more authentic because less pretentious 19th-century charm and a few nondescript urban centres, what I have so far seen of the rest of the country is flat, featureless and abysmally poor. This is where the other 80 per cent of the population live, eking out a subsistence living from a stubborn soil which they have yet to learn to cultivate. They are ground down by a version of Islam (the other major external influence in Senegal), which even my

Saudi Arabian colleague considers reactionary and which, it must regrettably be said, was protected and encouraged by the French for reasons of colonial administrative convenience . . .

[T]he deep imprint left on this country by the French has had profound consequences, not only economic but also political.

To take the economic consequences first, no one even pretends that this country enjoys economic independence. She is completely dependent on French aid, financial, commercial and technical. Such is the variety of aid involved, that even the French Aid Mission here appears genuinely unable to state its total value. It is generally estimated to be around £20 million per annum. While the basic reason for the continuation of aid on this scale is undoubtedly political, the French also expect to reap solid material advantages and in fact have succeeded in ensuring that a substantial proportion of their aid finds its way back to France . . . [F]or example, all the imported wheat and flour, 90 per cent of the commercial vehicles, 80 per cent of the tinned food and most of the textiles come from France. Not one single aspirin of other than French manufacture can be imported legally – not even from the other five Common Market countries. It is all beautifully and unobtrusively managed . . . The second instrument is that of massive technical assistance. There are still in this small country, dispersed throughout the administration in key positions of influence, about three times as many 'conseillers techniques' as there were Britons required to run the Indian Empire in the last years of the Raj . . .

The French have been here for over 300 years, the origins of their presence dating back to Richelieu. President

Senghor is proud to recall that in 1789 the people of St. Louis sent a remonstrance to the States-General at Versailles. Ever since 1848, the inhabitants of the four main townships in Senegal have enjoyed full French citizenship and the right to send a deputy to the National Assembly in Paris. By 1872 these townships had acquired self-governing status. In 1917 the privilege of French citizenship was extended to any Senegalese enlisting in the French Army and the end of the Great War saw black colonels in command of white troops. By 1939 nearly 80,000 Senegalese enjoyed French citizenship . . .

The psychological confusion which inevitably results from this spiritual and cultural identification with France extends to the Senegalese establishment, most of whom also completed their education in France and often, like Senghor, have French wives, own property in France and go there on annual 'home' leave, many still travelling on French passports. Consciously or sub-consciously, they continue to think and act as Frenchmen rather than as Africans. My Nigerian colleague regards them contemptuously as French 'slaves'. In running the country they have, by and large, taken over where the French left off, not only by maintaining the same administrative structure (our own former dependencies have often done the same), but by pursuing virtually identical policies. In other words, we witness here a continuation of the French colonial system under black auspices. It is a remarkable French achievement.

1. *deux chevaux*: Citroën 2CV (literally, 'two horses').

Gabon

'Bongo will not be moved'

ANTHONY GOLDS, HM AMBASSADOR TO THE
REPUBLIC OF CAMEROON, GABON AND EQUATORIAL
GUINEA, SEPTEMBER 1970

Christened Albert, the young President of Gabon changed his first name to Omar upon conversion to Islam in 1973. It was his surname, however, that ensured this Head of State always raised a smile among the English-speaking members of the Diplomatic Corps.

President Bongo received the credentials of the new British ambassador, Anthony Golds, after three years in office. Golds flew in from Yaoundé, the capital of Cameroon, where the British Embassy was situated, to endure this ordeal. The ambassador's First Impressions despatch captures well what Golds describes with understatement as the 'difficulties of non-resident accreditation'.

Bongo was often criticized by other Africans for being too sympathetic to the former colonial power, France, and to European interests in general, a stance Golds recognizes in the President's views on South Africa and Rhodesia. At a time when most freshly minted independent African leaders were wont to berate British ambassadors with long lectures about the evils of neo-imperialism, President Bongo was a one-off.

Golds's despatch was warmly but faintly condescendingly received in Whitehall as 'pleasant light reading', and given wide circulation. 'I recommend that this despatch be printed,' scribbled one senior clerk on the minute sheet. 'Especially in view of the forthcoming visit of President Bongo.'

'I endorse the recommendation,' wrote another, adding a flourish: 'I understand it is common practice for the President to refer to himself in the third person — "Bongo will not be moved", which can confuse strangers.'

The President's state visit to London in 1970 did much to cement his reputation as a comic turn. 'President Bongo's illusions of grandeur do only too often make him seem faintly ridiculous to outsiders,' wrote one of Golds's successors, Christopher MacRae, in a despatch from Libreville in 1980, looking back on the visit. 'Maybe, just as he feels constrained to wear high heels in public (to jack up his height of five foot or so),' wrote the Ambassador, 'so the small population of his country has to be compensated for, whenever he goes abroad, by a suite of fifty. Whatever the reason, this trait has hardly endeared him to Head of Protocol the world over.'

(MacRae's despatch, incidentally, also told of the demands placed on foreign ambassadors by Gabonese official nightlife – 'dances at President Bongo's marble palace, which went on until four o'clock, with armed guards on the gates to prevent the less energetic members of the Corps from sneaking off early'.)

Still in his early thirties, Bongo may indeed have been somewhat gauche when patronized by Mr Golds in 1970, but in the end it was the President who had the last laugh. Omar Bongo went on to lead Gabon for another thirty-nine years, and died in office as one of the world's longest-serving rulers – a Big Man (despite his small stature) of African politics. He became one of the continent's richest men, too, having misappropriated over many decades much of Gabon's oil wealth. Investigators were eventually able to trace thirty-three properties in France as well as millions *stashed in bank accounts in New York – assets linked to Bongo that were probably only the tip of the iceberg.*

Upon his death in 2009 Omar was succeeded as President of Gabon by his son, the equally memorably named Ali Bongo.

CONFIDENTIAL

PRESENTATION OF CREDENTIALS IN GABON AND SOME FIRST IMPRESSIONS

The British Ambassador in Cameroon to the Secretary of State for Foreign and Commonwealth Affairs

YAOUNDE,
4 September, 1970.

Sir,

I have the honour to report that, as instructed in your despatch PF 20126 of the 4th of June, 1970, I presented to President Albert Bernard Bongo, at Libreville on the 29th of August, the Letters accrediting me as Her Majesty's Ambassador Extraordinary and Plenipotentiary to the Gabonese Republic.

I enclose the text of the speech which I delivered on that occasion. Since President Bongo decided, in an abrupt access of bonhomie, to abandon his prepared reply midway and to improvise freely neither I nor his own staff have as yet any approved record of his words. Nevertheless they were, though syntactically obscure in places, essentially very friendly and welcoming. He particularly asked me to convey, together with his respectful greetings to Her Majesty, his warm thanks for the friendly interest which the United Kingdom was showing in Gabon. He claimed that this interest was all the more remarkable and meritorious because of the differences which there had been between us in the past. He did not specify what these were but seemed to imply that they had been as much the fault of Gabon as my country; that therefore the present ceremony was the conscious burying of some hatchet; and that Her Majesty's Government had shown great tolerance and generosity in not only sending him an Ambassador but even gifts as well (in the shape of Bedford lorries and Land Rovers). As proof of his own goodwill and gratitude he had decided to re-establish a resident Embassy in London and also to go on a private visit and see my country for himself.

This exchange of oratory took place, as does much else that concerns President Bongo, before the unwinking stare of television and ciné lights. Every detail of all the attendant ceremonial was likewise recorded. The result was reproduced by Gabonese television, with some skill, in a programme lasting about thirty minutes at the 'peak-viewing' time of 8 p.m. on that same Saturday.

The lights and cameras were present too in the President's private study, at the beginning and the end of my tête à tête with His Excellency. This lasted some fifty minutes and so, I was told, beat all previous records by a large margin ... [T]he President rapidly dispersed the formal atmosphere of the occasion by first calling for whisky and champagne and then bounding furiously across the room to silence his personal telephone, acting the part of an outraged A.D.C.[1] as he did so – 'No! The Chief of State cannot be disturbed ... How dare they try to interrupt? He is receiving Letters of Credence ... They must be told that His Excellency will speak to no-one. Say that the President of the Republic is not in!'

Thereafter, President Bongo fairly bubbled over with high spirits. He told me, as I have separately reported by telegram, of his plan to visit the United Kingdom on his return from the United Nations General Assembly and of his hope that he might have the honour of repeating to The Queen personally all the professions of renewed good will for Herself, for Her Government and for Her Ambassador which he had just been expressing to the latter ...

He praised the virtues of British vehicles and informed me that while in England he proposed to buy himself a Rolls Royce, that Queen of cars. He had noticed, on the Côte d'Azur, that everyone who was anyone – including the French – had a Rolls. Moreover hardly anything ever went wrong with a Rolls; and if it did a skilled mechanic – 'un vrai blanc' – was always sent out to deal with the problem. No bush-service for a Rolls! At this point the President summoned in several members of his staff to acquaint them of these verities and also to remind them that the Land Rover with which he had just been presented, as well as the Rolls which he was about to buy, were strictly for the personal use of the Head of State.

We discussed the question of possible arms sales to South Africa. The President warmly agreed that many 'sottises'[2] had been said on this subject ... he saw no reason why we should not sell arms to the South Africans in order to keep communists out of Africa ... He added that his fellow African leaders had neither the wit nor the strength to confront South Africa – nor Rhodesia. Apartheid was all wrong but you would never change the minds of the whites down there by trying to isolate them. The present attitude of the South African was little different from that of the French colonist in the bad old days. Until they saw it begin to happen, no Frenchman believed that a man with a skin as black as this (clutching his own wrist) could govern his own affairs like a man with a skin as white as that (clutching mine). After all if you want to tame a dog, you do not pick up a big stick (seizing a heavy blunt ornament from his table) and say 'Grrr, come here dog or I'll kill you!' (baring his strong white teeth in a highly alarming manner). You make friends with the dog and then you teach him. That is what must be done with the South Africans. They should be asked to see for themselves what Black Africa can do ... President Bongo also congratulated us on our Rhodesia policy, said that we were quite right not to use force, and informed me blandly that it was not possible for the Gabonese Government to dictate to people about trading with the Smith regime. Trade was a private matter with which Governments must not meddle. When I pointed out that this was scarcely Her Majesty's Government's policy over sanctions he hastily denied that any trade with Gabon was taking place – or, if there was, then no Gabonese were involved in it ...

The President thanked me for bringing with me, for Gabon television, an English-by-television serial (the 'Walter and Connie' series[3]). He said that he would arrange a private showing for himself at the Palace that very evening. He wanted everyone to learn English. Unfortunately His Excellency seemed to be under the impression that 'Walter and Connie' were a couple of free-lance crime investigators. The Director of Gabon Radio had to be called in to help me to disabuse him. Whereupon we understood the President to enquire whether there was not a famous B.B.C. 'feuilleton'[4] for television called 'Le Sein'[5] – or something similar! He would like to get a French-dubbed version of it and anything else like it. Neither the Radio Director nor I thought that we had heard of any such B.B.C. feature; though it might of course be I.T.V. Fortunately, after a little while we realised that he was talking of 'The Saint' and I undertook to enquire whether copies of it, and of certain other television serials were available for leasing to Gabon Radio.

After again inspecting the mighty troops of Titipu (who formed a very impressive guard of honour and gave a most tender Mozartian rendering of our National Anthem) I was escorted once more to my hotel by the numerous Presidential outriders, sirens blowing and flags flying. There the Gabon television recorded every canapé and bottle at what they described as the 'Grand Vin d'Honneur' which I offered to the President's and Foreign Minister's staff, to the Heads of local diplomatic missions and to the members of the small British community. They also recorded all the technical marvels of the president's Land Rover Dormobile – from its butane gas stove and expanding roof to its slogan Don du Gouvernement Britannique. On the television screen the vehicle appeared as long as a railway train and evoked many an 'ooh' and 'ah'. A number of Gabonese told us that they intended to try to buy one for themselves . . .

During my four and a half day visit I was accompanied by Mr Roger Westbrook, Third Secretary . . . In addition both of us were greatly helped by my son, Mr Richard Golds, who had come to Africa on holiday (from public-school teaching in Cornwall) but found himself temporarily drafted on to my staff – at the express desire of the President's staff, in order to keep the British numbers up. This followed the frustration of my Head of Chancery's efforts to attend by the failure of Air Afrique to honour a guaranteed connection. The whole occasion from this Embassy's point of view thus became something of an object lesson in the difficulties of non-resident accreditation and in the art of improvisation. Mr Westbrook and Mr Golds junior alternated in performing vis-à-vis the Gabonese, the duties of my personal secretary, Land Rover expert, cultural adviser, public relations officer and note-taker. Mr Golds junior was also offered and politely declined the post of Professor of English at the new University of Gabon (when formed). Finally he and Mr Westbrook were congratulated on having achieved in Gabonese eyes the status of 'petits frères' and assured of a permanent welcome in Gabon . . .

In view of President Bongo's prospective visit I will conclude with some brief personal impressions of him and of his country. In everything but stature he is larger than life. Physically he is short, slim and wiry, with alert and restless eyes and a fearsome bandit moustache (like Castro without the beard). He always appears full of energy though I am told that he eats very little. He orders his staff around with good-humoured ferocity and is unquestioned master in the Palace, the Government and the country at large. He is a stickler for protocol in public but readily dispenses with it in private and has a keen but not very sophisticated sense of humour. He takes perverse delight in upsetting the majority of the local diplomatic corps by insinuating that they are 'stuffed shirts' whose only function is 'le bla-bla-bla' as distinct from helping him to develop Gabon . . . In general he gives the impression of being shrewd, ruthless, competent and wholly self-assured . . .

I am sending copies of this despatch to H.M. Representatives at Lagos, Paris, Washington, New York (United Nations), Addis Ababa, Cape Town and Kinshasa.

I have the honour to be,

With the highest respect,

Sir,

Your obedient Servant,
A. A. Golds

1. *A.D.C.*: Aide-de-camp (literally, 'camp assistant'); a personal secretary assigned to a senior military officer or head of state.
2. *'sottises'*: Foolishnesses, stupidities.
3. *'Walter and Connie' series*: A global hit in the early 1960s, the BBC's Walter and Connie taught students through the power of television how to enunciate English verbs and nouns correctly in a range of everyday situations, such as 'At the Seaside' and 'Connie's Sewing Party'.
4. *'feuilleton'*: Serial.
5. *'Le Sein'*: 'The Breast'.

~

Namibia

'Like Guildford with sun'

BRIAN DONALDSON, HM HIGH COMMISSIONER
TO THE REPUBLIC OF NAMIBIA, 1999

SUBJECT: NAMIBIA: FIRST IMPRESSIONS

After a career spent mainly in Africa, Windhoek has come as something of a surprise. Urbanisation is as big a problem here as elsewhere in Africa, and the out of sight, cardboard city close to the former township of Katatura grows bigger by the day. But the rest of Windhoek is clean, well run and sophisticated, with modern, well stocked shops, supermarkets and department stores filled with apparently affluent shoppers. Its restaurants and busy pavement cafes are full of happy, smiling, well dressed people – both black and white – and there is hardly a tramp or beggar to be seen. Some of Windhoek's posher residential areas, built on barren, rocky hills, seen on more than 300 days a year under the deepest of clear blue skies, would not look out of place in Provence. To the British holiday-makers arriving here in increasing numbers it must look very much like Guildford with sun.

~

Madagascar

'A cross between nineteenth century Montmartre and medieval London'

BRIAN DONALDSON, HM AMBASSADOR TO THE REPUBLIC OF MADAGASCAR, DECEMBER 2002

From: Swift Incoming Telegrams (Machine 1)
Sent: Monday, December 16, 2002 8:14:12 AM

TELNO 145
INFO ROUTINE PARIS, UKREP BRUSSELS, UKMIS NEW YORK, WASHINGTON

SUBJECT: MADAGASCAR: ANNUAL REVIEW AND FIRST IMPRESSIONS

A late night arrival in Antananarivo has little to commend it. Facilities at the international airport are chaotic, and the customs officers even more unreasonable and avaricious than usual. The drive through dark, mean streets to the city centre reveals scenes both from nineteenth century Montmartre and medieval London – with only the occasional parked car or street lamp providing a reality check.

Daylight reveals a spectacular city sprawl of two million people, with tightly packed buildings on and around numerous hills, and extensive paddy fields – helping meet Madagascar's needs as the world's largest consumer of rice. Poverty is much in evidence, even in the city centre – where street dwellers are common, and two out of ten pedestrians still go barefoot. Slow-moving, impossibly heavy hand carts transporting timber and building materials block the narrow, traffic-bound cobbled streets, and street hawkers, both pavement-bound and mobile, add to the general impression of intense commercial activity and total confusion . . .

Madagascar has a long history of failure. But it would be a mistake to write it off as just another basket case. It is not. Despite all its problems, it has extensive mineral deposits, sapphires and emeralds; fertile soil; high rainfall (with a few exceptions); good stocks of fish and seafood; unique biodiversity – with all that means for the successful development of eco-tourism – and a willing, hard-working labour force. The root of Madagascar's problems over the past 25 years has been poor governance, due to costly experimentation with far left socialist policies, sheer inefficiency, corruption and unadulterated greed.

~

Malawi

'Petty tyrant, megalomaniac, figure of fun'

SIR ROBIN HAYDON, HM HIGH COMMISSIONER TO THE
REPUBLIC OF MALAWI, AUGUST 1971

'There is a problem about circulation,' reads a memo prefacing this despatch with its brilliant pen-portrait of Dr Hastings Banda. Haydon's despatch 'says a number of things about President Banda which can hardly be described as flattering'. The Office chose against tradition not to distribute the despatch, for fear it might leak. 'This sharply worded critique is eminently quotable,' wrote one official, who forwarded it on to a select group 'on a strictly "need to know" basis'.

Four decades on, and Britain's high commissioners in Malawi continue to shoot from the hip, London now less patient with Malawi. In April 2012 an electronic cable by Fergus Cochrane-Dyet, Britain's man in Lilongwe, leaked and was published in a Malawian newspaper, the Nation. *The High Commissioner criticized President Mutharika, the then Head of State, as 'ever more autocratic and intolerant of criticism'. The 'governance situation continues to deteriorate', wrote the British diplomat 'in terms of media freedom, freedom of speech and minority rights'.*

The Malawian government gave the High Commissioner seventy-two hours to pack his bags and leave the country – thereby vindicating in their response the very criticism Cochrane-Dyet had set out to make. Mutharika died and his regime collapsed in 2012.

There is something Victorian about Malawi though it is hard to define. There is a deal of cant, outward respectability and puritanism. Beneath the surface there is corruption and extortion, people are murdered, girls are bought and sold . . .

This outwardly placid, pleasant, rather cheerful little country is a dictatorship . . . Over everything there is the Flemingesque, slightly menacing figure of His Excellency the Life President, Ngwazi Dr. H. Kamuzu Banda. Is he statesman, fearless leader, beloved father of the nation, far-sighted realist, and man of peace and racial harmony in Southern Africa? Or is he an African Papa-Doc, a tycoon, petty tyrant, megalomaniac, figure of fun, hated oppressor of freedom? Is he mad?

I do not believe he is mad or even unbalanced, but I do think he is a bit of all the other things and that your attitude towards him depends on who you are. I should, I am sure, loathe and fear him were I a Malawian opposed to his policies.

I have seen a lot of him, and were he not the Head of State and I the British High Commissioner, I should enjoy talking to him; occasionally! He is highly intelligent, gets through mountains of work, and has the courage of his convictions. He can be very charming, has a good sense of humour, a great knowledge of history, knows many British personalities well, and can be fascinating in conversation. But I suspect his judgment and doubt his honesty; he is full of prejudices; he can be a crashing bore, he is ruthless and cruel. He is a tremendous old ham . . .

I have the impression that he is out of touch with his people who do not respond to the old speeches which are trotted out again and again. Recently, he spoke in public at inordinate length about the beastliness of the European habit of dancing with others' husbands and wives. Who really cares? Not the Malawians. The lack of enthusiasm from the crowds when the President appears before them has been an eye-opener to me. The police sometimes lock the doors of Kamuzu Stadium to keep the people in when the Kamuzu speaks. I think Malawians see him too often, at least in Blantyre and Zomba. The cheer-leaders, and ululating women are not incidental nowadays; they are essential...

His attitude towards Britain and the British is indeed intriguing. I think he is nearly obsessed by us. He proclaims on the one hand that he will not be pushed around by expatriate advisers and civil servants (which means Britons) and he criticises permissiveness in Britain. He is always reminding people that Malawi is no longer a colony as though that were a news flash. On the other hand, he says London is his second home, he can get sentimental about his days as a GP in Willesden, he speaks affectionately and in some awe of The Queen ... He is a bit mixed up about us, in truth.

~

Rwanda

'Clearly of a superior race'

JOHN BENNETT, HM AMBASSADOR TO BURUNDI AND RWANDA, APRIL 1964

This is a rather disgraceful despatch.
Around 800,000 people died in the Rwandan genocide of 1994. While the scale of the violence was unprecedented,

the struggle between Hutus and Tutsis had in fact erupted before. In the early 1960s, as the country emerged from Belgian colonial role, the long-downtrodden Hutu majority staged a revolution. The Tutsi elite, who under the Belgians had occupied a position of relative importance, were massacred in their thousands; those who survived fled to neighbouring Burundi.

When John Bennett arrived in Usumbura in 1964 this violence was still playing out. Dismayingly, his First Impressions despatch is less notable for its witness of these events than for its selective racism.

In preferring the Tutsis, the Ambassador was, it is true, swimming with the contemporary current. The tribe was already ascendant over the Hutu majority long before the colonial era, but it was the Belgians who systematized the relationship. Belgian ethnologists measured skulls – the Hutus, traditionally farmers, were said to have smaller brains – and judged the Tutsis superior for their taller frames and lighter skins. Using such dubious methods (and worse – ownership of ten or more cattle also made a Rwandan a Tutsi), the colonial administration divided the population into two groups and made every individual carry a racial identity card. It was this policy of divide and rule that laid the kindling for so much violence in the 1960s, and a generation later in the 1990s.

Subsequent scholarship has, however, found the genetic differences between Hutu and Tutsi to be small. The two peoples share the same language and culture, and the distinction that inspired so much killing appears to be primarily one of social class rather than ethnicity. Today, the Rwandan government says its people are of one blood, the Banyarnwanda. This despatch is striking testimony to

the ability of perfectly professional people to buy into the
ruling myths of their era, without (it appears) making any
serious independent evaluation.

CONFIDENTIAL

THIS DOCUMENT IS THE PROPERTY OF
HER BRITANNIC MAJESTY'S GOVERNMENT

JN 1015/3   *Foreign Office and Whitehall Distribution*

BURUNDI
April 13, 1964
Section 1

Mr. BENNETT'S FIRST IMPRESSIONS OF
RWANDA AND BURUNDI

Mr. Bennett to Mr. R. A. Butler (received April 13)

(No. 9. CONFIDENTIAL)   *Usumbura,*
April 4, 1964

Sir,

I have the honour in this despatch to record my first
impressions of Burundi and Rwanda. It was on the 23rd of
January that I arrived by air at Usumbura to find myself
immediately plunged into trying to analyse and sort out
the truth about the massacres of Batutsi in Rwanda – a
subject that was on the lips of everyone to whom I spoke.
As if it was not enough to be the principal topic of conversation in Usumbura, I had to receive a telephone call direct
from London from a leading newspaper within 48 hours

of my arrival asking for facts about the massacres. At that time, my ignorance of happenings within Burundi and Rwanda was almost complete, but I hope that I have been quick to sort out fact from fiction – and this was necessary – especially after an episode at my first lunch-eon when my hostess mentioned casually that if the fish I was about to eat was tough it was, according to her cook, because it had been feeding off the eyes of Batutsi which had been washed down into Lake Tanganyika! So it was that I was brought sharply up against the problem which was to exercise my attention in my first weeks in Central Africa . . .

Burundi and Rwanda are scenically two of the most beautiful countries I have ever visited. Fine high moun-tains, startling land-locked lakes, especially Tanganyika lake which comes to life at night with the fishing fleets and their acetylene lamps, impressive and impenetrable primeval forests and a countryside green and lush. Few countries can have such natural beauty. Animal and bird life abounds and collectors of wild flowers can have a heyday. Unfortunately it is not really possible to enjoy this natural beauty. Hotels are poor and offer no amenities except at the Kagera National Park. Roads are bad and it is a toil to drive over them – there are only 25 km. of hardtop road in both countries. Since both countries are over-populated, one cannot go off for a quiet picnic without being overrun by swarms of African children. Nothing, in short, has been done to develop either country for travelling or tourism, although there is undoubtedly a future in this field and as a result one suffers from general frustration.

As for the people, I find the local Hutu (80 per cent of the people) poor, dirty, ill-clad, prone to drink, unreliable, idle and dishonest. For me the Hutu has little charm. The Tutsi, on the other hand, is graceful and dignified, and is clearly of a superior race. (This does not mean that he does not drink and is not lazy.) The Tutsi is also of a different intellectual level, and only last week the Anglican Bishop mentioned that in his experience at his mission stations where Bahutu and Batutsi have equal opportunities, it is always Batutsi who come out on top.

I have been surprised to find an almost complete colour bar in both countries, not imposed by the 'whites' but rather by the 'blacks'. One never sees an African at any club – sporting or civic – although I am told that there are two African members of the Burundi Riding Club. I have yet to see an African at the home of a Belgian other than the Ambassador. At the homes of diplomats it is very much the exception than the rule to find an African among the guests. The Africans I am afraid in these two countries mistrust the 'white' face.

The fact that no newspapers other than mission vernacular are published in either country was unexpected, and virtually no book except the Bible has been published in either of the local languages. Other surprises have been that I have found no shops owned by Africans. All the shops in Kigali and Usumbura and other larger towns are run either by Europeans or Asians. Similarly, restaurants and hotels, bars and nightclubs are all owned by non-Africans ... Except for one small house which is being enlarged there is no construction work going on anywhere in the country that I have been able to see. The atmosphere is one of lethargy and nonchalance ...

I shall conclude with one or two anodyne remarks. Conditions of service in Central Africa are very different from conditions in other countries in which I have served. One has to go through a sharp adjustment in order to face the local scene and local problems. This comes the harder if one has not had previous service in Africa. For me it will be the first time that I shall have served in a country without being able to get to know the people. As I have said earlier in this despatch, the African of Burundi wants to keep himself to himself and I fear that there is little chance of my breaking down this barrier.

~

PART VII: MIDDLE EAST

Israel

'The Jews remain different from anybody else'

SIR BERNARD LEDWIDGE, HM AMBASSADOR TO THE
STATE OF ISRAEL, APRIL 1973

Israel was reborn 25 years ago and since then it has grown apace. Nearly three million Jews now live where there were only some thousands as recently as 1918, and only 650,000 when the State of Israel was proclaimed in 1948. These Israelis are fascinating people. At times they remind me of their ancestors in the Old Testament, for instance when I see them going up to Jerusalem *en masse* for the Passover. They go by car nowadays but they are obeying the ancient injunction. At times again they seem more like one's idea of 19th century Americans with their lack of distinctions in class and dress, their prickly egalitarianism, their abounding energy, and their indifference to the beautiful unless it coincides with the useful. But the population is not so predominantly European in origin as one might think. Nearly half of them were born in Israel, mostly of European parents it is true, while the rest come about equally from Europe and the Arab world. Those from Arab lands, particularly the Yemen, tend to be second-class citizens. Most of the levers of power are held by Ashkenazi Jews from Russia and Poland, but one cannot call them a ruling élite. Israel belongs to no continent. It is *sui generis*. Here, as elsewhere, the Jews remain different from anybody else . . .

The sustained military effort of the last 25 years has stultified the traditional Zionist dream of creating a new model society, egalitarian in spirit and rich in opportunity for all its citizens . . . It is not only the vision of equality that has been partially sacrificed to military needs. Beauty and elegance have gone by the board as well, and strictly utilitarian standards have been applied in building the State. Tel Aviv, thrown together in concrete without taste or plan, must be one of the ugliest cities in the world. Perhaps there are other reasons as well as military ones for the ugliness of Israel's modern towns and cities. The artistic gift of the Jewish people seems to be much more verbal than plastic. Israel produces writers, scholars and musicians in abundance, but her painters are indifferent and her architects are bad. The instincts of a nomadic race are still strong. Priority is given to the more portable forms of artistic expression. The Israelis build almost as if they were not sure how long they were going to stay here. In this they are conforming to the tradition of their race. The Jews of antiquity do not seem to have built much of importance except the Temple in Jerusalem, and even that was erected to house a mobile Ark. The historic buildings of religious importance in the Holy Land today are all Christian or Moslem. Apart from the Wailing Wall, the Jews hold in veneration only a few tombs, all of them probably spurious. To the Jews it is not so much a particular place, even Jerusalem apart from the Temple precinct, that is holy. It is the land itself.

~

'You never have to say things twice'

SIR JOHN MASON, HM AMBASSADOR TO THE STATE OF
ISRAEL, JANUARY 1977

(CONFIDENTIAL)   *Tel Aviv,*
                                   14 January, 1977

Sir,

I submit my first impressions of Israel after only one month in the country. There are two reasons for this: first I have always believed that first impressions should be just that, and not considered views; second, and more important, impressions crowd in so overwhelmingly and fascinatingly on the newcomer here that, if he does not set them down quickly, he will speedily find himself already into his eighth or ninth edition of them.

The problem for a newcomer is not to formulate his first impressions: I could dictate 20,000 words of them without hesitating. It is to select, to decide which particular shake of the kaleidoscope is most representative of the overall pattern ...

The land ...
The Israelis have both improved and damaged the appearance of their land. The irrigated agricultural lands, where the desert has been made to grow, are a joy to behold. They put the surrounding Arabs to shame. But the setting of Jerusalem, compared with when I last visited it, from Damascus, 13 years ago, has suffered from the extensive housing development since 1967. Moreover, the whole country, wherever the Jews have settled, tends to look, in my wife's words, like a dress that someone has made and started

to wear, without bothering to finish the hem. Tel Aviv is not exactly an eyesore, but there are few parts of it, or aspects of it, which are restful to the eye. Encampments, temporary or permanent, of the superbly efficient Israel Defence Forces, look like rubbish dumps. So does almost everywhere else.

I am perhaps being too harsh. Not all that the Israelis have built is bad: the campus of the Weizmann Institute is beautiful by any standards. It is just that it is so often a pity that the hem was not finished, nor, if my initial impression is correct, ever likely to be. Life in Israel may turn out to be full of drooping hems . . .

The people

I am baffled to know how to encapsulate my first impressions of the Jewish Israelis. On first acquaintance, they are the most stimulating and fascinating society in which I have ever found myself. I had expected life in Tel Aviv to be like life in Manhattan; but in a strange way it is not, I think because Manhattan Jews are more Americanised than one realises when one is among them. Life in Tel Aviv is in fact more intense. To my mind, although it is a comparison which I do not make to the Israelis, Tel Aviv less resembles Manhattan than Warsaw, as I knew it 20 years ago. Like the Poles, the Israelis have survived against all odds because to be Israeli, as to be Polish, is more important than anything else. Like the Poles, the Israelis love gossip, the more scurrilous the better, and speak well of their friends to strangers only after they have said something entertainingly unkind about them. We find them great fun to be with.

Members of my staff reading the last paragraph will think how much the new Ambassador has still to learn. Foreigners who have been here for some time tell me how infuriating the Israelis come to be. They finally get fed up with Israeli jostling, ill manners, aggression and incompetence. They say they have to get away from time to time for a break from the claustrophobic intensity of the atmosphere here, where no one ceases for one moment to bash one's ear . . .

It may be that in due course, like others, I shall be driven close to distraction by the pressures of Israeli society. For the present, I am content to enjoy the advantages. These include the fact that everyone one meets talks interestingly and interestedly, almost always in excellent English, about any subject under the sun. To sum it up in a sentence, the great joy is that you never have to say things twice; your interlocutor is with you or ahead of you.

~

Jordan

'There are, for better or worse, far more bagpipers than security men'

GLENCAIRN BALFOUR PAUL, HM AMBASSADOR TO THE HASHEMITE KINGDOM OF JORDAN, SEPTEMBER 1972

'I have always thought that Mr Balfour Paul writes supremely well,' wrote Anthony Parsons, then an Under-Secretary at the FCO in Whitehall, 'and this despatch is in his best tradition.' Another note in the file commends the despatch as an 'excellent contribution', and it was duly copied to the Foreign Secretary and, a rare distinction, to the Prime Minister. Another despatch from Amman by the same ambassador, albeit on a more light-hearted note, is on pp. 115–20.

Balfour Paul arrived in Jordan a year after a civil war. King Hussein's forces had taken on the fedayeen, paramilitary groups drawn from the vast numbers of stateless Palestinians in Jordan. Despite support from Syrian tanks, in July 1971 Yasser Arafat and his Palestine Liberation Organization were defeated and fled the country. The presence in Jordan, Lebanon, Syria and elsewhere of more than 4 million Palestinian refugees and their descendants remains a threat to regional stability even today.

'There would be no Jordan without the Hashemites,' wrote the Ambassador elsewhere in this abridged despatch, and 'no Hashemites without Jordan'. Both the country and its monarchy were, he thought, an asset to the West, and despite the recent war, Balfour Paul thought the Hashemite dynasty's 'genius for survival' would see them through. The Ambassador was right; King Hussein ruled without interruption until his death in 1999.

Pity, though, the poor Crown Prince. As junior partner and heir designate, Hassan gave King and country three decades of loyal service (putting to rest Balfour Paul's concern that through overwork Hassan might expire before reaching 'active middle-age') – only to be denied the throne. In 1999 the King on his deathbed wrote a letter accusing his younger brother of various misdemeanours and gave him the sack, passing the crown instead to his own son Abdullah.

The country's capital – a top-heavy symbol of the whole – sprawls over the bare and bumpy knuckles of biblical Ammon, like a rocky foreshore at low tide plastered with limpets awaiting, eagerly or apprehensively (for who can read the minds of limpets?), the next high tide. The two big camps of the first Palestinian diaspora, knocked up in the immediate neighbourhood in 1948, are now (one notices) absorbed and enveloped physically by the expanding city and are almost indistinguishable (save that the schools look better) from the rest. Physically but not, one fears, psychologically absorbed. For one thing that the luminous atmosphere of this harshly beautiful landscape – shadowless at noon, technicolour at tea-time – does not reveal is the psychology of the inmates of these or any of the country's other cellular and swarming clusters of Palestinian exiles, numbering one-half of the total population. Are they bees' nests resigned to making what little honey they can out of the sparse flora, or wasps' nests waiting to sting? ... Something or other, and something deserving our respect, keeps the mass of ordinary refugees above the deadline of despair: hope, one supposes, springing eternal – much as the women proudly continue embroidering their marvellous *guftans*, the only things in the camps that do not share the colour of the rancid soil.

But since for the present the Palestinians in Jordan, whatever their aims, are powerless to pursue them, I may as well turn to where power (in the limited sense applicable in Jordan) lies, on Jabal Hashemi. For despite the facade of Parliament and the Ministerial system (and there are men of quality in both), it is of course in the person of the King, and now also increasingly in that of his brother the Crown Prince, that authority is concentrated: Hussein and Hassan, vicar and the curate of this truncated Arab parish who have been ex-communicated by the Bishops of Confrontation but who continue to serve the Mass (or the masses) faithfully after their own dissident doctrine.

The first thing that strikes one about them, apart from

their resilience, their dedication, and their shirt-sleeves, is how harmoniously they complement each other, the division of parish work between the pair suiting their respective turns of mind. The King concerns himself with external affairs and public relations, the Crown Prince with internal affairs, planning and economy. (The middle brother, Mohammed, having inherited from his hapless father not only his gentle charm but also his less marketable features, has been put out to grass, though his functions as Head of the Tribal Council are not purely honorary.) King Hussein needs, so to speak, no introduction. His hair is thinner and his work schedule even more devastating than in the descriptions of my predecessors; but his sense of destiny is unchanged and his addiction to water-skiing keeps him physically a match for it, presenting as he does, when stripped on his beach at Aqaba, the physique of an Olympic featherweight. Prince Hassan, on the other hand, has surely altered since last presented. I have seen no sign of the earlier abrasiveness. As a man to meet and talk to, he outclasses the King. ('C'est un enfant intelligent' was the testimonial given him some years ago by General de Gaulle – not a man to toss off testimonials lightly.) At 26 his powers of intellectual concentration, though his ideas may not be original, are formidable, his jokes sophisticated, his English distinctly more fluent than mine. But his average work-day is apparently 14 hours and he allows himself no physical relaxation. Bullets apart, I would demand a higher insurance premium on his survival into active middle-age than I would for the King. As for the rest of the Hashemites (the impressive Chief of Staff, Zaid bin Shakir, excepted) they recall Eliot's Prufrock – 'ones that will do To swell a progress, start a scene or two . . .' – Rosen bin Krantz and Gilden bin Stern al Hashemi . . .

In the past 30 years I have served in many Arab countries, have experienced Arab kindliness in all of them, and am well aware how little substance may lie behind it. I have never met it in more startling degree than here. It may even be that Jordanians really rather like the British. After many visits to Jordan over the years I still detect, fancifully perhaps, something in the make-up of its citizens that distinguishes them from other Arabs. (It is the only Arab country in which – years back – I have been arrested and the only one in which the case would have been dismissed, and coffee ordered instead of imprisonment, simply because I was a Briton and pleaded guilty in Arabic.) My Tunisian colleague also credits the Jordanians with a superiority over other Arabs, of an unexpected kind. 'The rest of us,' he said to me, 'always fix even the most important appointments for *hawali as-s'a ashera* (*about* 10 o'clock). We are a nation of approximators,' he went on; 'and that is why, for instance, our anti-aircraft shells never actually quite hit those aeroplanes. The Jordanians are different. They are punctual, therefore precise and practical. They do what they set out to do. Must be the British influence', he added.

Thinking over the Tunisian's tribute later that day while I waited three-and-a-half hours in the King's ante-room, I found myself unable for the moment to share his admiration for Jordanian sense of time. But maybe there is something in the rest of his tribute. Even the ubiquitous policemen give the impression, unprecedented in other Arab countries, of actually being there for a purpose – quite apart from their amiable disposition to spring (more or less) to attention, shake one by the hand and exchange the time of day. Not that the purpose is sinister. Despite all the khaki and gun-barrels, Hashemite Jordan is emphatically not (as so many of its Arab neighbours are) a police State. There are, for better or worse, far more bagpipers than security men . . .

I certainly look forward to my assignment with interest. And a country where, in the tense aftermath of the Munich horror,[1] the cricket elevens of the Palace and the British Embassy assemble to find the ground staff moving up and down the pitch not with rollers but (as if it were the most natural thing in the world for groundsmen to be doing) with mine-detectors, can hardly be dull. My own innings, short but painful, left me with the feeling that the pitch would have been a good deal less explosive if it had been rolled instead. There is doubtless a moral somewhere.

You will recall, Sir, that just after all the King's horses and all the King's men had been observed (by Alice) running confusedly through the woods, and further fighting for the Crown was about to break out all round the Town, an Anglo-Saxon Messenger arrived. Being somewhat out of breath, the Messenger asked the King if he would be good enough to stop a minute. 'I'm good enough,' said the King, 'only I'm not strong enough'; and he asked first for one ham sandwich, which he devoured greedily, and then for another. 'There's nothing left but hay now,' the Messenger said, peeping into the bag (or Bag). 'Hay then,' murmured the King faintly. Perhaps there is a moral somewhere there too.

1. *Munich horror*: The 1972 Olympic Games were marred by an atrocity, the killing of eleven Israeli athletes and support personnel by

Palestinian terrorists. The Munich massacre happened just three weeks before Balfour Paul wrote his despatch.

~

Syria

'A land of revolutions – and earnest revolutions at that'

SIR JAMES CRAIG, HM AMBASSADOR TO THE
SYRIAN ARAB REPUBLIC, DECEMBER 1976

Readers of Parting Shots *will recall Sir James Craig's terrific valedictories from Dubai and Damascus. The leading Foreign Office Arabist of his generation, Craig first served as ambassador in Syria. Three years in Damascus bred in him a deep dislike of the regime in power, but Craig retained the affection he felt for the country itself throughout his long career in foreign service. In 2011 he told us that in fact he regards Syria as his favourite country. The Ambassador's mystification at Syrians' willingness to tolerate their joyless despotism has its resonances as we go to print.*

CONFIDENTIAL

FOREIGN AND COMMONWEALTH OFFICE DIPLOMATIC REPORT NO. 13/77

NFY 014/4   *General Distribution*

SYRIA
20 December, 1976

SYRIA: FIRST IMPRESSIONS

*Her Majesty's Ambassador at Damascus to the
Secretary of State for Foreign and Commonwealth Affairs*

(CONFIDENTIAL)   *Damascus,
                                                  20 December, 1976*

Sir,

Hardly first impressions, for 26 years have passed since I came
to Damascus as a young student and walked, every evening
between the afternoon and the sunset prayers, through the
streets of the old town. In those days I could sit in one of the
old-fashioned cafes watching the women swing by in their
veils and the men in their tarboushes and baggy trousers,
and – with determination rather than delight – smoke the
hubble-bubble and sip the traditional sherbets. Ah, bliss was
it in that dawn . . . The romanticism which you may detect
in those purplish phrases has gone from my mind. Just as
well; for it has gone from Damascus too. Syria in the interval
has been a land of revolutions – and earnest revolutions at
that – prouder of its cement factories than of its mosques and
bazaars, known for its rigid ideologies and its secret police,
its Regional Command Councils and its Five-year Plans.
How different from the life of our own dear caliphs.

I had been told before I arrived that six years ago, with
the advent of President Asad, a reaction had set in. The
doctrinaire policies of the rather presbyterian Ba'ath Party
had been modified by a new, pragmatic liberalism: speech
was freer, government was more tolerant, Ministers were
more accessible; the famous merchants of Damascus and
Aleppo, sharp as needles, were once again free to buy and
sell and cheat and profit. My first thought, when I had

settled in, was that I had been deceived. The atmosphere of Damascus seemed to me pretty much as I had pictured an Eastern European capital: in the quarter where I live hard-faced (and rather rude) men in civilian clothes stand on every street corner, carrying sinister sub-machine guns; few consumer goods are on sale and there are sudden shortages – of candles, of bread, of glass; the electricity breaks down frequently; there are too many soldiers and policemen for a Westerner's liking; although in the old town the remnants of antiquity distract you from the shabbiness and the dirt, the new quarters are simply a dump; streets, hotels, shops are drab and tasteless; the Parliament is a timid claque, the Press a Government hand-out, unreadable and, I suspect, unread; the graces and entertainments that adorn Western society do not exist.

But I was unkind. I have remembered, after the first surprise, that many of Syria's deficiencies are endemic to the Middle East, whatever the political regime: there are no graces and no readable newspapers in Saudi Arabia, which is hardly a Socialist revolutionary country. And I find that everyone I meet, without exception, is agreed that things are better now than they were before Asad took over.

So at last I have reached some conclusions. Damascus is not the old oriental town of labyrinthine alleys and Turkish baths and over-laden donkeys. That is dying and will soon be dead, except for a few monuments preserved like the Tower of London in the aspic of the Department of Antiquities (itself a new and welcome phenomenon). Nor is it the levantine beehive of private enterprise which, without Palestine and the Ba'ath Party, it might have become. Some of that will survive because the Syrians are mercantile people (how do they tolerate the stuffy old

Ba'ath?). But the free for all days are gone for ever. Yet neither is it the stern, puritanical, authoritarian, repressive don't-talk-of-frivolities-we-are-all-dedicated-to-the-cause regime of the 'sixties . . .

[M]y strongest single impression (and one shared by all my colleagues, Arab and foreign alike) is of the shortage of news and of informed comment. I have already mentioned the papers: their news pages contain little more than the President's diary and the usual overblown slogans about struggle and national destiny and shouldering our responsibilities . . . Ambassadors, alas, are equally in the dark. Only half a dozen Syrians at the top know what is really going on – and they are not talking. So the Government's case is seldom properly presented and meanwhile everyone can listen to Radio Jerusalem.

Still and all, Damascus is an exciting place to be. Parts of the countryside are very beautiful and the whole of it is an archaeologist's dream. The Syrians are a hardy and likeable people, with a zest for life and progress. The amount of interest, and admiration of Britain has surprised me, given the estrangements between us over the past 25 years. Even the Ba'ath leaders I have met have been friendly and amiable (though I should not like to be alone with some of them on a dark night). I hope we may find ways of responding.

I am sending copies of this despatch to Her Majesty's Ambassadors at Beirut, Amman, Cairo, Baghdad, Tel Aviv, Washington and Moscow and to Her Majesty's Consul-General at Jerusalem.

I have, etc,
JAMES CRAIG.

～

Lebanon

'A kind of perpetual Nescafé society'

SIR PAUL WRIGHT, HM AMBASSADOR TO THE
REPUBLIC OF LEBANON, MARCH 1972

I must confess that hitherto I had never been able to take the Lebanese entirely seriously. Poised uneasily between Europe and the Orient, Christianity and Islam, the country, for all its beauty, seemed not really to belong anywhere. It appeared to be inhabited by a type of quintessential wog with a rich patina of French chic, ready to trade with anyone in any commodity at his own price, existing in a kind of perpetual Nescafé society, hoping that the problems of the real world would somehow disappear if not looked at too closely, and concentrating on the sensible occupation of making money. 'Always count your fingers after shaking hands with a Lebanese,' as they say in the souks. Added to this, it must be admitted, there was in my case, a certain respect for the historical antiquity of the coastline, a misty glamour surrounding the names of Tyre and Sidon, due perhaps to the strange prominence given in our history books to the arrival of the Phoenicians in Cornwall sometime during the second millennium BC.

It was to be expected that this somewhat superficial and *simpliste* view would be considerably tempered by the experience of living and working in the country, even for the few months that I have been here. And although certain aspects of the picture remain true there is, of course, more to Lebanon and the Lebanese than that. To begin with, the beauty of the country is far from being only coast deep. The Beka'a, lying between the two mountain ranges, is surely one of the most beautiful places on earth . . . The Lebanese, it is true, are hard bargainers and slick operators. But they have great charm, a refreshingly uncomplicated zest for life and, above all, tolerance . . .

[I]nvestment is far below that required for healthy growth. Indeed the Lebanese economy, in spite of many advantages of geography and temperament, seems to be in some ways a self-perpetuating confidence trick of a kind most dear to Lebanese hearts: a legalised near-fiddle in which wealth is somehow produced by fast talk and waving arms and by being that much quicker-witted than the next man. There is nothing much wrong with this so long as it lasts; but it is a precarious basis for long-term development in an increasingly competitive world.

Qatar

'One vast building site'

COLIN BRANDT, HM AMBASSADOR TO THE
STATE OF QATAR, MAY 1978

BRITISH EMBASSY,
DOHA QATAR,
014/2   1 May 1978

Sir

FIRST IMPRESSIONS OF QATAR

A 14th Century Cotswold wool merchant once inscribed over his new house:

> 'I praise God, and ever shall
> It is the sheep hath paid for all.'

Though the praise in Qatar may be faint – or absent –
it is certainly the hydrocarbon molecule 'hath paid for
all' here and should continue to do so well into the 21st
Century.

The wonder, as Dr Johnson would have observed, is that
Qatar should have existed at all. Until the development of
oil, this long low, desert peninsula, jutting out into the
Arabian Gulf like a sore thumb was only sparsely settled –
by Bedouin tribes who came in overland from Saudi
Arabia, and seaborne arrivals from elsewhere in the Gulf
and India. Even in 1959 Doha was still only a modest little
town of 50,000 people, with few roads or other services,
and only the most rudimentary attempt at civilisation.
Twice in the previous 150 years, such small fortunes as
Qatar had enjoyed were broken by events in the world
beyond: piracy was put down by the British Navy in the
19th Century; and pearling was destroyed by Japanese
imitation pearls, and the post-war depression, in the first
decades of the 20th. During the worst days of the last war,
poverty and hunger had reduced Doha's population to
perhaps less than 10,000.

Oil has changed all that. Doha has grown and prospered
mightily since the 1960's – especially in the four years since
OPEC quadrupled the world's price of oil – and is now a
thriving town of some 200,000. Where once the camels
were driven off the runway of the primitive little airport to
allow the daily 'Dove' to land, the Tristars and Boeings
thunder in across the harbour at regular intervals, skim-
ming the roof of the luxurious new Doha Club, (which

itself would not look out of place in Monte Carlo). The chrysalis of old Doha has split irretrievably, spilling modern hotel and office blocks along the reclaimed waterfront Corniche Road, and projecting the latest cars along the wide dual carriageway avenues radiating out from Doha, which at night transform what was once desert into long necklaces of light. From the confines of the original Doha one vast building site now spreads to the horizon in various stages of activity under the tower cranes (today's fertility symbol), replete with all the ugly detritus of cast-off civilisation . . .

All this has been paid for (or is due to be paid for) by the proceeds from Qatar's two oilfields . . . Moreover, a belatedly benign Providence has now been found to have awarded Qatar a glittering consolation prize of huge deposits of offshore as well as onshore gas . . .

The irony of the situation is that all this material wealth has emerged at the feet of such a minuscule number of people, in a small, backward, tribal and Bedu society. It has been a fascinating experience to see how that society has so far coped with the wave of wealth, and to assess its chances of survival without too intense a strain on this small body politic.

Basically, it is the 50,000 or so native Qataris who are the natural heirs to all this wealth. If one can generalise, they appear on the surface to be a good-natured, soft-spoken lot, happy to cash in on their new found fortunes for all these are worth, and content to enjoy the Divine Right of Qataris to a privileged cut at the State's revenues from oil. So Qatari nationality is still a jealously guarded meal ticket with many social and commercial advantages attached. Many of the Qataris have jobs in the Administration (where they are frequently 'carried' by their Palestinian or British expatriate staff) or the modest-sized Armed Forces. Even more are engaged in business. They make quite good businessmen ... [O]n the surface, they seem to bear no resentment against the foreigner, whether on ideological, social or political grounds. (The Palestine problem has nothing like the emotive power it has in other Arab countries.) But basically they have the mean streak of the camel-trader. And doubtless thanks to experience gained abroad a nucleus of the younger generation here has come to regard European women as fair game for harassment, which is causing us problems at present.

At the top of the Qatari social scale, the Ruling Family, the Al Thani, are virtually a law unto themselves, and dominate all Governmental and business activity. Viewed dispassionately they seem, with a few exceptions, an unattractive bunch, possessing little natural ability or power of leadership. I see them collectively as the local equivalent of The Mob. Prolific propagators, (if nothing else) they are now one of the largest and most widely-dispersed ruling families in the Gulf ... Since they control the Army, the Police and the Ministries, no-one can hope to best them. Their extravagances in new Palaces, farms, cars and boats go unchecked. And their attitude to marriage and women continues to be medieval. Wives and women are acquired frequently and almost casually, though any public immodesty in women is officially viewed with pious horror, (and alcohol is still a fruit forbidden to the populace at large).

~

Yemen

'Like a dilapidated farmyard'

MICHAEL EDES, HM AMBASSADOR TO THE YEMEN
ARAB REPUBLIC, DECEMBER 1971

According to a traditional Arab saying, Yemen is 'the birthplace of the Arabs'. Perhaps. But certainly it is an extremely ancient country. It has been continuously inhabited for a very long time ... If Yemen is an historian's delight, she is also a photographer's, let alone a mountaineer's. Much of its total area (some 75,000 square miles, or about the size of England and Scotland combined) is dominated by high mountain ranges, rising in places to well over 10,000 feet. These ranges, which form Yemen's massive central backbone, run right through the country from Saudi Arabia in the north to the People's Democratic Republic of the Yemen in the south – a distance of some 400 miles ... [T]he views from these and the high passes below them are, quite literally, breathtaking. I have not seen anything more lovely or dramatic, the Alps not excluded. It is in a sense sad, if selfish, to think that Yemen is bound in time to attract the tourists, that the awesome solitude of her magnificent mountains will not stay undisturbed for too much longer ...

Those Yemenis who survive the infant mortality rate of about 50 per cent and the quite ghastly diseases from which this country suffers, develop into tough, wiry and on the whole, little people with a well-deserved reputation for endurance and bravery in war. The climate in the Central Highlands and Middle Heights is conducive to hard work and the Yemenis are the hardest working folk in the Peninsula. They generally indulge their craving for 'qat', a mildly narcotic plant grown in abundance here, in the afternoons and evenings, i.e. after work. Its adverse effects can perhaps be rather exaggerated. Of course, given the basically inhospitable nature of their country, the Yemenis have always had to work just to survive. But they combine this attractive quality, so uncharacteristic of Arabs elsewhere, with quick-wittedness, intelligence, kindness and humour of a high order. Yemenis often remind me – dare I say it – of the Scots. They even have their Calvinist equivalents . . .

Finally, Sir, I should perhaps try to convey some flavour of the kind of life in which my staff and I at present live, move and have our being here. In doing so, I shall have to stress the sheer rurality of it all. The rubble in the streets, the endless dust, the pungent smells and general squalor – these are all too like a dilapidated farmyard. As elsewhere in the Arab world, the city 'cleansing department' is mainly staffed by packs of semi-wild pye dogs which do their work – and howl incessantly – by night, with the able assistance of the buzzards and crows by day. A decrepit, toothless tribesman lovingly feeds, by hand, his camel in the morning just outside my gate. Another severed ox head – but at least it is not a man's – lies rotting in the road outside the Ministry of the Interior, as tribal expiation for some offence against the customary law. A fox was seen untroubled in Independence Square not so long ago. But there are some compensations – the perennial sunny days, the sunsets over Sana'a and the surrounding hills, the crisp, cold and starry nights and the early morning call to prayer, unless distorted by modern electronic gadgetry.

I am sending copies of this despatch to Her Majesty's Ambassadors in Cairo, Jedda and Aden.

I have, etc.,
MICHAEL EDES.

~

PART VIII: COMMUNISM AND ITS AFTERMATH

The Soviet Union

'Either we live with the Soviet Union or we die with them'

SIR CURTIS KEEBLE, HM AMBASSADOR TO THE
SOVIET UNION, JULY 1978

In the early 1970s East–West relations were looking up. Détente bloomed, with the first of the Strategic Arms Limitation Talks (SALT) leading to a treaty limiting anti-ballistic missiles, and the Helsinki Accords promoting mutual understanding in Europe.

But by 1978 when Sir Curtis Keeble arrived in Moscow, the limitations of détente had become clear. The USSR continued to sponsor the spread of Communism in the Third World, while America, shamed by Watergate, had lost prestige in Vietnam. In rhetoric and outlook new leaders such as President Carter sought to challenge rather than conciliate the Soviets. Renewed fears in Washington over a perceived 'missile gap' saw American military spending rise sharply as the decade wore on. Not to be outdone, by the early 1980s 15 per cent of Soviet GDP was being spent on defence.

Relations were at a low ebb. Acknowledging this, and the scant prospect of their improvement, Keeble used his First Impressions despatch to describe the essence of the Soviet regime as he found it, trapped in deadlock with the West. The despatch is notable for the light it casts on the psychology of the Politburo, the 'tightly knit little group of conspirators' around Brezhnev who through a blend of suspicion, fear and secrecy exercised total control on policy in the USSR.

The file shows that Sir Reginald Hibbert, then Deputy Under-Secretary at the Foreign Office, commended Keeble's despatch to ministers, while cavilling at some of the Ambassador's language, minuting that 'it can be danger-ous to use emotive adjectives such as "evil" in relation to the Soviet Union'. (President Reagan would of course have disagreed.) The problem in handling the USSR 'is not the degree of its evilness', wrote Hibbert, 'but the degree of danger which it constitutes'. A very Foreign Office view.

Nevertheless the despatch is notably pacific in its tone and implicit policy advice. Britain at that time was gripped by a debate about whether the West should 'match' Soviet aggression with a bellicosity of its own, or whether efforts should be bent towards calming tensions. Keeble's concili-atory tone is underpinned by an argument that was surprisingly little heard at the time, but which later came to be decisive: that the Soviet economy was failing anyway. These, remember, were the years in which the Leader of the Opposition, Margaret Thatcher – whom Moscow had dubbed the 'Iron Lady' – was striking a note some thought warlike, others precautionary. Keeble is not on her side here.

A year after Keeble wrote his despatch, the Cold War became chillier still. The USSR invaded Afghanistan, plun-ging East–West relations into a deep freeze which saw sixty-five countries boycott the Moscow Olympic Games in 1980.

Despite the Ambassador's protestations about lack of access to Soviet decision-makers, by the time he left Moscow in 1982 Keeble had in fact established quite close

relations and was able to count the Russian Foreign Min-
ister, Andrei Gromyko, as a personal friend. As a parting
gift Gromyko gave the ambassador and his family a tour
of the inner sanctum of the Kremlin, somewhere few for-
eigners had ever set foot. One can imagine the satisfaction
this must have given Keeble, a glimpse behind the imperial
'facade' which in this account seemed so impenetrable.

CONFIDENTIAL

BRITISH EMBASSY,
MOSCOW,
12 July 1978

THE RT. HON DR DAVID OWEN MP
etc etc etc

Sir

FIRST IMPRESSIONS OF THE SOVIET UNION

I was in two minds about offering you the traditional first
impressions. The Soviet Union and its system of government, its personalities and its policies have been subjected
to more than enough expert reporting, analysis, comment
and controversy. First impressions from here run a greater
than normal risk of being superficial, platitudinous or plain
wrong. But even so they are perhaps worthwhile. The relationship between the Soviet Union and the West is in a
peculiarly uneasy state. It matters that we should get it right.
It matters that we should make as good a guess as we can
about the way this country's policies will develop. So, with
all possible reservations, I offer the impressions made on
someone who first set foot in Moscow three months ago.

I am told that one of the Tsars, when receiving foreign Ambassadors, kept a bowl of water handy so that he might wash away the taint. Perhaps the story is apocryphal. But it well illustrates the position of an Ambassador in Moscow today, indeed, in some respects I envy my predecessors. They at least met the Tsar. I have not yet met his successor or, for that matter, the Prime Minister, Foreign Minister or any member of the Politburo . . . I have had easy access at Deputy Minister level within the Foreign Ministry, and at Ministerial level in those technical Ministries which have business with Britain. Russians stream into the Embassy on every social occasion. I can visit factories, mines and hospitals. Yet there remains a sharp contrast between the amiable but unrevealing working contacts and the virtually total exclusion of foreign Ambassadors from contact with the real centres of power in the Soviet Government and party. There is, of course, nothing new in this. The Marquis de Custine's observations on Russia in the 1830s are rather over-quoted, but his comment that one might 'over run the Empire from one end to another and return home without having surveyed anything but a series of facades' is depressingly valid today. It is applicable also to the Soviet citizen, but he is perhaps less bothered about seeing behind the facade and into the process of policy-making. Fortunately, because the facade is maintained with great care, close scrutiny can give quite a good idea of the nature of the building. After all, when the astronauts first set foot on the moon they found few surprises.

The obsession with secrecy and the sharp distinction between the formulation of policy and its proclamation are not just a source of frustration to foreign observers. They are in themselves factors in determining the policies which emerge because they lead to policies which reflect a conspiratorial view of both domestic and international affairs. One has here the odd sensation of dealing at one and the same time with an age-old Russia and a newly legitimised revolutionary regime. The instincts of the two sometimes conflict and at others coincide with alarming force . . .

If the new arrival is struck by the force of Russian tradition, he is struck every bit as forcefully by the total grasp of Soviet power. It was tight central control which made possible the establishment and maintenance of a Leninist state. Sixty years of development may have reduced the element of irrational terror, but not the obsession with power and security. To oppose that power is to threaten the basic structure of the state . . .

The combination of tight central control, absolute secrecy and repression of individual expression is not just an evil way of running a country. It is also not peculiarly efficient. In the Soviet economy it has produced results with which we have long been familiar . . . A centrally planned economy is by its very nature ill-equipped to respond to the vagaries of consumer demand, so the qualitative deficiencies are not surprising. What is remarkable is that even today there should be such absolute shortages of everyday items. A former Pakistan colleague of mine once described Communism as a car with only bottom gear – fine for getting out of the mud, but not much good on a motorway. The Russian economy is now on the motorway. Expectations rise when one gets onto the motorway and the leadership are aware that they are not being fulfilled. One is conscious of a vast amount of engine noise, not much acceleration and rather hard seats . . .

It is Soviet foreign policy that has recently given rise to the greatest degree of concern in the West. What is their principal objective, security or expansion? Everything that has happened since I have been in Moscow has shown that they covet both. I think the obsession with security is dominant. It is a folk memory from Russian experience, reinforced by the appalling experience of 1941–45. That experience – though I hesitate to make the comparison – has seared them as it seared the Jews. I do not think we should judge their arms policies by rational western standards. Where their security is concerned they seem in fact to be guided by emotion rather than reason. It is a state of mind which needs to be handled with firmness and patience.

Clearly, however, Soviet foreign policy is not just the foreign policy of a super-power obsessed with the need for security. One has the impression that Mr Brezhnev and the elderly men around him see themselves at one moment as the statesmen ruling a super-power, at the next as the guardians of an ideology determining the future of mankind and then suddenly as a tightly knit little group of conspirators menaced on all sides. They are influenced not merely by their own habits and emotions formed over the sixty years of Soviet power. They are also carried forward by the impetus of an elaborate machine which in part they control, but which also in part controls them. I do not suggest that it does so directly or that on really major issues there is any risk of their being unable to control events, but rather that the machine serves them with a view of the world which they have been conditioned to expect and that they feed back to it responses conditioned in part by their own philosophy, in part by habit, in part by an assessment of Soviet interests and in part by the danger of challenging any of the basic tenets on which their power rests. The end result is that a desire to negotiate sensible agreements, like SALT II,[1] seems from time to time about to founder under the weight of suspicion, fear, distortion and polemics which it has to carry . . .

The Prime Minister posed the basic problem when he said, 'Either we live with the Soviet Union or we die with them.' If we are going to live with them at all satisfactorily we need to overcome the mixture of fear and aggressiveness which inspires their policy. We need in fact to make them realise that they face no external military threat, that the real external ideological threat is largely a reflection of their internal repression and that the biggest single step they could take towards their own well-being would be to humanise their system . . . The time may not be far off when the leadership will begin to see that their ideology, a sick and ageing doctrine conceived for the conditions of primitive 19th century capitalism, lacks any effective international appeal. If at that point they also see themselves as encircled geographically and threatened militarily they will be more dangerous than they are today . . .

So, infuriating though the rulers of the Soviet Union are, I hope that we shall be able to keep on the kind of quiet steady course we have been pursuing. We should not refrain from speaking our mind about Soviet repression at home or abroad, from exposing Soviet hypocrisy, from resisting Soviet expansion. We should not be deterred by the infinite Soviet capacity to bore and to insult . . .

We may appear to reap little reward . . . [W]e shall get no dramatic victories in human rights, but we may help to bring about a detente which means something, to move to a slightly safer rather than a significantly more dangerous world, and to ensure that when this rather nasty system decays, as it will, it does not bring us down with it.

I am sending copies of this despatch to HM Ambassadors in Washington and Peking.

I have the honour to be

Sir

Your obedient Servant
Curtis Keeble

1. *SALT II*: Brezhnev did in fact sign this second Strategic Arms Limitation Talks treaty in 1979, a year after Keeble wrote his despatch.

~

Cuba

'*Shabby gentility*'

RICHARD SYKES, HM AMBASSADOR TO THE
REPUBLIC OF CUBA, JUNE 1970

(CONFIDENTIAL)   *Havana,*
                                               2 June, 1970
Sir,

In 1948 a benevolent Personnel Department chose Nanking, at that time the capital of China and the seat of Chiang Kai-shek's Government, to be my first post overseas. Within a few months of my arrival the 'People's Liberation Army' had carried all before them and the Government of Mao Tse-tung was ruling from Peking. To some more generous-minded than brash post-war entrants there was a tang of Wordsworthian bliss in the air. Reality proved different. But it was a stimulating experience; and it was therefore with lively interest that I found myself, some 20 years later, accredited to another unorthodox Communist regime, my first impressions of which, in accordance with custom, I now have the honour to convey . . .

Has Cuba found the Utopian solution for which liberal sentiment has been seeking ever since the Russian and Chinese revolutions so clearly turned sour? Should middle-aged parents confess their errors, and admit that their children in glorifying Fidel and Che have found the right road? Of course not. Cuba is no Utopia. And though parents may still be wrong, Fidel and Che are no reliable guides to the New Jerusalem.

The price Cuba is paying for the achievement of its Government is a heavy one. I have yet to travel much outside Havana (though I doubt if things are so very different in the provinces) and so must judge largely from my experience of the capital. It presents a sad sight. The visual impact of the city on a new arrival is essentially one of seediness – of shabby gentility and of having come down in the world . . . In its corrupt and capitalist heyday Havana must have been beautiful. But now every building badly needs paint. Elderly vehicles lacking silencers and exhaust gaskets make a hideous noise. There are pot-holes in every side street (and many main ones) which never seem to be filled in, and the piles of rubble on the pavements have obviously been there for months. There are queues everywhere – for food, for clothing, for the ice-cream parlour when there is ice cream. There are queues today for tickets permitting you to queue at a restaurant tomorrow. The small shopkeepers were nationalised in 1968 and all distribution is now by the State. There is no starvation (I see stale bread in dustbins from time to time) but food is far from plentiful and clothing scarcer still. People are shabbily if adequately dressed. There is little elegance but no rags. The weather helps here of course. A short straight dress for a woman and a shirt and slacks for a man are adequate climatically. But I passed a shoe shop the other day with a notice which read 'This branch is open on Fridays from 7.30 p.m. to 11.30 p.m'. There are no bars; and no night clubs except on Saturdays and Sundays, and very few of them. I have yet to discover where, if you are an ordinary Cuban, you buy a ball of string, a packet of envelopes, a needle and thread. I do not think you do.

~

Hungary

'They lack animation'

SIR LESLIE FRY, HM AMBASSADOR TO THE PEOPLE'S
REPUBLIC OF HUNGARY, JANUARY 1955

In the Parting Shots *radio series we had great fun spotting the predictions made by British ambassadors in their valedictory despatches which ended up proving wide of the mark. In 1967 our ambassador in Bangkok confidently predicted that 'the days of the* coup d'état *are probably over for good', only to see the military sack parliament four years later (since then Thailand has seen eight further successful or attempted coups, the most recent in 2006). In 1965 Lord Harlech, Britain's ambassador in the US, predicted President Johnson would serve eight more years in* the White House; the fates tempted, Johnson of course stood down at the next election. We found another miss from 1988, when Sir Bryan Cartledge was Britain's ambassador in Moscow and Gorbachev's perestroika was already transforming Russia. The Ambassador thought change needed a 'timescale of twenty years, perhaps of a generation' to bear fruit. 'I do not believe that Gorbachev and his allies can bring about a moral, social, psychological, political and economic revolution in the Soviet Union more quickly than that.' Fifteen months later the Berlin Wall came down, though maybe Cartledge's doubts about psychological change were right.

Sir Leslie Fry's despatch from Hungary is in a somewhat similar vein. He saw in the population 'apathetic resignation' to Communist occupation and foresaw 'no hurtful kicking against the pricks'. But, just twenty months after he wrote those words, the same Hungarian people whose courage the ambassador so scornfully doubted mounted a spontaneous nationwide revolt. The Hungarian Uprising of October 1956 stunned the world. Within days the government fell, and the new liberal revolutionaries announced they would withdraw from the Warsaw Pact. Their optimism was short-lived of course. The following month Soviet tanks rolled back into Budapest, crushed the uprising, and installed a new government loyal to the USSR.

'Prediction is very difficult,' said the physicist Niels Bohr. 'Especially about the future.' The wisest diplomats avoid it altogether. As another old Moscow hand, Sir Rodric Braithwaite, sees it: 'The only people who have ever been able to predict the future are Roman augurers, by cutting up chickens.'

Sir,

I have been in Hungary for two months, near enough to the term usually regarded, I believe, as the normal period of gestation for a report on one's first impressions of a new post; and the end of the year seems in any event to mark a point of time beyond which I may no longer look on myself as a newcomer. I therefore have the honour now to submit this conspectus of my impressions.

Budapest cannot be despoiled of its beauty. The scars of extensive war damage which still disfigure it could be healed. The shabbiness of streets and houses, the untended gardens, could soon be put to rights. These things, and the paucity of traffic on the roads, are the first to impress the senses; but they are almost as superficial as the red stars which form no pleasing addition to the more prominent public buildings.

It is the people themselves who make the second and much deeper impression. They lack animation. Even the children, seemingly well cared-for, are unnaturally subdued, at any rate in public. Almost the entire nation, soldiers and sportsmen apart, gives the appearance of physical and mental dejection. Well it might. Power (under Moscow) is in the hands of Mr Rákosi, veteran Stalinist, one of the few survivors of the old guard of Communist leadership in Central Europe. Food is expensive although of indifferent quality, and meat, bread and eggs are frequently scarce: the common belief is that everything is going to Russia. Shoddy consumer goods are displayed with more art than prodigality in shop-windows; prices are extortionately high, wages low. Living accommodation is grossly over-crowded, public transport is antiquated and insufficient. Highways are poor, while most of the byways outside the capital are no better than rutted tracks. Schools and hospitals are drab and ill-equipped. Such new buildings as I have seen appear to be hastily constructed, utility-pattern affairs. The press, perhaps needless to say, is rigidly controlled and sickening in its adulation of the U.S.S.R., 'the liberators' to whom all thanks are due. To a country proud of its history, the Eastern bastion (as the Magyars used to claim) of Western civilisation, the red flags flanking the Hungarian tricolour wherever it appears must be a bitter affront. Above all, though the police and military forces are not in much public evidence, fear of indictment, deportation or worse is everywhere . . .

The Magyars are not Slavs; indeed, they have long regarded themselves as a master-race born to rule Slavs. They have strong links with the West, and a background of Western culture. They are sensitive and artistic, with mental resources and a lightness of spirit greater, I suspect, than those of most of their present associates. They are volatile and, not least among their characteristics, they have a keen sense of humour. They are not, in brief, of the stuff of which reliable Party members are made: the active supporters of the regime are still placed at no more than 5 to 10 per cent of the population.

Foreign domination, however, is no strange event and the national genius (which does not appear to include the frequent production of leaders) is for survival rather than for successful revolt. Even if courage were among the more notable Hungarian qualities, the geographical features necessary to a Resistance movement – mountain, forest or seaboard – are lacking; and even if there were no Soviet troops in Hungary, she has a common frontier with Russia. There will accordingly be no hurtful kicking against the pricks. Rapid advantage will be taken ... of any laxity of control from Moscow, but it is highly improbable that a bold hazard will be attempted. Apathetic resignation, the compromise of 'go slow but don't strike', sums up the general attitude.

◈

Bulgaria

'A sense of slight inferiority'

DESMOND CRAWLEY, HM AMBASSADOR TO THE
REPUBLIC OF BULGARIA, FEBRUARY 1967

CONFIDENTIAL

THIS DOCUMENT IS THE PROPERTY OF HER BRITANNIC MAJESTY'S GOVERNMENT

NG 1/2   *Foreign Office and Whitehall Distribution*

BULGARIA
13 February, 1967
Section 1

Mr. CRAWLEY'S FIRST IMPRESSIONS OF BULGARIA

Mr. Crawley to Mr. Brown. (Received 13 February)

Sir,

There can be few more interesting contrasts than a transfer direct from a small African country such as Sierra Leone, to a small European Communist country such as Bulgaria. Here there are for us no racial nor colour nor immigration problems, no imperialist past to live down *vis-à-vis* the natives of the country itself, no non-official British community to act as a listening post or to support in its difficulties, no questions as to whether we are or are not extending as much economic or technical or defence aid as we materially could or morally should. One does, however, find the familiar situation of a comparatively backward agricultural country, not naturally very richly endowed otherwise, trying to develop industrially too fast. One watches one's Russian colleague at social functions, rather larger than life, surrounded by attentive Bulgarians, and one hopes that he is being put through his paces for ever more assistance as would be the lot of any British High Commissioner in any new, post-war Commonwealth country. If he is under such pressures, he at least has the advantage over us that such controversies as may exist are conducted in private. In any event, there is ample evidence of Russian economic and technical aid to this country on an impressive scale . . .

It is therefore inevitably with a sense of less direct involvement that I have the honour to submit my first impressions of an East European country. Unlike some of my more distinguished colleagues at present serving in Communist posts (but, judging from their biographies, in common with some six of my eight post-war predecessors), I arrive immaculate from previous service in any East European country. One's total ignorance is not even impaired by any great historical funds, as it were, of mutual Anglo-Bulgarian knowledge. This has never been a country of which many of our compatriots have known much, or in which more than a few have ever lived for long. One has read Mr Gladstone's pamphlets on the Bulgarian atrocities;[1] of the diplomatic achievements of that great Times correspondent, J. D. Bourchier;[2] of King Boris[3] and his passion for railway engines. One is aware that the first classic example of a Communist take-over after the war took place here, and that in order to win a war it is wise to note first which side Bulgaria joins before joining the other. The Bulgarians, on the other hand, equally ignorant of us but being an eminently practical people, are more inclined to recall Lord Beaconsfield's association with the Treaty of Berlin[4] rather than his adversary's liberal prejudices; that the British bombed their capital during the last war; and that they are supposedly dedicated by political conviction to work for the elimination of our own chosen way of life. This is not, in short, a very promising stock-pile of mutual understanding . . .

Early December of a continental winter is not, of course, the best time to arrive. Touring, though possible, is not as rewarding as at other seasons of the year; industrial and especially agricultural workers are, one finds, inclined to hibernate, regardless of norms and productivity targets. This gives one, however, all the more leisure to explore Sofia itself, a spacious, but hardly the 'elegant city' as recently defined in The Times. Allowing for their dour and not conspicuously personable qualities, Bulgarians seem to be, generally speaking, a sturdy, orderly, amiable and usually friendly people, albeit with a peasant caution, and a peasant suspiciousness of strangers. It also strikes me that there is something of an undue diffidence, almost a sense of slight inferiority, in their national make-up, which has to be carefully taken into consideration. Communism does not seem to rest too heavily on them; they are accustomed through the ages – as is their persecuted but resilient Church – to shrug off their rulers and to bend to the prevailing wind. There is more in the stores, a more plentiful public transport system, more signs of reasonable social and financial well-being than somehow one expected. Appearances are admittedly drab, and accommodation continues to be of comparatively low standards. The city – at any rate in winter – would be only half as drab if there was anything approaching the standard of town lighting of any Western city; if such filthy, smog-spawning, brown coal was not consumed in such abundance; if the exteriors of buildings were kept reasonably decorated; if people did not usually wear such dark clothes; or if such simple and relatively inexpensive skills as that of shop window-dressing were not so lamentably neglected.

Only the Press in its infinite tedium – compulsive reading that it entails – exceeds one's worst forebodings. But culturally the Bulgarian is very much alive. In a country of some eight million people, mostly agricultural or industrial workers, the opera, the concert, the theatre, the ballet, and above all choral singing, flourish exceedingly ... I must confess that I have enjoyed such modern Bulgarian painting and films as I have seen more than I am told I should. Even their sculpture similarly gives pleasure by the very immensity of, for example, the Communist human form. There is a certain masochistic and nostalgic satisfaction to be derived from surveying colossal statuary, some of it erected in honour of the Russians during a period when so much of the rest of the world was busy demolishing monuments to the British and other former imperial peoples.

1. *Bulgarian atrocities*: In 1876 Gladstone was stirred out of semi-retirement and into print by the massacre of 15,000 Christians in Bulgaria. His famous pamphlet *Bulgarian Horrors and the Question of the East* laid into the ruling Turks ('elaborate and refined cruelty ... abominable and bestial lusts'), and into his nemesis, Prime Minister Disraeli, who had dismissed reports of the killings as 'coffee-house babble'.

2. *J. D. Bourchier*: In 1913 the Balkan correspondent of *The Times* acted as a go-between in the negotiations that ended the Balkan Wars. Bourchier vocally, but ultimately unsuccessfully, opposed peace treaties that saw poor Bulgaria cede territory, first to Romania, and then in 1919 – after the First World War (in which Bulgaria was once again on the losing side) – to Greece and Yugoslavia.

3. *King Boris*: Boris III ruled Bulgaria from 1918 to 1943. A true railway nut, when the Orient Express passed through Bulgaria, King Boris insisted on driving it.

4. *Treaty of Berlin*: In 1878 the Congress of Berlin redrew the map of the Balkans, and saw Bulgaria humiliated, losing Macedonia to the Turks. Bulgaria's efforts three decades later to remedy the situation led to the Balkan Wars. Lord Beaconsfield was Benjamin Disraeli, who signed the treaty for Britain. His liberal adversary was Gladstone – see note 1 above.

∽

Yugoslavia

'If two Englishmen constitute a club, three Serbs constitute a civil war'

SIR ARCHIBALD WILSON, HM AMBASSADOR
TO THE SOCIALIST FEDERAL REPUBLIC OF
YUGOSLAVIA, NOVEMBER 1964

Yugoslav individuals seem to be, if such a thing is logically possible, more unique than others. Most diplomats need only hear the noise in their own kitchen to conclude that, if two Englishmen constitute a club, three Serbs constitute a civil war. The racial differences in Yugoslavia, of course, aggravate the problem. At the Belgrade Opera House, it is possible to hear a Slovene tenor holding the principal role in Italian against a flood tide of Serb around him, on the ground that he does not know the language of his capital. An almost arrogant self-confidence is apt to go with this individuality. It has been said that the first word normally uttered by a Yugoslav baby is not 'Mama', or even 'Papa', but 'Znam' ('I know', and by extension 'I don't need telling' or 'I know better than you'.) This self-confidence remains very much alive in Yugoslavia to-day. I was treated to a good example of it recently, when I answered the questions of an old Macedonian peasant about my identity. 'You foreigners,' he said, 'talk about Ambassadors. We Yugoslavs call them Consuls.'

~

Latvia

'Comically awful Embassy premises'

RICHARD SAMUEL, HM AMBASSADOR TO LATVIA,
APRIL 1992

The fall of the Iron Curtain led Britain to move swiftly to reopen embassies in the newly independent states in the Baltic and elsewhere. This brought career opportunities for up-and-coming diplomats sent to run the revived British missions. As (for the most part) relatively young, first-time ambassadors, they put up with the poor living and working conditions.

In 1993 John Everard, for instance, had as his first embassy in Minsk a small shabby room furnished 'student bed-sit style' inside the former East German Consulate. Seen in these surroundings the new British Ambassador to Belarus seemed more like a 'village cricket captain', according to the Independent, *'than emissary of a great nation'. The locally engaged administrative staff supporting HM Ambassador shared a desk tucked away under the stairs. Richard Samuel's first impressions despatch from Latvia describes a similar scene.*

British Embassy
Riga
15 April 1992

The Rt Hon Douglas Hurd CBE MP
Secretary of State for Foreign and
   Commonwealth Affairs
Foreign and Commonwealth Office
London SW1

Sir,

FIRST IMPRESSIONS OF LATVIA AND CHRONOLOGY FOR 1991

When Soviet forces invaded Latvia in June 1940 they ordered all diplomatic missions out of Riga, including the British Legation. Its staff left in good order, but had to leave the building as it stood, still identified as the Chancery by a brass plate inscribed in Latvian and English, with the crest of HM King George V. The Russians then took the building over, but unknown to us, the nameplate was kept in safe hands throughout the Soviet period. Last month the 'Twenty One Club' of Riga, a political association, organised a presentation ceremony at which it was returned to us, resplendently polished, with a graceful speech about our two countries' traditional friendship from the Chairman of the Foreign Relations Commission of the Latvian Parliament. At another ceremony two months before that, the Riga Municipality formally transferred back to us the old Legation building itself, in Riga's equivalent of South Kensington. Both events are of a piece with the welcome the Latvians have given us since the Embassy, after fifty-one years' absence, opened its doors – more precisely our hotel bedroom doors, on 5 October . . .

The often uncertain expressions I encountered last autumn when I said where I was going encourage me to begin with a snapshot of this attractive if troubled country. Even to those in the UK who knew something of them before the summer, the Baltic States must have seemed small, remote, and never likely to impinge much on our own affairs. In fact their populations, taken together, equal that of Sweden; Latvia itself, with its 2.7 million people, is greater in size at least than Switzerland or the Netherlands and is physically closer to the UK than an EC applicant such as Finland. Furthermore, if the UK's interests here are perceived in London as less than vital, this seems not to be the case for important partners of ours like Denmark, Germany and Sweden.

Riga itself is a green and handsome city, whose fine pre-war buildings and old town in the Hanseatic style have more than enough presence to face down the shoddy and pretentious Soviet additions of the post war period. Lenin's overbearing monument was carted off as soon as possible after the coup in Moscow. The city centre is once again dominated, unchallenged, by the Freedom Monument from the first republic; amazingly, the Russians never got round to demolishing it.

The undulating and fertile Latvian countryside, despite areas of industrial pollution, has much undramatic beauty, with lakes, rivers and extensive forests of birch and pine. With their own distinctive and archaic Indo-European language, closely related only to Lithuanian, the Latvians have managed to preserve a rich musical heritage and folk traditions despite hundreds of years of colonisation by Swedes, Germans, Poles and Russians. The vitality of that culture made Latvian independence possible after World War I, and is the reason for its recovery last year. Certainly their two modest decades of independence before World War II do not make the Latvians feel any less a part of European civilisation than nation states with a much longer history. Their economic and political objective now is to rejoin the European mainstream as soon as they can overcome the enormous problems they now face . . .

Where does the UK now stand in Latvia and how should we develop our relations in the coming months? The Latvians were gratified at the speed of our response to their independence. Our recognition of it on 27 August, together with other EC states, was rapidly followed (on 1 September) by the Prime Minister's meeting with the Baltic Prime Ministers in Moscow and by the Minister of State's visit to Riga (as well as to Tallinn and Vilnius) on 4/5 September. A resident Embassy followed within a month and though our cramped and dingy rooms in the Riga Hotel made for almost comically awful Embassy premises for the first four months, we are now enjoying the spacious if temporary facilities of the former Communist Party Central Committee offices – a nice irony. We hope to move into the refurbished Legation building in Alunana street in stages, beginning this summer. The political symbolism of that return means much to the Latvians . . .

~

PART IX: EMPIRE AND COMMONWEALTH

Australia

'Australia is "the lucky country" all right'

SIR DONALD TEBBIT, HM HIGH COMMISSIONER
TO AUSTRALIA, SEPTEMBER 1976

CONFIDENTIAL

FOREIGN AND COMMONWEALTH OFFICE
DIPLOMATIC REPORT NO. 342/76

FWA 014/5   *General / Economic Distribution*

AUSTRALIA
20 September, 1976

AUSTRALIA: FIRST IMPRESSIONS OF "THE LUCKY COUNTRY"

*The British High Commissioner at Canberra to the
Secretary of State for Foreign and Commonwealth Affairs*

(CONFIDENTIAL)   *Canberra,
20 September, 1976.*

Sir,

'Here perhaps, more than anywhere, humanity had a chance to make a fresh start . . . Nothing in this strange country seemed to bear the slightest resemblance to the outside world; it was so primitive, so lacking in greenness, so silent, so old.' Alan Moorehead: *Cooper's Creek.*

'The immigrants . . . found it no land for loving at first sight. Only time would make friends of the unbending gums whose branches with their thin perennial leaves spread stiffly above the reach of man.' Mary Durack: *Kings in Grass Castles.*

'And the sun sank again on the grand Australian bush – the nurse and tutor of eccentric minds, the home of the weird, and of much that is different from things in other lands.' Henry Lawson: *The Bush Undertaker.*

'It is a country that is rich in mines, wool, ranches, trams, railways, steamship lines, schools, newspapers, botanical gardens, art galleries, libraries, museums, hospitals, learned societies; it is the hospitable home of every species of culture and of every species of material enterprise, and there is a church at every man's door and a race-track over the way.' Mark Twain: 1897.

'When I invented the phrase in 1964 to describe Australia, I said: "Australia is a lucky country run by second rate people who share its luck." I didn't mean that it had a lot of material resources . . . nor did I mean the Bondi Beach syndrome . . . I had in mind the idea of Australia as a derived society whose prosperity in the great age of manufacturing came from the luck of its historical origins . . . In the lucky style we have never "earned" our democracy. We simply went along with some British habits.' Donald Horne: *Death of the Lucky Country,* 1976.

From a distance, Australia looks like a straightforward, uncomplicated, homogeneous, prosperous kind of place; from the inside, the reality is surprisingly complex.

Materially, Australia is 'the lucky country' all right. It has so few mouths to feed, such an abundance of agricultural and mineral resources and so much room for development. Only with gross mismanagement could it bring upon itself a serious balance of payments problem. Despite the problem of the aborigines, it still has a more or less homogeneous population: there is no good reason why the 'new Australians' who have come in since the Second World War from countries like Italy, Greece, Turkey and Yugoslavia should not assimilate well in time with the older Australians of predominantly British and Irish stock and the million or so who have themselves come from Britain since the war . . .

Australia is a friendly place. Mark Twain said what he met here was 'English friendliness with the English shyness and self-consciousness left out'. That is accurate but there is more to it. The Australian personality and the Australian way of life have been created out of British stock and inherited British attitudes by the battering and baking of a remote, harsh, yet ultimately fruitful, environment. It has been a triumph of mind – and of character – over matter. Yet the victory has left scars: the Australian is genuine and full of good will but externally rough; generous but conformist; courageous and a good mate rather than a special individual; a loyal upholder of group values but one who sometimes makes poor distinctions between them. Like ourselves, the Australians are pragmatists; but pragmatists who, given the right cause may turn into heroes or may equally cut off their nose to spite their face. An interest in sport, natural enough in its way, is incredible in its intensity and is an emblem not only of virility but almost of respectability. For all that, the Australian girth grows larger over the age of 20 as players join spectators and easy living softens the traditional impression of the Australian as a tough bushwhacker. There is a need to be respected and even to be loved; but this is made harder to achieve because Australians, to an unusual degree, combine thinness of skin with forthrightness of expression, offering to the foreigner, as Jan Dawson pointed out, 'a baffling mixture of arrogant nationalism and self-deprecatory comment'. Paradoxically, it has probably been all the harder for Australians to strike an easy natural balance between their heredity and their environment because Australia has never had to fight for her political freedom. Consequently the very things that some Australians cherish as their birthright are seen by others as irrelevant or even as antiquated wrappings of their infant tutelage.

The environmental element too is divisive. The original, authentic Australia is the Australia of the bush and of the outback. The large, modern and increasingly sybaritic coastal cities with their advanced and opulent life style provide a startling antithesis to the background of the farm and the mine. Physically, the Australian continent is over 30 times the size of the UK, yet with only a quarter of its population ... [I]n Australia, distance breeds differences and misunderstanding more often than it lends enchantment ... 'The tyranny of distance' has separated Australians not only from each other but from nearly all the inhabitants of the globe with whom they have most in common. Australia is placed in a corner of the world where she feels no natural, spontaneous sense of identity with her neighbours, apart from New Zealand. There are significant overtones in the advertising slogan of the national airline: 'Quantas [sic] will fly you to the world'.

~

Pakistan

'Despite any line on the map, the same India'

MAURICE EADEN, HM CONSUL-GENERAL IN
KARACHI, DECEMBER 1975

*Eaden arrived in Pakistan fresh from a posting in Belgium,
another country whose sense of identity rather bled into
that of the neighbours next door. In Karachi the Consul-
General was much taken with the existential question of
whether, since splitting from India, Pakistan had managed
to establish itself as a nation as well as merely a state.*

*Writing back, R. J. O'Neill of the South Asian Depart-
ment offered an answer: 'Is not the final reason for the
existence of Pakistan the fact that there is now, at least, no
alternative?'*

*'That is putting things very low,' admitted O'Neill. 'But
may it all not be rather like being Belgian? It is not very exciting, but who would really want to throw in his lot with
any of the neighbouring states?'*

CONFIDENTIAL

1/2   31 December 1975

Sir Laurence Pumphrey KCMG
British Embassy
ISLAMABAD

Sir

IMPRESSIONS OF KARACHI AND SIND AFTER SEVEN WEEKS

Coming to Karachi after three years in Brussels and before that a spell in Bombay has been and is a fascinating experience. After seven weeks, as after one day, the abiding impression is one of familiarity. The same hooded crows, parakeets, kites and hoopoo birds as in our garden in Bombay. The malis, dhobis, chowkidars and the Goan drivers all so familiar. The same shanties and mansions, ceiling fans, tenements and white paint in the cantonments and the civil lines, the same trees and the circuit houses. And despite any line on the map, the same India.

Differences of course there are – the most noticeable in the city being the almost complete absence of women from the street scene, with a consequential drabness and loss of colour. The physical setting is quite different – there torrential monsoon rains, here desert. And no sacred cows here to hold up traffic (but plenty in the bureaucracy). One could list a good many more such differences but somehow they all seem rather peripheral and detract little from the basic oneness which is perhaps best illustrated by the mosques covered by a small forest of small poles with little red and green flags making them look just like Hindu temples.

Perhaps the most familiar aspect of all, and certainly the pleasantest, is the ease of social contact with educated Pakistanis, in business, in government and in the professions, and with their wives. This stands out all the sharper after three years of unfruitful struggle to get to know Belgians. I cannot speak of pre-1971 Pakistan[1] nor of present day India but my guess is that getting on with Pakistanis is now easier than with Indians. Defeat has removed much of the arrogance the Pakistanis may have had. Victory certainly had the opposite effect in India in the months I was there following the Bangla Desh war . . .

I have the distinct feeling that a good many leading Pakistanis are in regard to their country like the agnostic who badly wants to believe and recites the creed several times a day without, however, ever really becoming convinced. They are good Muslims and are naturally doing their best to get what they can out of their wealthy co-religionists. But their real interest is in the Sub Continent. Early on in almost every conversation I have with a Pakistani I meet for the first time, I am asked 'Have you been in this part of the world (i.e. the Sub Continent) before?' They show polite interest in other parts of the world. What really interests them is India. There is little we can do to promote better Indo/Pakistani understanding, in fact to try would probably be counter-productive. But when it happens I hope that we shall cheer.

1. *pre-1971 Pakistan*: The Indo-Pakistan War of 1971 ended with Bangladesh – East Pakistan as it was – seceding from the western rump. It was a humiliating defeat for Pakistan, which saw a third of its army become prisoners of war in India.

~

Barbados

'This windblown island of boredom'

JOHN BENNETT, HM HIGH COMMISSIONER TO
BARBADOS, DECEMBER 1967

The Barbadian in many ways continues to live in the shadow of the end of nineteenth-century England. The pace is slow – hippies and flowers are absent – mini-skirts are rare – crime is minimal – Sunday sees the family walking to their place of worship (the choice is large with at least 16 active denominations) – gambling and night life, except for the infamous Harry's are absent – cricket is the main relaxation. The country remains firmly democratic and is one of the few ex-colonial territories which has absorbed the democratic customs and institutions of Whitehall. The Bajan is prepared to fight hard to retain them. The 'whites' live apart from the 'blacks' but, to date, this poses no particular or acute problem. Her Majesty – Queen of Barbados – continues to enjoy a very special place in the hearts of all the people, regardless of colour or creed. Through the monarchy the Barbadians, with nostalgia, look to the Mother Country. There is much truth in the saying that Barbados is 'Little England'.

So, in many ways, Barbados is an anachronism in this modern world and not quite part of it. The slow pace, the honesty, the stability have a certain charm, but also disenchantments, since, with little or no stimulations – cultural, economic or political – the average Bajan is a bore, narrow-minded and self-satisfied. The atmosphere was well described in a recent writing of Mankowitz when he referred to Barbados as 'this windblown island of boredom'.

~

The Cayman Islands

'This is no tropical paradise'

KENNETH CROOK, HM GOVERNOR OF THE
CAYMAN ISLANDS, JANUARY 1972

When Kenneth Crook became Governor of the Cayman Islands in 1972 it was clearly still a very hands-on job. His predecessors in the role had learned the nitty-gritty of how to run a country in the Colonial Service. Unfortunately for Crook that anachronism had been abolished six years earlier. While Crook's own career path in the Diplomatic Service had been stimulating, knowing how to navigate the complex politics of Bangladesh and Pakistan was of little use in the Caribbean.

Sir Athelstan Long, the previous governor (1971–2), told us he suspects Crook 'may have been given a rather flattering picture by the Secretary of State in order to get the post filled'.

'It obviously did not live up to his expectations,' said Long. 'None of the comforts of a diplomat, and no time to write clever and well-phrased despatches and letters giving wise advice to London – plus no expatriate support staff. He was very much "The Boy on the Burning Deck", with problems and responsibilities which must have been completely new and rather overwhelming.'

The Cayman Islands are still a British possession. Under the latest constitution, enacted in 2009, ultimate legislative and executive authority still resides in the Governor – who remains an FCO appointee.

George Town,
26 January, 1972

Sir,

Governors do not I believe usually write first impressions despatches. But it was suggested to me that you, Sir, and the office as a whole, might find some interest in the first reactions of a pair of Diplomatic Service eyes and ears (two pairs, if you count my wife's) to this basically colonial situation. I have the honour, therefore, to submit the following first thoughts.

It is hard to be sure whether they derive from comment made when I first heard of the posting a year ago, comment heard when I visited the place in June (disguised, like Nanki-Poo,[1] as a second trombone), or things learned since I arrived. However this may be, one thing stands out. This is no tropical paradise. I could enlarge, in terms of a magnificent but mosquito-ridden beach; of a fairly new but rather ill-designed and sadly-neglected house; of a pleasant but very untidy little town; of swamp clearance schemes which generate smells strong enough to kill a horse; of an office which will one day ere long collapse in a shower of termite-ridden dust . . . But enough! The point is made.

This is certainly an odd appointment for a Diplomatic Service officer, and the main difference which at once emerges concerns responsibility. How many of my colleagues, like myself, contemplating the inanities of some Head of State to whom they had the misfortune to be accredited, have said to themselves 'If only the fool would do so and so, how easy it would be.' But have they really thought how it feels to *be* the fool in question? One minor and very superficial example will illustrate the point. My wife, faced with roads likely to daunt a Sahara explorer, said aggrievedly, 'Why don't they do something about this?' And got the terse if ungrammatic reply, 'Not they – me!' It makes a difference! I might also invite my colleagues to try running a Parliament in the best Westminster tradition, in which one Member leaves, and as a result throws the entire Finance Committee into confusion for want of a quorum, because he has to drive the school bus – which he owns. It seems a bit unfair to have to learn at one and the same time *(a)* how to run a Parliament, *(b)* how to bend its rules so as to get it out of such self-created messes. What extraordinary demands modern diplomacy makes of her servants!

1. *Nanki-Poo*: In *The Mikado*, Gilbert and Sullivan's 1885 comic opera, the love-lorn son of the Emperor goes disguised as a wandering minstrel.

~

The Gilbert and Ellice Islands

'But a stroke of green between an immensity of sea and sky'

JOHN SMITH, HM GOVERNOR OF THE GILBERT
AND ELLICE ISLANDS, NOVEMBER 1973

You won't find the Gilbert and Ellice Islands in a modern atlas. As with so many other former British possessions, the coming of independence saw the old colonial names disappear. A string of tiny islands in the Pacific a thousand miles north of Fiji, they were hard to find on the map even before the late 1970s, when independence saw the Gilberts incorporated into Kiribati, and the Ellice reborn as a separate country, Tuvalu.

Judging by this despatch, John Smith seemed to like the locals more than he did his subordinates in the colonial administration. Back in Whitehall the final paragraph presented a problem to Mr J. Nicholas in the Pacific Dependent Territories Department, who was tasked with having the despatch printed and circulated to all diplomatic posts. Fearing that the full version would cause 'great offense' to the officers concerned, and spark off an 'anti-Smith campaign', Nicholas took the rare step of asking the Governor to amend his text before having it printed. Smith acceded to the request to end his despatch with a 'fairly non-controversial statement' instead. We print here the original version.

The Governor's views on resettlement were also somewhat maverick. Smith supported the aspirations of many of the islanders to emigrate in search of work, and believed that a lack of economic opportunity, combined with population growth, would see most of the atolls deserted within fifty years. Today, with less than a decade to go, this prediction looks set to be confounded.

The spectre of uninhabited desert islands has not gone away altogether, however. At just 4.5 metres above sea level, Tuvalu is perilously vulnerable to climate change. Rising sea levels over the next few decades threaten to poison the water table and force the islanders out for good, with New Zealand the most likely destination. At the United Nations Climate Change Conference in Copenhagen in 2009, Tuvalu rejected a compromise deal on carbon

emissions. 'We are being offered thirty pieces of silver to
betray our people,' the country's representative Ian Fry
told the conference. 'Our future is not for sale.'

CONFIDENTIAL   13 November 1973

The Right Honourable
Sir Alec Douglas-Home KT MP
etc etc etc

Sir

GILBERT AND ELLICE ISLANDS IN 1973 – FIRST IMPRESSIONS

Sir Arthur Grimble[1] has written so ably and so popularly about these remote and unusual islands that it is as impossible for a newcomer not to feel intimidated about offering first impressions as it is to arrive without preconceptions. But just as the Grimble who emerges from the files is not quite the sympathetic and kindly man who emerges from his books, so, too, the islands and their peoples are no longer quite the same as those with whom he first came into contact half a century ago. The record deserves re-examination and first impressions are of value because the absolute sameness of atoll ecology and equatorial climate quickly blunt the edge of perception, while the background of sun, surf and sand encourage the unwary to fall into the mood of island life which remains so relaxed that the only thing I have been pressed to do as governor is to attend parties . . .

For years it was assumed that it would be possible to graft on to the traditional economy and culture only the barest trimmings of the western world. Over centuries the Islanders had evolved a pattern of life which made their chosen atoll homes tolerable at a level of existence which would seem affluent to the poorer peoples of South East Asia . . . There is an abundance of fish, coconuts, pandanus and 'taro' which provide a balanced diet, shelter, and the accoutrements of culture. Born into a world in which the land is but a stroke of green between an immensity of sea and sky the Gilbertese have achieved their highest expression of art in the construction of canoes. Capable of great turns of speed the sailing canoe has reduced the loneliness of atoll existence, kept the people together and enabled a homogenous culture to survive.

But it has not been possible to contain the intrusion of the Western world with its whalers, traders, missionaries and finally colonial administrators. Exposure to an external economy has introduced exchange where it was hardly needed, encouraged specialisation which was previously tolerated only as demonstration of exceptional skill in canoe building or dance, and brought incentives to a society by custom suspicious of the individual who stepped out of line . . .

While seafaring and commercial fishing can provide additional employment and income the natural limitation of resources sets not only a level on the standard of living but a time scale as well. The population, despite a widely understood and accepted control programme, is growing apace . . . It is now time to seek opportunities not only for other external employment but for settlement as well. The total population is not large. It could be absorbed in a single year's immigration quota into Australia and still leave room for as many again . . . Whole island communities are hefty dumplings for a racial stew pot, but I have yet to meet the young Gilbertese or Ellice Islander who has seen something of the outside world who does not want to go back there and who would not, if given the chance, opt to settle . . . potential migrants would be English speaking, accustomed to the rule of law and Western democratic institutions, cash motivated and of proven assimilability. A group already happily settled in Melbourne through marriage may be pioneers of a new pattern of migration which will probably leave most of the atolls uninhabited fifty years hence. The alternative is for the rest of the world to pay for the technology necessary to keep the Gilbertese at home. It is an alternative which could quickly degrade and reduce a decent and deserving people into decadence . . .

If the road ahead is difficult, it is also exciting. I would be more sanguine about the challenge if the expatriate civil service were not predominantly contract and, encouraged by remoteness and a narrow way of life, in many cases unduly obsessed with its own conditions of service. Recruitment attracts some running away from an unpleasant reality and others inspired by cultural romanticism or touristic interest. There is little of the commitment and perception which once characterised Her Majesty's Overseas Civil Service. Britain's understandable inability in these days to service a dependency with the staff it deserves is in itself a compelling reason to persuade the Gilbertese and the Ellice Islanders to stand on their own feet and make independence their goal.

I have the honour to be Sir

Your obedient Servant

John Smith
Governor

1. *Sir Arthur Grimble*: Commissioner of the Gilberts in the 1920s, Grimble spent most of his career on small islands in the outer reaches of the empire. In a series of colourful books Grimble described the Stone Age myths and rituals of the Kiribati people, who once used him as human bait to catch a giant octopus.

~

The New Hebrides

'In bed with the French . . . Two things to do . . . We have tried sleeping and it is time for the other'

ROGER DU BOULAY, HM RESIDENT COMMISSIONER
IN THE NEW HEBRIDES, JANUARY 1974

Vanuatu, an archipelago in the Pacific, won its independence in 1980. Before that, as the New Hebrides, it was administered by Britain and France in a joint condominium, a form of government unique in the colonial world.

At the top, British and French 'Residents' exercised equal control. Further down the ranks the principle of dualism was taken to farcical extremes. For each French bureaucrat or technician, Britain posted an exact equivalent, so that the staffs of the two residences were almost totally symmetrical. The tiny administration was burdened with two currencies, two education systems, two police uniforms and two different legal codes (in the event that the rival judges disagreed, a nominee of the King of Spain would be asked to arbitrate).

The diplomats on the ground tasked with implementing this byzantine fudge tried their best. Du Boulay's despatch was titled 'First Impressions of a Franco-British Partnership

That Works – After a Fashion'. His successor as British Resident in Vila, John Champion, was less kind, describing having to split every decision with the French as 'wasteful and inefficient', and the Condominium as an 'absurd predicament'.

On the political side Du Boulay's fears of unrest below the surface were well founded. A few weeks before Vanuatu gained its independence a breakaway faction on the island of Espiritu Santo seized the airport and hoisted the flag of the Republic of Venerama, their own putative state-within-a-state. The ensuing struggle saw rebels armed with bows and arrows defying the Condominium government, and was soon tagged 'The Coconut War'. Troops sent from Papua New Guinea eventually brought an end to the quaint insurrection.

CONFIDENTIAL

FOREIGN AND COMMONWEALTH OFFICE
DIPLOMATIC REPORT NO. 84/74

FWA 014/5   *General Distribution*

NEW HEBRIDES
2 January, 1974

NEW HEBRIDES: ANNUAL REVIEW AND FIRST IMPRESSIONS OF A FRANCO-BRITISH PARTNERSHIP THAT WORKS – AFTER A FASHION

The British Resident Commissioner in the New Hebrides to the Secretary of State for Foreign and Commonwealth Affairs

New Hebrides,
2 January, 1974

Sir,

The first thing that strikes the newcomer to the New Hebrides is how much there is to be done. The real development is only just starting; in most fields we are still in the law and order, care and maintenance stage. It is also as salutary to the recruit from the Foreign Service to be reminded that we actually have to run the place, keep the peace and mend the drains and build the future – something more than analysing and reporting on how this is being done or not done by others – as it is interesting to find that negotiating with the French on running the colony presents all the problems and frustrations, and requires all the same qualities, as negotiating with them on [European] Community problems.

Only slightly less striking at first glance is the difficulty of the task, in this remote and scattered group of islands, with few natural resources but the sea and sunshine, rain and coconuts; with more than 100 different languages among less than 100,000 people; with little or no traditional system of authority or hierarchy on which to base a system of indirect rule; and with a climate and custom that conspire to make inaction the easiest option. Then there is the Condominium – or more specifically the French. In some ways the most surprising discovery for the latter-day Captain Cook is that in this corner of the Pacific we and the French have been achieving, over the past 60 years, a partnership that actually works in practice and has succeeded despite all difficulties in delivering the goods . . .

The Condominium may be the second clumsiest system of government yet invented – after Brussels – and it is easy to make fun of it (as almost every recent foreign observer, in *Stars and Stripes*, and the BBC and *le Monde*, has most amusingly done). But to my mind the surprising thing is, not how badly it works, but that it works at all. The system of dual control makes an already difficult task almost impossible. Like an aircraft with dual controls and two separate, but equal, pilots, the machine will only keep flying if both agree on where they are going and how they will get there. Yet historically there has been no such agreement. The British Government got sucked into the South-West Pacific against their will and proclaimed policy to protect 'the natives', curb the excesses of the British (mainly Australian) traders and settlers, prevent the exploitation of one by the other and exclude the French from sole control. They gave their Resident Commissioner a relatively free hand . . .

The French by contrast came here to spread the blessings of French language and culture, to promote the interests of their settlers and to help them to exploit the natural resources of the group including its indigenous inhabitants. They seldom stinted money and delegated financial control, but kept political control decisively at the centre. Their aim was first to make the New Hebrides totally French – by harassing, boring and frightening the British out – and then to keep it that way.

These disagreements have obliged us to perform the aeronautically impossible feat of keeping the machine stationary in mid-air while the pilots bickered over the controls and charts. But it has kept flying – partly because of necessity and the good sense of the officials on the spot, and also because the requirements of administration were until recently minimal; but mainly because of the docile good nature, the lack of sophistication, education, social cohesiveness and elementary political organisation of the New Hebrideans themselves. There was no pressure from below, and, provided things were quiet and expenditure kept within bounds, none from above or outside . . .

Matters will not stay like this. The bay which shelters the port of Vila is, I am told, an old crater lake, and, according to some, but not the better, authorities, the island in the middle of it on which I live is the remnant of the volcano's core or plug, a sort of giant champagne cork, in fact. Although many volcanoes in the Group are still active, it is unlikely, I understand, that I shall be suddenly translated into the upper atmosphere with a Krakatoan pop (to form part of the Western sunsets in the ensuing months). But the daily earth tremors remind us that the crust is thin and the fires burn beneath. We could do worse than bear this in mind when we survey the political scene . . .

For better or worse, then, we have been, and should remain, in bed with the French. There are only two things you can conveniently do in bed. We have tried sleeping and it is time for the other. I believed before I arrived here that the key to progress lay in Paris, and everything I have seen since confirms me in this view. The trick must be to persuade Paris to move . . . When I asked earlier this year . . . what the [French Foreign] Minister wanted from the New Hebrides, the answer was essentially, *Tranquillité*. Nothing must be allowed to obstruct the extraction of nickel from New Caledonia and the development of the H-bomb in the central Pacific. The best way, it had been thought in Rue Oudinot,[1] of achieving this desired tranquillity was to resist political advance, encourage French settlement ... and lock the New Hebrides firmly into the French system. It is now clear at least to some of the French on the ground that this will not work ... We have to persuade the French to take the small but giant step on political evolution that will unlock the door to reform across the board. Once we start along the road towards self-government, the process will take on its own momentum ...

A normal report on first impressions of a dependent territory would, I daresay, deal exclusively with the political, economic and social scene. My report naturally covers these things, but its theme is Franco-British partnership (that essential word for which there is no French equivalent), because that is what the Condominium is about, and that is what dictates and determines its progress. May I therefore end with a reference to the first of my predecessors, Mr King, the only one unfortunate enough so far to have got himself into the history books? Of him it has been said that 'he maintained a politeness in the face of many provocations as invariable as his inertness, and displayed a reluctance to discommode his French colleague if it was at all possible to oblige him, which exasperated his fellow British ...' Another observer of the scene at the beginning of the century remarked that ' ... the British officials all seem weighed down with the immense responsibility of sustaining the *Entente Cordiale* ... The French on the other hand do not worry about the matter at all and are out for all they can get ...'

It could, I suppose, be maintained that these remarks apply as well today as they did in 1906; and I must declare my prejudice when I say that I love the French even in their colonies as much as I am exasperated by them. But my aim will be to ensure that this particular piece of history does not repeat itself precisely, and that if we strive to emulate the *suaviter in modo* of our predecessors, it will be accompanied by a great deal more *fortiter in re*.[2]

In one other respect, too, I must disclaim any ambition to emulate Mr King: he held his appointment for 17 years.

I have, etc.,
R. W. H. du BOULAY.

1. *Rue Oudinot*: The Paris boulevard, home to the French Ministry of Foreign Affairs.
2. *suaviter in modo ... fortiter in re*: 'Gentle in manner', 'resolute in execution'.

3. Envoi

The Falkland Islands

'The blunt question . . . do 2,000 people matter?'

SIR JAMES PARKER, HM GOVERNOR OF THE
FALKLAND ISLANDS, JANUARY 1980

'Mr Parker,' wrote Robin Fearn, head of the FCO's South America Department, 'tends to look at the problem from the Islanders' viewpoint.'

Argentina invaded the Falkland Islands in April 1982. James Parker was the penultimate governor of the British dependent territory before the war. In 1980 the shooting was still some way off, and Britain and Argentina were in talks over the future of the islands. In his valedictory from Port Stanley, declassified for the first time in 2011, Parker calls on the British government to stand firm.

Britain's successful defence of the Falklands is nowadays (in most quarters) a pillar of national self-esteem. It has achieved such importance to British pride that is hard to believe that in stating the case that the UK should negotiate robustly with Argentina before the conflict Parker actually blotted his copybook with his superiors at the Foreign Office.

Parker saw a need to defend Britain's strategic and economic interests in the South Atlantic, as well as to protect the wishes of the Falkland Islanders. In the file Fearn notes critically that the Governor considered the islanders a 'viable and solid community', albeit one hamstrung by what Parker saw as neglect by the British government. It seems HMG disagreed.

Argentina was bellicose in stating her claim to the islands. Instead of negotiating with 'apparent detachment', Parker calls on British ministers to tackle the dispute 'on the same terms'. But Fearn argued a different line. British policy was for a 'compromise political solution' with Argentina. In HMG's cold-eyed assessment, the cost of sustaining the islands against 'determined Argentine pressure' was unaffordable.

'We must try to ensure,' wrote Fearn after Parker returned home, 'that the new Governor retains a more objective view of his mission and of the need to bring the Islanders to recognise the narrow options open to them and to us.' In the measured prose of the Foreign Office, this is serious criticism. It failed in its objective. The next governor, Rex Hunt, in place when Argentina invaded, was equally staunch in his defence of the islanders.

History suggests that, at least tactically, it was Parker who was right, and Fearn wrong. For it was General Galtieri's misinterpretation of conciliatory British attitudes that encouraged him to invade. Critics cite the decision in 1981 to withdraw from service the Royal Navy ship HMS Endurance, Britain's only naval presence in the South Atlantic, as suggesting to the Argentinian junta that the UK was unwilling and perhaps unable to defend the Falklands.

That was of course a misunderstanding. The eventual British victory energized Margaret Thatcher's premiership and boosted Britain's international status.

In the South Atlantic it was Argentina that was beaten. But back home in Whitehall the Foreign Office lost the Falklands War. At King Charles Street, Britain's biggest military success of the 1980s saw resignations, recriminations and a lengthy formal inquiry.

Three days after Argentinian troops seized Port Stanley in April 1982 the Foreign Secretary, Lord Carrington, and two of his ministers stood down. Ever since then critics have sought to lay blame at the door of the Diplomatic Service, claiming dozy civil servants failed to alert ministers as Argentina moved on to a war footing. If so, Sir James Parker would not have been among them.

But the reality was more complex. The negotiations in the late 1970s between Britain and Argentina were expected to result in administrative and economic cooperation over the Falklands. But the ultimate aim for London was to alter the nature of the dispute from confrontation to partnership, and thus actually help to preserve, rather than end, British sovereignty in the South Atlantic.

As an institution the Foreign Office had clearly invested heavily in this strategy. The documents show that within the debate, the FCO – and Fearn – occupied one end of the spectrum: favouring a negotiated settlement with Argentina, as opposed to defending the status quo at all costs.

But by 1981 the drawbacks of the negotiation strategy had become apparent. Contrary to the popular myth of the FCO sleeping on the job, diplomats were by then warning ministers that the Argentinians might invade if they decided the British government was not negotiating on sovereignty in good faith.

Officially, the FCO was exonerated after the conflict. The Franks Committee, which investigated failings in the *run-up to war, said the decision to invade 'was taken by the Junta at a very late date' and thus 'could not have been foreseen'. And crucially for Fearn it dismissed as 'without foundation' the damaging allegation that the Foreign Office had pursued a policy of its own, separate from that of elected government ministers, aimed at 'getting rid of the Falklands'. That would certainly be overstating it. But the spat chronicled here between the Governor and the office does suggest a private FCO view in Whitehall.*

CONFIDENTIAL

28 January 1980

The Right Honourable
The Lord Carrington PC KCMG MC MP

My Lord

LAST IMPRESSIONS OF THE FALKLANDS

At the end of this month I will leave the Falklands after three intense, sometimes trying, but mostly happy years living among the Islanders as their Governor. Glancing through the despatches of my 20-odd predecessors a few, it seems, left with no regrets, and one or two had even had enough and were glad to go. Others had become so attached to the place they were sorry to leave, some with hope a better future might be possible for the Islanders if things turned out well, and many with concern about what that future might really hold for them. My own feelings are a mixture of the last three, and my concern is deep.

On my arrival, at short notice, just before Christmas in December 1976, I had little time to put my first impressions into clear thought. My immediate task was to calm down the decidedly emotional state the Islanders had got themselves into in the preceding year or so, when everything seemed to go wrong and apprehension about the future was high . . . The negotiations, in which their Councillors have been kept informed at every stage, have gone on at lengthy intervals since then, with no marked result so far . . .

What are my abiding impressions of the Islands as I leave them? A bare, rugged, isolated and unspoilt landscape, with abundant wildlife, mostly around the often strikingly dramatic coasts. A climate that is much maligned and which, while it sometimes produces bleak miserable days of rain and wind, mostly offers the clearest skies and brightest sunshine anyone could wish for. Some of the kindest, gentlest, most hospitable people in the world, gossipy, like all scattered island folk and occasionally slyly sharp in their humour, but not intentionally malicious. Hardworking, very versatile in their talents and skills, and with a better understanding of the world outside than the formal education of some of them would incline one to expect. Tolerant of human frailty, and with their social problems quietly under control. Intensely proud of their Falklands heritage, but totally loyal and totally British in their way of life, appearance, manner and outlook. Although so close to the South American mainland they have taken in none of its culture or habits. Historically they have had little to do with it . . . In earlier days, frequent shipping, the mail, the telegraph and periodic leave visits sufficiently bridged the 8,000 miles from Britain . . .

[L]ooking back over the colony's history it is sad to see all the opportunities that have been lost to it. From the beginning, and throughout most of the last century, the cause can be seen in the lack of interest by successive British Governments in maintaining the place as very much more than a strategic foothold in the South Atlantic, across the Cape Horn route . . . More people, more investment and more resource development would have made a power of difference, both politically and economically. The Islands are still fairly prosperous; they could be more so, were it not for the now stultifying effect of the Argentine claim . . .

[The] greater part of a Governor's time is taken up by the day-to-day maintenance of the community's services . . . it is a necessary part of the job also to devote time to the planning of the further improvement of those services, alongside long term schemes for urban and rural development – just as if the place had the longest of all futures. And then the cold thought comes: that all this work and planning could be set at naught because of the need to meet the emotional and nationalistic demands of a country, Argentina, 400 miles away across the sea, which should have more to concern itself in the social, economic and political problems that face it inside its own frontiers. Is it then wrong to hold out the illusion of hope to the Islanders?

This brings us to the blunt question. If an irksome dispute with a country we may not much care about, but which has no scruples about its behaviour, can be ended, should we allow less than 2,000 Islanders to prevent it, just so that they can continue in their happy way of life without any change in their status? What, as one senior Argentine diplomatic official, perhaps not uncharacteristically, put it to a visiting journalist, do 2,000 people matter anyway?

It ought to be possible to answer that by asking why should not these people matter, and why should they not be allowed to go on living in a way which does no harm to anyone. The stark answer to that one seems to be that, leaving aside a flurry of emotion over an alleged historic wrong, the Argentines are determined to strengthen their position in the South Atlantic, and thence in the Antarctic, by totally usurping ours, which we have not seemed too concerned to maintain.

I cannot see any way of disinterestedly reconciling the wishes of the Islanders with the demands of the Argentines ... It might clarify thinking considerably if Britain were to drop her attitude of apparent detachment, assess her advantages and interests, and openly meet the Argentines on the same terms in the dispute as they have chosen for themselves ...

What are our interests in the region, apart from that of just protecting the Islanders? We know there are substantial marine resources ... There may also be oil and other seabed minerals, as well as those possibly under the ice. It is all wildly speculative at present, and it may take many many years for the right technology to be developed to reap what harvest there is. But other eyes are now fixed on those prospects, and no country is going to give up its position in the Antarctic and adjacent areas while those prospects remain. Except, it sometimes seems, Britain, which history has given the best of all bases; just because it is an 'uninhabited rock' we have even looked like loosening our grip on South Georgia, where we have an unassailable and vital position. One cannot imagine the French, for example, doing the same; they are clearly going to stick to their similar vantage point at Kerguelen, come what may.

In time, if things go badly for the Islanders in the negotiations, the Falkland Islands could also become a collection of uninhabited rocks, the Islanders having left, and few Argentines wishing to come in. That would be to no-one's gain. It would indeed be a tragic loss if this unique little democratic showpiece of a community, with all the history that lies behind it, were to vanish from the earth just because of national ambition on the one side and on the other because policy, or so I think, got off on the wrong foot several years ago. But although I began this despatch on a note of pessimism, I will end it optimistically; I am hopeful a solution can be found, and the Falklands will survive . . .

I am sending a copy of this Despatch to HM Representative at Buenos Aires.

I am

Sir

Yours faithfully
J. R. W. Parker

~

Iceland

'It is scarcely an exaggeration to say that Iceland is part of the British Isles'

KENNETH EAST, HM AMBASSADOR TO THE REPUBLIC
OF ICELAND, MARCH 1981

Character, as they say, is destiny. And Kenneth East's observations on the Icelandic character and its opposing tendencies do seem somewhat prophetic.

The Ambassador was struck, for instance, by Iceland's love affair with borrowed money, in its early stages in 1981 as the country's economy transformed away from fish to less tangible goods. This ill-starred romance was to hit the rocks finally in the 2008 financial crisis, with the collapse of Iceland's banks, brought down by their unfeasibly large foreign debts, and eventually of its entire economy which had to be rescued by the IMF.

East was also perceptive in seeing how Icelanders, as 'outliers', were both drawn to and repelled by Europe. The British as good Europeans should try to make the Icelanders 'feel they belong'. The official who received East's despatch in Whitehall, David Gladstone, judged it to be 'a fine example of an ambassador's craft . . . I cannot fault his reasoning or his conclusions.' Gladstone argued Britain should do 'everything in its power' to prevent Iceland – 'effectively part of our own backyard' – from 'drifting away . . . into the American embrace'. Iceland's response to this dilemma, a policy of mid-Atlantic neutrality, was another characteristically stubborn trait that did not survive the 2008 financial crisis. In 2009, Iceland decided it could no longer risk plucky isolation and, setting its face firmly east, applied to become a member of the European Union.

Character analysis aside, East's main occupation in Reykjavik was mending fences. When he arrived in 1975 Britain and Iceland were waging low-level naval warfare against one another in the climactic round of an ugly fisheries dispute which became known as the Cod Wars. The catch that Iceland relied on for most of its foreign currency earnings was increasingly finding its way into the nets of foreign trawlers. Iceland's response was to declare an Exclusive

Economic Zone beyond its territorial waters in which British ships were forbidden to fish. The gradual and seemingly arbitrary extension over the years of the zone's perimeter led to a series of clashes, with shots fired, nets cut and ships rammed. In 1976 Britain finally backed down and agreed to abide by the 200-mile limit. It is surely no accident, therefore, that when Kenneth East was in need of a rhetorical device to capture the bumpy history of British–Icelandic relations in his final despatch he should alight on the topography of the seabed.

'Mr East has done an exceptionally good job of repairing broken relations,' minuted Gladstone. 'He will be a hard Ambassador to follow.'

CONFIDENTIAL

WRC 014/3 DS(L) 1701

Departmental Series
Western European Department
DS No. 12/81

<u>VALEDICTORY DESPATCH</u>

(Her Majesty's Ambassador at Reykjavik to the Secretary of State for Foreign and Commonwealth Affairs)

Reykjavik,
12 March 1981

My Lord

Six years is a long sojourn in a mini-post and carries a high risk of 'clientitis' – that blurring of the vision in which one's hosts are increasingly seen at their own valuation. Perhaps that is why the theme of this report is that Iceland, its people, and our relations with them, matter, even though we have no hope of returning to fish their waters. The Country Assessment Sheet which I inherited (before the final Cod War) placed defence above fisheries as our primary interest, and everything that has happened since has magnified its importance and the consequent need to cultivate the keepers of this strategic portal.

The Icelandic character is not always admired in Whitehall. Colleagues from Ministries concerned with the sharing of natural resources – fish, air traffic, ocean bed – usually regard Icelanders as greedy, obstinate and shameless in asking for special favoured treatment. This impression is less than fair, but understandable. Having survived against all the odds, Icelanders regard themselves as a chosen people. But they are not organised in a way that facilitates negotiation. With no military experience in their history, they have never had to develop chains of command. Disputatious Parliamentary and legal traditions go back to the founding of the nation, but the executive branch is younger and less certain. Everyone tends to function as an individual, and to be wary of being committed, especially on paper. To procure internal agreement within coalitions is often delicate and time-consuming, and when it comes to projecting it outwards so that it can interact with the position of another state, finding compromises and adjustments, the difficulty is squared. Like Roman Legionaries, Icelandic delegates would rather confront the enemy than their own headquarters, and stone-wall or evade until the other side gives way. It took a hundred years of barnacle tactics to wear out the Danes and thirty years to get us off the fishing banks.

Before the age of the steam trawlers, Icelanders were (and still are to a certain extent) a nation of sheep farmers. Nowadays, the service sector absorbs twice as many workers as fishing and agriculture put together and most Icelanders are owner/occupiers of cosy urban dwellings. The present generation has experienced a social revolution, but traditions are strong (there are even stories of people breaking the law by keeping sheep in the basements of Reykjavik houses because they could not contemplate life without them). Attitudes of the peasant subsisting in marginally habitable conditions virtually outside any cash economy are mixed up with those of the inflation-happy flat dweller raising a bank loan to buy a package holiday on the Costa-del-Sol. Visitors to Iceland at the time of our fisheries dispute alternated between sympathising with the Icelanders because fishing was all they had, and being scandalised by their spending.

Below this ferment, Iceland is endowed with protein and natural energy, an educated homogeneous population, a strategic location and plenty of empty space. Barring natural disasters, to which it is prone, it is a good risk. So much the better for us, because it is scarcely an exaggeration to say that Iceland is part of the British Isles. Old-fashioned maps were content to show the sea as blue and inhabited by monsters. But if, as we increasingly should, we use maps which range from white shallows to azure depths, we see that in an age where the use of submersibles will become routine, the way through the Shetlands and the Faroes to Iceland and Greenland is little more than a bicycle ride. It is a mere series of historical accidents that dealt out the various parcels of land to different monarchs. As the British Museum's Viking Exhibition brought home, it was formerly just one trading/raiding settlement area. Iceland happens to be that link of the chain we inhabit which joins us to North America.

Icelanders would not, of course, care to be claimed as part of us, any more than do the Irish. They are a nation with a very distinct personality, and their pride is in inverse ratio to their numbers. But geographical facts remain while technology changes and our priorities should reflect both. It is important to have healthy, well-behaved neighbours, especially if they are relatives and you live in a terrace.

Without scaring the Icelanders into isolation (bearing in mind that their independence is as newly won as 1944 and that they were brought up in the faith of neutralism) the problem is one of making them feel they belong in the right company and that their security and economic needs could not be better met elsewhere. The fulfilment of these needs has moved Iceland westwards, first from dependence on Denmark to dependence on Britain (Himmler's agent sent to gather the 'Saga Island' into the Nazi fold was disgusted to find it for practical purposes a British Colony) and then to strategic dependence on the United States when Britain alone provided insufficient refuge and strength. At the fringes were advocates of joining the British Empire and others of becoming an Atlantic Hawaii. But mainstream opinion through four decades, while accepting United States strategic dominance as unavoidable . . . has sought a point of balance. This involves close links with Britain and the Nordics, the widest attainable diversity of markets, and the pursuit of independence within the structures of NATO and EFTA-EC. We must hope these structures will continue to satisfy Iceland's needs, though we may speculate whether the whole chain of Faroes, Iceland and Greenland will see itself and be seen as remaining an outlier of Europe or whether the gravitational pull of North America will ultimately prove to be irresistible.

~

Sweden

'The leisured, antiseptic society'

SIR JEFFREY PETERSEN, HM AMBASSADOR TO THE
KINGDOM OF SWEDEN, JULY 1980

Petersen gave over his final despatch, written on his retirement from the Diplomatic Service after thirty-two years' service, to an analysis of the Swedish welfare system.

With a new Conservative government in power in Britain, the file shows that Petersen's critique of the 'Swedish model' was well received in Whitehall. 'This is a subject of interest to us in the UK as pioneers of the Welfare State,' wrote Peter Vereker in the Western European Department. 'The picture Sir Jeffrey paints as to where the Swedish experiment is leading them is an unattractive one . . .

'The leisured, antiseptic society which the Despatch described clearly has many undesirable characteristics,' Vereker went on. 'Perhaps there are advantages, for those of us who have not yet achieved Swedish levels of income, leisure and elimination of unemployment, in being rather further away from Utopia.'

Sweden, once the cynosure of the social engineers now has social as well as economic problems. Apologists for the 'Swedish model' are inclined to attribute the former to the difficult economic climate of the past decade. But acute though the effects on Sweden of the oil crisis and the difficult external trading environment have been, I believe that deeper and more permanent influences have been at work in the sphere of social development and that these are likely to prove historically more significant. We are seeing now the effects on two generations of Swedish society of the world's first outwardly harmonious and successful attempt at using democratic procedures to graft a system of socialist welfare policies into a highly evolved, essentially capitalist economy. Although there is room for much argument about the nature of the phenomena and the causal chains which have led to them, I believe that there is now enough evidence to justify concern at some of those effects.

I must first re-affirm the view, expressed in my 'first impressions' that there is an immense amount to admire in what has been achieved. If real trouble befalls a Swede it would be difficult, nowadays, to blame this on official indifference or material deprivation of any kind. In sickness and unemployment, in bereavement and other uninvited, as well as much self-inflicted, misfortune recourse to money to alleviate hardship and to services designed to repair personal and domestic damage is available to all . . . Wages and holidays are generous and secure. Health services are efficient, if impersonal, and sickness benefits cover absence from work from the first day. Great efforts have been made to improve working conditions . . . The old are very generously provided for. I am tempted, not for the first time, to quote Miss Katharine Whitehorn's[1] observation that the trouble with countries like Sweden is that once you have put all the sensible social ideas into practice you are left with only the silly ones. The social debate during my time here, lacking more urgent topics, has often come perilously close to the latter; for example the proposal to pay mothers an hourly rate for looking after their own children. Even in 1980, therefore, to have been born in Sweden is (to borrow a phrase from, I believe, Cecil Rhodes) to have drawn first prize in the lottery of life. And yet . . .

Absenteeism from work, not counting the recent strikes, is currently running on average at well over 20 per cent. Among schoolchildren the level of scholastic achievement is falling and consumption of alcohol has reached epidemic proportions. The teachers' trade unions have defended the decision of their members at a few badly affected schools to absent themselves on certain working days when it is known, because of a conjuncture of holidays or particular celebrations, that a proportion of their pupils will appear in class unmanageably drunk. Teachers report that an increasing number of children have little meaningful contact with their parents and that many are left to their own devices even at weekends. The new high-rise housing complexes round the large cities, many of them built during the affluent days of the 'sixties, have become the major centres of crime. Both tax avoidance and tax evasion are major industries.

Already in 1976, shortly before they lost power, the Social Democrat party had held a conference to go into the question of why, with all the advances of the past 20 years, it was a matter of common observation that most Swedes grumbled and complained more, not less, than an earlier and less fortunate generation. The basic reason is, I suppose, that human beings lacking grave or urgent problems to occupy their thoughts are that way inclined. To quote Miss Whitehorn again, '. . . never mind whether affluence brings happiness: the prospect of affluence always does'. By world standards Swedes are already decidedly affluent and it is hard to see how in general they could become more so. Many of them see nowhere else to go. Harder work, more responsibility, can only bring higher taxes and few compensating benefits. Lacking the stimulus of a rewarding climb ahead many Swedes resort to the common outlets of grumbling, gambling and drink.

1. *Katharine Whitehorn*: British journalist, who wrote a column at the *Observer* for nearly forty years (1960–96).

~

Norway

'Not even the sun penetrates in winter let alone the outside world'

SIR ARCHIE LAMB, HM AMBASSADOR TO THE KINGDOM OF NORWAY, DECEMBER 1980

Lamb's final despatch before retiring after forty-two years in the Diplomatic Service was warmly received in Whitehall as 'an excellent example of the genre'. David Gladstone, head of the Western European Department at the Foreign Office, wrote of Lamb: 'He has plainly found the Norwegians an unsympathetic people to deal with, insular and borné.'

Norwegian diplomacy towards the US Government ... has been inept ... Defence Minister Stoltenberg's visit to Washington in June marked a new low in the US Government's sympathy for the Government of Norway, the latter's wetness having exasperated Washington. The Norwegian Government cobbled together in September a deal ... for stockpiling heavy equipment for a US Marine Force in Trøndelag in mid Norway, 300 miles south of where it was expected to be and 600 miles from the frontier with the Soviet Union. This must be seen as a small but significant triumph for Soviet diplomacy ... Their success was signalled in an article by State Secretary Hoist of the Ministry of Foreign Affairs published by the Norwegian Atlantic Committee: 'Norway has emphasised that the size and location of any allied prepositioning in Norway will be limited so as not to constitute any real threat to neighbouring countries.' So, in Mr Hoist's Norwegian book, you demand your allies' full support but restrict their ability to give it ... 'All for Norway' is the Royal motto of The King of Norway: it sums up the Norwegian interpretation of the North Atlantic Alliance ...

[T]he average Norwegian politician is essentially a person of narrow horizons. He (and she) come from and represent small constituencies, often tiny communities in fjords and valleys where not even the sun penetrates in winter let alone the outside world. There are few Norwegian politicians with whom one can enjoy a satisfactory discussion of The World Today. They still represent and personify 'Little Norway' and are resistant to persuasion ...

$\sim$

Ivory Coast

'The shadow is so often, deliberately, taken for the substance'

THOMAS SHAW, HM AMBASSADOR TO THE
REPUBLIC OF CÔTE D'IVOIRE, FEBRUARY 1967

In a file at the National Archives, Shaw's valedictory is tagged together with a handwritten note from a senior clerk, commenting that it was 'an interesting, if somewhat jaded despatch'. His Excellency plainly did not like Ouagadougou.

I have wondered from time to time whether the British interests we try to serve really have any need of us. Only seven years ago there was not even a British Honorary Consular presence in the Ivory Coast, Upper Volta or Niger . . . One could of course let Parkinson's Laws have their head and generate activity for activity's sake. But it seems more sensible to accept that the raison d'etre of an Embassy such as this is an act of limited but respectable presence. And at least here we perform the act in three countries . . .

Apart from anything else I have had frequent personal cause in the last three years to bless the system of multiple representation. Many African capitals offer little compensation for what may be the limitations and frustrations of diplomatic work there. Change of scene, climate and environment are a valuable safeguard against parochial distortions of all kinds. The moist miasmal monochrome of the lagoon country can be exchanged for the dust and blue skies of the Sahel; the cheerful openness and fecklessness of the northern peoples, touched by the dignity and discipline of Islam and the need to work, are a useful antidote to the stay-at-home, indolent, reserved complacency of the urban Ivoirien; a few days in Ouagadougou enable one to appreciate the real economic achievement of President Houphouet's[1] regime in the Ivory Coast, and the orderly well laid-out cleanliness, even the brash and glossy modernity of Abidjan, with its new office buildings and its pink and white villas proliferating among the palm trees like so many exports from the world of Jacques Tati's 'Mon Oncle'.[2] The fate of a Head of Mission confined to Ouagadougou is not enviable, and a system which permits it scarcely humane.

I would not go so far as one of my diplomatic colleagues who observed on leaving Abidjan 'at least I have learned how little there is to learn', but I cannot say that three years' observation of what has gone on in the Ivory Coast, Upper Volta and Niger leads easily to conclusions, still less to prognostications.

There is a story long current here of a scorpion who came to a river which he urgently needed to cross. But he found no means of doing so until he met a crocodile whom he begged for a lift across. Before agreeing, the crocodile wanted an assurance that the scorpion would not sting him in midstream. 'But if I did' replied the scorpion, 'you would die and I should be drowned; of course I won't.' Half way across the river the scorpion did in fact sting the crocodile, who, as he died, cried 'Why, why did you do it?' 'C'est l'Afrique' replied the scorpion. And together they sank to the bottom of the river . . .

I left tropical Africa once before after 3½ years with few regrets. I cannot claim to feel many more now. A couple of years ago I was sitting alone in the bar of the hotel in one of my four capitals[3] finishing the last bottle they possessed of a well-known brand of stout. I watched the African barman take down a vase of flowers from a bracket on the wall, carefully renew the water and put the vase back in its place. The flowers were artificial. After three years it is I think time to leave a part of the world where the shadow is so often, deliberately, taken for the substance.

I have, &c.
T. R. SHAW.

1. *President Houphouet*: See note 2, p. 221.
2. *'Mon Oncle'*: Jacques Tati's 1958 film poked fun at the questionable French modern architecture of its time.
3. *four capitals*: As well as Abidjan (Ivory Coast), Ouagadougou (Upper Volta) and Niamey (Niger), for his first two years in West Africa Shaw also had to represent HMG in Abomey, the capital of Dahomey. In 1965 Dahomey broke off relations with the UK, making Shaw's job slightly easier. Dahomey is today known as Benin, and Upper Volta as Burkina Faso.

~

Cambodia

'More of a retinal sensation than a coherent picture'

SIR LESLIE FIELDING, HM CHARGÉ D'AFFAIRES IN
PHNOM PENH, SEPTEMBER 1966

Another example of how a well-penned despatch can be the making of a diplomatic career.

In 1964 an angry mob torched the British and American embassies in Phnom Penh. Once the women and children were evacuated, Leslie Fielding was flown in to take charge. Heroic, perhaps. Or perhaps not; Sir Leslie himself believes he was picked for the post as 'an expendable fall guy'. Either way, given the circumstances, Fielding could count on there being at least a small group of interested – not to say concerned – readers in Whitehall of the reports he was to send from Cambodia over the next two years.

Nevertheless, as Fielding scribbled off the customary valedictory despatch before packing his bags in 1966, it was hardly to be expected that a routine report from a young and very junior diplomat would have gone very far up the Whitehall tree. And yet, on obtaining his personnel file recently from the Foreign Office via a Freedom of Information Request, Fielding was amazed to discover that his 1966 despatch had in fact reached the desk of the Prime Minister.

Harold Wilson was impressed. The file contained a memo sent back to the Foreign Office relaying his verdict: 'First class – it tells me more than a hundred telegrams. Where is this chap going now?'

The Foreign Secretary's office took the hint. 'Fielding is being posted to Paris as one of the two First Secretaries in Chancery,' they replied to Number 10. 'As you know, this is a job on the way to stardom.' (True enough; Fielding ended up in Brussels, as Director General of the European Commission's Diplomatic Service.)

History, of course, was not to be so kind to Cambodia. Neither was Prince Sihanouk's rule to continue unchallenged, as Fielding expected. Just four years after Fielding's despatch the Prince was deposed by his parliament while on a foreign trip. He was briefly restored as titular Head of State by the Khmer Rouge in the mid-1970s, but ended up a prisoner of the regime, and fled into exile in China and North Korea, as Cambodia descended into genocide. Sihanouk was eventually reinstated as King in 1993 and abdicated peacefully in 2004. Fielding's instinct – that the King was a survivor – proved sound. And, give or take a date or two, the hope he expresses when signing off, that he would still be alive when this despatch entered the public domain, has been fulfilled.

In retirement Fielding has once more taken up the pen, using his time in Cambodia as the inspiration for a film script. His most recent work in non-fiction is a serious look at some big international issues and the tools diplomats use to tackle them (Mentioned in Despatches – Phnom Penh, Paris, Tokyo, Brussels: Is Diplomacy Dead? *(Boermans Books, 2012)*).

DU 1015/21   *Foreign Office and Whitehall Distribution*

CAMBODIA
23 September, 1966
Section 1

CAMBODIA: SOME FAREWELL IMPRESSIONS

Mr. Fielding to Mr. Brown. (Received 23 September)

(No. 23. CONFIDENTIAL)   *Phnom Penh,*
20 September, 1966.

Sir,

When I was invited at less than two weeks' notice to proceed to Phnom Penh in order to assume temporary charge
of a sacked Embassy, no one foresaw that circumstances
would require me to conduct the Mission for nearly two
and a half years. For this reason, I did not trouble your
third predecessor with my first impressions of Cambodia.
As some aspects of this country have always remained a
mystery to me, the valedictory despatch which I now have
the honour to compose must still be considered more of a
retinal sensation than a coherent picture.

As long as he remains Head of State, the Kingdom of
Cambodia is Prince Norodom Sihanouk. He is at once the
most attractive and most infuriating of Asian leaders.
Attractive, because his profound concern for his people,

his dynamism and sheer native wit make him a national leader of international standing. Infuriating, because of his extreme sensitivity to criticism, his resistance to well-meaning advice, the unpredictability of his day-to-day conduct of affairs and the urchin-like quality which prompts him to hand out mockery and abuse on all sides.

Fortunately, the Prince has visibly slowed down over the past two years. The intractable problems with which he is faced, the various reverses with which (perhaps for the first time in his life) he has been confronted, and the growth of criticism at home, all have left him a quieter and (hopefully) a wiser man. Some say he is becoming a burnt-out case. But my astrological faculties assure me that the Mandate of Heaven has not yet been withdrawn from the God-King.

Norodom Sihanouk is likely to control the destiny of the Kingdom for as far ahead as we can see ... [T]here remains no individual rallying point for dissent, no common courage or conviction among the critics and no sign of a possible move towards change. Sihanouk's skill in handling his people gives daily proof that he is still the one man who can control the factions and unite the nation.

I have found that nation by and large a likeable lot. There is a strong mixture of Chinese blood, and more than a tincture of Siamese, in the veins of the upper class, whose lively but mixed-up members tend to be a little humourless and complexed. But the underlying hysteria of the Chinese races is alien to the easy-going, dark-skinned Khmer. They are a more primitive and occluded people than their neighbours and one sometimes has the frustrated impression of dealing with a pack of amiable simians (just as they privately think of us as long-nosed wonders from outer space). But their ethnocentricity, pride and deep Buddhist persuasions are the roots from which Sihanouk's own policies of nationalism and neutrality draw their strength. Their country is a natural buffer-State on the long cultural and political frontier between the Indian and Chinese civilisations, between East and West in South-East Asia.

But Phnom Penh shivers to the shock of all kinds of conflicting ideologies and interests. Overshadowed by the Viet-Namese conflict, Cambodia is a field in which it is prudent that a modest British diplomatic effort should be deployed. We were wise not to break off relations after the Embassy was attacked by the mob in March 1964, and it has been worth it to have slogged on through the mud towards at least the illusion of green fields beyond. There is no inherent hostility towards the West and certainly none to the British in this country. Sihanouk's tantrums are of a feminine nature; they can be soothed with manliness and a well-timed box of chocolates. It is perhaps less awkward for London than for Peking that Monseigneur should be a capricious mistress who will not be bought for money or ever be taken the slightest bit for granted.

In retrospect, and on the human plane, the fare has been rich. Loyal allies (not least the Australians) and a small but enthusiastic staff; international intrigue; an exotic court complete with a ballerina princess in the limelight and the old narrow-eyed Rasputin in the gilded shadows; the varying beauties of tropical nature, from the dark tiger-jungle to the white-sanded sea; the brooding solemnity of the Angkor temples and the fun-loving company of their modern Deva-Raja,[1] Norodom Sihanouk. These have left me with no dull moments and few sad ones; I shall be sorry to step back through the looking glass into normality. It is all worth several books, but the Official Secrets Act and the chastity of diplomatic intercourse would prevent their publication.

There remains a handful of grey despatches printed in the Indo-China volume. To be circulated to officialdom around 1972, this *magnum opus* will eventually be released to an eager public on what I calculate may be my 80th birthday. I hope that I shall still then in some sense enjoy the honour of being, as to-day, your obedient servant.

I have, &c.
LESLIE FIELDING
(Chargé d'Affaires).

1. *Deva-Raja*: King of the Gods. This deity supposedly protected the Khmer Empire, which ruled South-East Asia in the Middle Ages from its capital, the temple city of Angkor.

~

Vietnam

'Some pigs more equal than others'

BARONESS PARK, HM CONSUL-GENERAL
AT HANOI, OCTOBER 1970

Despatches from Vietnam rarely disappoint. Daphne Park's valedictory from Hanoi is no exception, giving a vivid account of the difficulties Western diplomats experienced living and working 'in Limbo'. As the representative of a country – Britain – which did not recognize North Vietnam's claim to statehood, Park was granted only the most basic privileges in Hanoi.

The Consul-General's empathy for the plight of the ordinary Vietnamese also leaps from the page. But Park's own story is actually the most interesting of all. She was a spy.

Daphne Park spent thirty years in MI6, ending up as Controller of intelligence operations for the Western Hemisphere, which meant North America, South America and Canada. While in Hanoi she ran agents as a senior controller for the intelligence service, cultivating contacts over bottles of brandy at 6.00 a.m., and would fly with her top-secret reports out of the country in a light aircraft so as to evade surveillance. But Park's most successful field of operations was Africa. In the 1960s she combined her spying with postings to the Congo – where she narrowly escaped execution by firing squad – and, as High Commissioner, to Zambia.

Baroness Park died in 2010. She used her formidable reputation in Africa to good effect: according to her obituary in The Times Park was held in such awe by leaders across the continent that she could gain access to them whenever she wished.

In her undercover work she used the opposite tactic. In the Congo, Park smuggled Lumumba's private secretary, a would-be defector, out of the country in the boot of a Citroën 2CV. Her explanation was simple: 'Nobody ever takes 2CVs seriously.'

FOREIGN AND COMMONWEALTH OFFICE
DIPLOMATIC REPORT NO. 525/70

FAV 1/24 *General Distribution*

NORTH VIETNAM
25 October, 1970

HER MAJESTY'S REPRESENTATIVE IN LIMBO: A VALEDICTORY

The British Consul-General in North Viet-Nam to the Secretary of State for Foreign and Commonwealth Affairs

(CONFIDENTIAL) *Hanoi,*
25 October, 1970.

Sir,

The Residence was formerly a house of ill-fame. Handkerchiefs are boiled in the saucepans, other dirty clothes in the dustbin. When the household cat disappeared, opinion was divided whether she had been eaten by the neighbours or the rats. When even more water than usual flooded the bathroom floor, and even less (though more noisome) water came from the tap, and the plumbers eventually came, they withdrew for three days to attend cadre meetings before removing the dead rats they found in the pipes. No rodent extermination service exists because, officially, rats have been eliminated. Unfortunately the rats do not know this. When Ambassadors come to dinner and it rains, the drawing-room floor is covered with buckets and saucepans to catch the water from the ceiling. The major-domo at the Residence has been at some earlier time an inmate of a mental institution; the misfortune is that he was ever released. Nearly every necessity of life must be imported, though only upon receipt, after some months, of import permits listing each jar of herbs, each bundle of toothpicks. The Director of Customs has sometimes refused a permit, or proposed to allow in only part of the order, on the ground that Her Majesty's Representative 'has had enough this year' and does not need it. The presents most prized by local staff, when they dare to accept them, are razor blades, bicycle repair outfits, bottles (empty) and Aspro. Locally produced records of 'people's song and dance', bought in the State shop, are confiscated by the Customs on departure unless their export has been approved by the Cultural Commission.

The small but fortunate number of those who have served here will find no difficulty in guessing that this despatch comes from Hanoi. They too have been Non-Persons, issuing visas on affidavits, and yearly Queen's Birthday invitations to Viet-Namese, who do not come, on cards without crests. They have received warnings not to enter forbidden areas, but no map defining them. Out of tender Viet-Namese regard for their lives and health they have yearly been refused a bicycle, as well as being denied access to the swimming pool, the International Club, the diplomatic shop, and, for nine years, permission to travel outside the city. But like me, most of them have wanted to come here and have left with some regret – though never quite enough to ask for another year. The very great political interest of the post is still not enough to account for its fascination; I have tried therefore in this valedictory despatch to define the peculiar flavour of Hanoi, and to communicate what it is possible to learn about the North Viet-Namese from the sheer physical fact of living here.

The disagreeable and restrictive features of life in North Viet-Nam which I have cited are no more than incidental, though they wear away time, temper and sometimes health. The real hardship lies in the fact that, surrounded by Viet-Namese, we can know none of them. It is in part our non-recognition of North Viet-Nam which creates this special vacuum round us, and it is a wise policy which limits our tour here to a year: it might be difficult to report objectively for longer. Yet even if the end of the war should bring about the establishment of diplomatic relations and hence the relaxation of the present restrictions upon us, isolation from the Viet-Namese will continue, I believe, to be the rule. The unconsciously arrogant reserve which the Viet-Namese display at home, even towards their friends, will be increasingly reinforced by the defensive security processes of a Communist society. The shooting war over, the ideological war will go on, and there are few grounds for believing that Communism has been a temporary expedient here and that the rulers of North Viet-Nam are merely waiting to slough their Communist skin and appear in fresh and uncommitted nationalist colours. It may be a long time before this snake changes skins again.

The diplomatic heaven

Very few weeks pass in Hanoi without a national day, an army day, or a day to commemorate some Socialistic event. On those days, at 7 p.m. precisely, the long line of official cars disgorges diplomats and cadres at the International

Club. Between March and October, when the temperature in the shade may stand at 110 degrees, and the humidity at an unvarying 98 per cent, shirtsleeves are worn, and like unhappy overheated penguins a long way from water, the Socialist Ambassadors line up at the top table on the right of the host and the Dean,[1] flapping their paper fans: on the left stand the Viet-Namese. The arc lights burn, the mosquitoes whine, as the speeches are made – in Viet-Namese with no translation, in Bulgarian, or Polish, or Russian, with Viet-Namese translation only – and the diplomats cautiously clap, with one eye on the Dean. Toasts are offered and a curious Nuts in May ceremony is observed; first the diplomats file past the Viet-Namese, clinking glasses, then the Viet-Namese return the compliment. After that both parties eat, wise diplomats confining themselves to the soup and the bread, the rest laying up worms and worse; the tables groan with dishes full of what at best may be sliced dog, of pork rolls, and mudfish from the paddies, and bright yellow icecream. These rituals last two or three hours. Throughout, the Viet-Namese stay on the left, the diplomats on the right of the hall; and crossing over is not encouraged. These occasions represent, in microcosm, the co-existence without contact which is diplomatic life in Hanoi.

The Socialist diplomats, at first merely baffled by the bland unpenetrability of the Viet-Namese, soon find it hard to conceal resentment at being taken for granted. Like the large, damp, crumbling crates of machinery from Eastern Europe which lie month after month in marshalling yards or at the roadside, they stand about in bulky awkward groups, and the whole colonial effect is absurdly enhanced by the pith helmets still favoured by so many

Viet-Namese. The Soviet Ambassador, guttering in the heat like tallow, mutters to the Mongolian: 'Ah, how wonderful it would be to be cold, and see snow.' Inward-looking, the 'Socialists' are more alien from the Viet-Namese than the most ruthless 'imperialist' could be, and without the common denominator of Marxist jargon, as well as aims, it seems doubtful whether there could be much communication between them ... Socialist diplomats in Hanoi complain often and with justice that they see less of the country than visiting delegations: they are unable to meet even the Viet-Namese who have been trained for years in their universities and have learnt their languages, and meet Ministers chiefly when the Viet-Namese want something ...

The Viet-Namese hell?

North Viet-Nam, like any Communist country, is run by the Politburo, and the most powerful members of this small body, all now in or approaching their sixties, may be seen, and sometimes heard, at receptions. Their speeches become basic texts for study by the cadres, industrious but individually expendable worker bees, unlikely to be queens, who, like their leaders, stand in ritual shirtsleeves on the left at each reception. Outside the hall, the Viet-Namese live in a different world. Diplomats and foreigners, driving to and from receptions, cease very soon to see them except as cyclists bent on suicide. Living in Limbo, we are nearer to them, for we walk far more, and especially at night when the children who in daylight pursue us shrieking Lien Xo (Russian), and leave us black and blue with inquisitive pinches, are gathered round the family brazier on the pavement, eating their rice, or are already asleep. Young and old, like battered bundles, sleep in the hottest months on the steps of the Ministry of Foreign Trade, on the pavement, in doorways, anywhere out of the stifling courtyards and the houses where they live, a family to each room. The rats run over them as they sleep, fight over scraps of garbage, and sometimes drown, in the water which gathers in the open concrete shelter-holes; and at flood time when the drains overflow and the streets for a while are two or three feet deep in rushing water, they swim along in the brown muddy flood with leaves, twigs and rubbish. There are rats even in the cinema.

Yet the squalor, the filth and the evident poverty are dominated by the intense vitality of the people and their capacity for survival. It looks out of the wizened faces of the old women, yoked to carts piled with coaldust, or balancing baskets on their shoulders, and those others who sit at the pavement edge selling sunflower seeds and nuts, strings of live crabs, a chili or two, slices of watermelon or sections of grapefruit or, further up the scale, stock a bootlace or two, thread, some cheap celluloid goods, envelopes, paper fans, paper knives made from crashed United States aircraft and nit-combs. The families camped all night at the bus and railway stations, drinking green tea or soup, may wait there for days. They are patient, but not torpid; and they do not beg. The children seem tireless, whether they are playing hopscotch, football with an old clog for goalpost, flying kites or spinning tops made from turnips. Boys hang round the one-man bicycle repair stands which in Viet-Nam take the place of garages; the more enterprising earn a little money pumping tyres with the family bicycle pump. The girls collect twigs and dry leaves and grass to take home for fuel. The babies ride in neat wicker chairs strapped to the carriers of their mothers' bicycles, often almost extinguished under a large straw hat . . .

Two nations – the cadres and the rest – co-exist in North Viet-Nam. In the State shop one counter sells precious bicycle spares to cadres at specially low prices, and supplies never run out. Another counter sells the same range to the public who do not hold cadre ration cards: charges are higher, the goods are often not available . . . To the Viet-Namese the concept of some pigs more equal than others is not new . . .

Only a very strong and enduring people could survive, and with such pride and energy, the unremitting struggle that must be needed merely to stay alive in North Viet-Nam. It is almost impossible to imagine how it is done, on an average wage, with allowances, of 70 Dong a month to feed a family of four, on a staple diet of rice and farinaceous food, supplemented by minute quantities of sugar, meat and fat. Yet the miracle of self-respect and survival is performed every day. The houses belonging to the collective masters, are crusted with grime, but each window has its hanging garden, carefully tended, and on holidays shirts are white, and the children have firecrackers. On days of socialist labour or of emulation, when the whole population turns out to mend the dykes or carry earth for roadworks, the people are gay: they probably find such events a great deal less boring than the solemn and drab little street meetings conducted by the cadres on most evenings. Though it would be difficult to think of a place more totally devoid of diversion and amusement for the population than Hanoi, young teachers and medical assistants are constantly working their way back to the city from the horrors of village life, even in the Delta, with cries of nostalgia for the lights of Town . . .

Conclusion

When I arrived here 13 months ago buffaloes grazed on the grass in front of the Consulate-General, the factory defence militia practised unarmed combat and grenade throwing there, an occasional battered *cyclo-pousse*[2] creaked past carrying a family and its chattels, and at night the bats swooped and the cicada were noisy. None of this has changed. But the sentry outside the Algerian Embassy has planted a garden round his sentrybox, Hanoi is full of new lorries, the shape of Ho Chi Minh's mausoleum is under debate, and the State Plan for 1970 has allowed the Residence roof to be mended; my successor will not need to catch the drips in the drawing room. A new kitten appeared at the Residence this month, and may one day kill rats if it survives. We have moved a few steps out of Limbo for we have been allowed to travel, and perhaps even hell is a little less hot than before. The children are back from the country and Hanoi is a year further from the war. I do not yet know, and neither do the Viet-Namese, whether that means they are a year nearer to peace.

I am sending a copy of this despatch to Her Majesty's Representatives in Saigon, Washington, Paris, Moscow, Vientiane, Phnom Penh, Bangkok, Peking, Tokyo, Canberra, Wellington and Ottawa and to the Political Adviser to the Commander-in-Chief at Singapore.

I have, etc.,
DAPHNE PARK.

1. *Dean*: All of the foreign diplomats gathered in a particular country together make up the Diplomatic Corps. So as to avoid unseemly arguments about who is the most important, ambassadors place great

stock in precedence. The post of Dean therefore falls usually to the longest-serving ambassador in that capital, from whichever country – except in some Catholic countries, where the position goes to the Papal Nuncio, representing the Vatican. The Dean speaks for the Corps on formal occasions.

2. *cyclo-pousse*: Bicycle-powered rickshaw.

$$\approx$$

Brazil

'*I am content to be dismissed as a disgruntled maverick*'

KEITH HASKELL, HM AMBASSADOR TO THE
FEDERATIVE REPUBLIC OF BRAZIL, 1999

The KCMG (Knight Commander of the Order of St Michael and St George) is often the gong given to diplomats for long and loyal service to Queen and country, especially if they have served as Head of Mission to an important country. Eighteen of Keith Haskell's nineteen immediate predecessors as Ambassador to Brazil were made Sirs, as was his immediate successor. But Haskell retired in 1999, after thirty-eight years' service, without the customary honour.

Reading his valedictory it is not hard to find possible cause for this omission. The despatch came in two parts, one of which bore the eye-catching title 'WHAT'S WRONG WITH THE DIPLOMATIC SERVICE'. Among the litany of organizational failings Haskell describes are that his bosses in Whitehall lack relevant experience and should have their jobs abolished, that many ambassadorial appointments were blatant stitch-ups, and that the Foreign Office had too many elected ministers who were a burden to serve. Haskell sent his despatch to all diplomatic posts, a readership of several thousand.

Whether merited or not, the long list of charges the ambassador lays at the door of the FCO bureaucracy amply supplies something which government ministers say they value above all in reporting from British diplomats in the field, and that is candour.

INFO ROUTINE HM TREASURY, DTI, DFID, ECGD, BANK OF ENGLAND
INFO ROUTINE WASHINGTON, UKMIS GENEVA, UKREP BRUSSELS

SUBJECT: BRAZIL VALEDICTORY

I leave Brasilia and the Service today, after over 4 years in Brazil . . . It is the fifth largest country in the world, with the fifth largest population, 2700 miles from north to south and the same from east to west. I am proud to be the first British Ambassador (and possibly the first from any country) to visit all its 27 States. Much of my time has necessarily and rightly been spent with leading businessmen in Sao Paulo and Rio. But I have also visited the Yanomami (often described as the world's most primitive people) in the jungles of Roraima. I have swayed to the emotion of a 100,000-strong football crowd in the Maracan Stadium. And dressed in shocking pink tights and a costume bedecked with huge sea-shells and mermaids, I have paraded with a top samba school during the Carnival in Rio. So my experience is broader than that of some less active colleagues, who spend their time immured in this remote and artificial capital.

When I first came to South America in 1975, it did not present an attractive picture. Virtually all its major countries suffered from military dictatorships, closed economies, bloated bureaucracies, corruption and widespread abuses of human rights. The continent was rightly low on the list of priorities for British government and business alike. But there has been a profound change in the ensuing two decades . . . So it is a pity that perceptions in London have often not caught up with reality. Partly this is because so few people have actual experience of South America. We have had some 20 Ministerial visitors, from Governments of both major British parties, since my arrival: to the best of my recollection, every one was a neophyte. More significantly, all were surprised by the size and sophistication of Brazil: especially its southern cities, which resemble Barcelona or Naples far more than the cities of other Third World countries. The Chairmen and Chief Executives of major British companies, when they can be persuaded to forsake their usual haunts, feel likewise. Unfortunately, governmental policy seems often to be driven by officials with no knowledge or understanding of today's Brazil.

Brazil's current President, Fernando Henrique Cardoso, is very good news for Brazil . . . a look at where Brazil stood when he took office on 1 January 1995 will show how much has been achieved in rolling back the boundaries of the state, privatisation, facilitating foreign investment and stabilising the currency . . . Progress would have been even faster were it not for the austerity measures imposed on the country by successive phases of the Asian economic crisis, culminating in the enforced devaluation of the Real last January. Though at that moment the future looked bleak, I was confident that Brazil would weather

the storm and said so. This led Treasury and other com-
mentators in London to criticise this Embassy's reporting
as unsound. It is a matter for some satisfaction that hind-
sight has proved us completely right, and I hope this will
be remembered the next time pundits in London reach an
unjustifiably gloomy assessment of a situation which they
do not properly understand . . .

SUBJECT: VALEDICTORY: WHAT'S WRONG WITH THE DIPLOMATIC SERVICE

When I joined the then Foreign Service in 1961, its members serving overseas were paid only four times a year.
Those working in London had their offices heated by open
coal fires. Even quite large posts endured the drudgery of
enciphering and deciphering telegrams with code books
and one-time pads. Ambassadresses whose role models
were the memsahibs of the Raj were at liberty to tyrannise
junior members of the staff and their wives (note: wives,
not spouses: a female officer who married had to resign
from the Service). Close protection teams were unknown,
but the first Embassy in which I served had a cupboard full
of ancient .303 rifles and .45 pistols with which to defend
ourselves against riot and revolution, like our predecessors
in the Legation at Peking during the Boxer Rebellion.

So I am aware of and appreciate the benefits of change.
But in recent years change seems to have been increasingly
in the wrong directions . . .

EXCESSIVE CENTRALISATION AND BUREAUCRACY

The FCO has five full-time Ministers: far more than other
countries of comparable importance find necessary. It is

of course true that British Ministers carry a far greater burden of Parliamentary and constituency duties than their counterparts elsewhere. It is also true that it is helpful to have Ministers who can specialise in certain geographical areas and types of work, (though the advantage is lessened if they have little power to take decisions). But servicing this plethora of Private Offices carries a bureaucratic cost.

On the official side, the picture is the same. The PUS[1] has five Deputies (not counting the Legal Adviser): other Foreign Ministries find it possible to manage with three, for political, economic and administration issues. Except for the occasional self-contained task (such as the creation of British Trade International), for which a temporary appointment could easily be made, the other two DUS[2] posts add little value and could be eliminated, with their functions transferred to Director level.

Reducing the number of DUS posts would also enforce reform of the Board of Management, which to judge by the reports of its deliberations sent to overseas Posts has no clear role to fulfil. It would also enforce changes to the No 1 Board, which recommends appointments to the highest ranked and most desirable Missions. If the Board were to include Ambassadors from one or two European posts (or from further afield on leave) and, even better, some outside members, it would be in less danger of appearing like a self-perpetuating oligarchy. A similar reform would be desirable for the other Boards as well. The further one travels from London, the stronger one finds the suspicion that their decisions tend to be taken on a wink and a nod, and candidates serving overseas are disadvantaged . . .

[T]he bureaucratic load overall has greatly increased.

As Ambassador in Lima, with a total of 9 UK-based staff of whom only 6 were from the DS,[3] I once counted up the number of reports, returns, forms and other pieces of paper which the 9 of us annually had to complete and send back. Including all the paperwork connected with the accounts, and individual items like family certificates and applications for children's journeys, the total was 3700. One bag brought us news that the Annual Personnel Security Certificate had been dispensed with, but that after our monthly consular visit to the 6 British drug-smugglers in jail a single report on their condition was no longer acceptable: we had to report separately on each. Down 1, up 60.

POOR RELATIONS WITH OVERSEAS POSTS

I do not want to return to the days of book cypher or the unlovely and temperamental Noreen. But the speed and capacity of modern communications systems creates a temptation to micro-manage which few Directors or Heads of Department can resist. Heads of Mission are no longer given general guidance on what to say and do and encouraged to use their initiative: they are told in precise detail exactly what to say, when and at what level. This adds to the burden of staff in London, who spend longer and longer hours drafting ever more detailed instructions and lines to take, while leaving those in the field feeling no better than a ventriloquist's dummy. 'You spoke well' was a frequent accolade in the days when an Ambassador had to rely on his own intelligence and understanding: it is rare nowadays because the scope for initiative is rare . . .

I suspect that part of the problem lies in the limited

overseas experience of senior officials in London. The FCO has 6 members of the Board of Management and 13 Directors (excluding non-career staff). Only one of the 19 has ever served in Latin America (a single posting to Havana 30 years ago), and 3 in Africa. But 12 of the 19 have been in Brussels, 5 in Washington and 5 in New York: and 9 of them (almost 50 percent) have spent more time in London than overseas. Properly to understand the difficulties of small posts, you have to serve in one . . .

CONCLUSION

I have addressed this despatch to all classified posts not out of vanity, but because the issues I have mentioned tend to be muttered about in private rather than stated openly in public: this inhibits reform. I hope that as many readers as possible will tell the Administration whether or not they agree in general with my criticisms. If they do, the Administration may for once have to take note. If not, I am content to be dismissed as a disgruntled maverick.

38 years is more than long enough to spend in a single job. I am lucky in that while quite a lot of it has been physically dangerous, much has been fun and very little has been boring. Like so many of my colleagues, I owe a truly enormous debt of love and gratitude to my wife, who has stood by my side in every situation from State banquets to a fusillade of pistol shots from a Libyan revolutionary (he missed). We now have time to stroll together and smell the roses (and perhaps slash the heads off a few more nettles . . .) .

HASKELL

1. *PUS*: The Permanent Under-Secretary is the head of the Diplomatic Service. He runs the FCO, answering to the Foreign Secretary.
2. *DUS*: Deputy Under-Secretary.
3. *DS*: Diplomatic Service.

∼

The Vatican

'A torpedo and a burning deck'

GEOFFREY CROSSLEY, HM ENVOY
EXTRAORDINARY TO THE HOLY SEE, MARCH 1980

My thirty-seven years on the Foreign (and Commonwealth) Office pay-roll have been rich at least in adventure and incident. I recall a torpedo and a burning deck, typhoid, a Jewish terrorist attempt to bomb the Paris Embassy, a Greek guerrilla minefield, Malayan jungle snipers, a meeting on the coast of the South China Sea with Norodom Sihanouk[1] campaigning against communist guerrillas, a glide up the Laotian Mekong in the Royal Pirogue, the receipt in my German letter-box of a sample of excrement in a paper bearing a swastika, involvement in the frustration of Qassim's attempt to grab Kuwait,[2] being blown off the air-strip while landing in a tropical storm in Nigeria, being hit over the head in a howling mob of Zanu terrorists on my lawn in Zambia, saving the child of the French Ambassador from a crocodile infested river, drifting on the Zambesi with broken-down engine towards the Victoria Falls, and oh how they thundered, practising pistol and machine gun fire with my guards in Colombia, and hoping for the best in a harassed Rome. Our service still offers lively adventure in addition to work which as well as being varied is particularly rewarding to those who remember that diplomacy is about people.

1. *Norodom Sihanouk*: King (and sometime Prime Minister) of Cambodia; see also pp. 362–5.
2. *Qassim's attempt to grab Kuwait*: General Qassim ruled Iraq after a military coup, and in 1961 laid claim to Kuwait. Troops deployed by Britain, and then the Arab League, saw off the threat.

Picture Credits

1. US Army Signal Corps, courtesy of Harry S. Truman Library.
2. Courtesy of Douglas Stuart.
3. National Archief/Spaarnestad Photo/Het Leven/Fotograaf onbekend.
4. Bayerische Staatsbibliothek München.
5. Getty Images.
7. Malcolm G. Dennison Photograph Collection, No. MGD-003, as posted on www.JEPeterson.net <file://www.JEPeterson.net>.
8. AFP/Getty Images.
9. Doug Pensinger/Getty Images.
10./11. The Estate of Alan Davidson/Jennifer Davidson.
12. Michael Rougier/Time and Life Pictures/ Getty Images.
13. Courtesy of Jay Smith, stamp dealer, www.JaySmith.com <file://www.JaySmith.com>.
14. Hulton Archive/Getty Images.
16./17. The Principal and Fellows of Somerville College, Oxford.
18./19. Courtesy of Lorna-Jane Winn.
20. Dmitry Kostyukov/AFP/Getty Images.

Index of Diplomats

Index of Countries

MATTHEW PARRIS & ANDREW BRYSON

PARTING SHOTS

'There is, I fear, no question but that the average Nicaraguan is one of the most dishonest, unreliable, violent and alcoholic of the Latin Americans'
Roger Pinsent, Managua, 1967

Up till 2006 a British Ambassador leaving his post was encouraged to write what was known as a valedictory despatch, to be circulated to a small number of influential people in government. This was the parting shot, an opportunity to offer a personal and frank view of the host country, the manners and morals of its people, their institutions, the state of their cooking and their drains. But it was also a chance to let rip at the Foreign Office itself and to look back on a career spent in the service of a sometimes ungrateful nation.

Combining gems from the archives with more recent despatches obtained through the Freedom of Information Act, *Parting Shots*, based on the successful BBC radio series, is a treasure trove of wit, venom and serious analysis. Astute and often gloriously non-politically correct, they shed light on Britain's place in the world, and reveal the curious cocktail of privilege and privation which make up the life of an ambassador.

'Wonderful . . . a glimpse of that lost world of private eloquence and erudite candour' Matthew d'Ancona, *Evening Standard*

MATTHEW PARRIS

A CASTLE IN SPAIN

'So infectious is his enthusiasm for L'Avenc and the dramatic, unvisited landscape of Collsacabra, that I wanted to leave at once [to explore it] . . . And it's all just a few miles away from the Costa Brava!'

Christopher Hudson, *Daily Mail*

Walking in the Pyrenees one spring morning Matthew Parris stumbled upon a magnificent ruined mansion standing on the edge of a line of huge cliffs. Later he was to discover that parts of the house dated back to the 14th century though it had not been completed until 1559; and that it had survived two massive earthquakes before falling into disrepair in the early 1960s.

A few years later, seduced by 'one of those foolish challenges that grip us in middle life', Parris bought the house, L'Avenc, and set about restoring it to its full glory. This delightful book chronicles it all: the original discovery, the attempts to discover its history, and then the long effortful years trying to bring it back to life in the face of scepticism from family, friends and Spanish neighbours. The original edition of *A Castle in Spain* was published in 2005 when the renovations were a work in progress; this new edition triumphantly records all that has happened since.

'Stands apart . . . This Englishman's castle might have started as a dream, but it has ended up being an extraordinary reality' *Sunday Times*

'A class of its own' *Guardian*

He just wanted a decent book to read ...

Not too much to ask, is it? It was in 1935 when Allen Lane, Managing Director of Bodley Head Publishers, stood on a platform at Exeter railway station looking for something good to read on his journey back to London. His choice was limited to popular magazines and poor-quality paperbacks – the same choice faced every day by the vast majority of readers, few of whom could afford hardbacks. Lane's disappointment and subsequent anger at the range of books generally available led him to found a company – and change the world.

'We believed in the existence in this country of a vast reading public for intelligent books at a low price, and staked everything on it'
Sir Allen Lane, 1902–1970, founder of Penguin Books

The quality paperback had arrived – and not just in bookshops. Lane was adamant that his Penguins should appear in chain stores and tobacconists, and should cost no more than a packet of cigarettes.

Reading habits (and cigarette prices) have changed since 1935, but Penguin still believes in publishing the best books for everybody to enjoy. We still believe that good design costs no more than bad design, and we still believe that quality books published passionately and responsibly make the world a better place.

So wherever you see the little bird – whether it's on a piece of prize-winning literary fiction or a celebrity autobiography, political tour de force or historical masterpiece, a serial-killer thriller, reference book, world classic or a piece of pure escapism – you can bet that it represents the very best that the genre has to offer.

Whatever you like to read – trust Penguin.